Child
Development

For Andrew, Sean, Sarah, June, and Lucinda—the new generation.

Child
Development
Myths and Misunderstandings

Jean Mercer
Richard Stockton College of New Jersey

Los Angeles • London • New Delhi • Singapore • Washington DC

For information:

SAGE Publications, Inc.
2455 Teller Road
Thousand Oaks, California 91320
E-mail: order@sagepub.com

SAGE Publications India Pvt. Ltd.
B 1/I 1 Mohan Cooperative
  Industrial Area
Mathura Road, New Delhi 110 044
India

SAGE Publications Ltd.
1 Oliver's Yard
55 City Road
London EC1Y 1SP
United Kingdom

SAGE Publications Asia-Pacific
  Pte Ltd
33 Pekin Street #02-01
Far East Square
Singapore 048763

Printed in the United States of America

Library of Congress Cataloging-in-Publication Data

Mercer, Jean.
Child development : myths and misunderstandings / Jean Mercer.
  p. cm.
Includes bibliographical references and index.
ISBN 978-1-4129-5646-8 (pbk.)
  1. Child development. I. Title.

HQ771.M47 2009
305.231—dc22   2008036217

This book is printed on acid-free paper.

09 10 11 12 13   10 9 8 7 6 5 4 3 2 1

Acquisitions Editor:	Erik Evans
Editorial Assistant:	Lara Grambling
Production Editor:	Catherine M. Chilton
Copy Editor:	Cheryl Duksta
Typesetter:	C&M Digitals (P) Ltd.
Proofreader:	Annette Van Deusen
Indexer:	Diggs Publication Services
Cover Designer:	Janet Foulger
Marketing Manager:	Stephanie Adams

Contents

Topically Organized
Table of Contents

Part II: Health and Physical Development

Part III: Social and Emotional Development

Part IV: Cognitive Development

Acknowledgments

The author would like to offer her sincere thanks to the staff of the Richard Stockton College Library for many years of friendly and efficient help and to Erik Evans and Lara Grambling of Sage for their cheerful encouragement. Also many thanks to my husband, Mike, for being a dude with a good attitude.

Sage Publications would also like to thank the following reviewers:

Sarah Jane Anderson
Mount Ida College

Christine F. Delgado
University of Miami

Nancy E. Dye
Humboldt State University

Roseanne L. Flores
Hunter College, CUNY

Robert G. Harrington
University of Kansas

Debra Lively
Saginaw Valley State University

Armeda C. Reitzel
Humboldt State University

Anne R. Schutte
University of Nebraska–Lincoln

Introduction

Claims About Child Development

Everyone has some knowledge about children because everyone has been a child. Most people have also observed other children and have heard adults talking about children. As a result, students arrive in a child development course with a lot of background knowledge, not as the "blank slates" they would be for a course in Russian, introductory physics, or the Victorian novel.

Students entering a child development or developmental psychology course bring more than observed facts with them. All of us have *theories* of child development based on our observations, the connections among these observations, and the ideas we have picked up in school or social settings. For example, almost every person has a way to explain juvenile delinquency—and chooses either genetics or family experiences as the cause. These explanations come from individuals' theories about child development. Very few people can state their theories in words, but the theories are there, and they exert a strong influence on expectations about development.

So far, this sounds like a good arrangement. Students come to study child development, not "from scratch" but with some knowledge and thoughts already in place. How can this not be good? The answer is this: Not all past observations are completely accurate, and not all theories are good descriptions of the rules of development. In other words, people can "know" a great deal that cannot be substantiated by systematic research. As is often the case, the problem is not what students don't know but what they know that isn't true. Most people who study developmental psychology find that they need to examine their own beliefs and assumptions, throw out some of what they've always thought, and make way for information supported by good evidence. If your old assumptions are in conflict with new information, you may not thoroughly understand or remember the new information.

Surprisingly, people who have their own children already do not necessarily have more accurate information than beginning students do. A survey of parents conducted by one of the premier associations for education about early development, Zero to Three, showed that parents performed especially poorly on understanding of social and emotional development (DYG, Inc., 2000). The power of old, inaccurate information is a real problem for everyone who needs to know about child development.

This book comprises a series of essays on common but inaccurate claims and beliefs about childhood growth and development. These essays serve to call students' attention to the assumptions they bring to a child development or developmental psychology course. Careful examination of your own assumptions—the "facts" that everybody knows but that are not true—is an exercise that can help prepare you to understand some important issues in the study of development. You will find that the examination process is important because of the complexity of the modern view of developmental change. As is frequently noted among developmentalists, developmental psychology isn't rocket science; it's a lot more complicated than that. When material is complicated, one has to be especially careful to resist falling back on "what everybody knows."

Types of Mistaken Claims

Naturally, not all incorrect claims about child development are of the same type. A range of inaccuracies exists, from completely invalid ideas to incorrect conclusions drawn from correct information.

Some beliefs about development are so off base that one can call them *myths*—ideas that are so far from what research evidence shows that they are essentially a superstition. To use an example from another topic, most cultures have creation myths, which are old stories that explain the origin of the world. Although the stories are interesting and enjoyable to hear, they do not stand up well to close examination. One story tells of an anthropologist who questioned a person who believed the world rested on the back of a giant turtle. The anthropologist asked, "And what's under that?" The person replied, "Another turtle." The anthropologist repeated the question and received the same reply. After the anthropologist's repeated questioning, the exasperated informant declared, "It's turtles, turtles, turtles, all the way down!" Myths about child development do not stand up to examination any better than the "turtles, turtles, turtles" explanation, but nevertheless these myths are so deeply entrenched in U.S. culture that they are not easily dismissed. For example, the belief that children learn moral values by experiencing punishment for mistakes is generally accepted, but it is probably not correct, nor is the idea that learning right from wrong is a simple matter.

Some erroneous beliefs about child development are *mistakes*, which are based on errors in research design or conclusions, leading to much-publicized statements that are difficult to correct. For example, in the early days of crack cocaine use, statements about the terrible problems of "crack babies" were common, but later work showed that good environments and early intervention corrected many of the difficulties the babies might have had as a result of prenatal drug exposure.

Some erroneous claims are based on a *misunderstanding* of complex issues and are often related to mistakes in the definition of words. Ideas involving the use of the terms *bonding* and *attachment* are often good examples of such beliefs. As an essay in this book shows, people who make claims about bonding and attachment often assume meanings for these terms that are different from their technical use. These claimants also often believe measurement of these behaviors is easy and the discovery of all of the factors involved in emotional development is uncomplicated.

Some erroneous beliefs are related to *missing information*. Strange though it may seem, researchers are still very far from having all of the basic data that will show people how development proceeds. For example, it is common to hear explanations for child behavior couched in the term *brain development*, but in fact there is very little information about normal brain development or how it relates to behavioral and cognitive change. At the time of this writing, research related to this concept in brain development is being conducted by studying developmental changes in 500 typical children (Waber et al., 2007). Also, though we may hear "it's genetic" or "it's in the DNA" as explanations for children's behavior and cognition, we need to remember that there are many questions to answer about the role of genetics in development.

"Seductive Ideas"

In the late 1990s, the leading developmental psychologist, Jerome Kagan, published a book with the intriguing title *Three Seductive Ideas*. Although Kagan's book is not quite as juicy as its title suggests—these ideas would not be much help if you wanted to seduce someone—*Three Seductive Ideas* addresses some important issues for our consideration of child development claims. Seductive ideas, according to Kagan, are assumptions that are so attractive to people that they quickly give the ideas credence and fail to give them the examination they require. They are ideas that people respond to with an immediate "yes, of course" and can confuse an examination of claims about child development. Kagan referred to one of his seductive ideas as the love of abstraction. *Abstraction* is a necessary tool for forging an understandable conclusion out of many pieces of information, but it can prove dangerous when people abstract excessive simplicity out of complication and are thus unable to tell the difference between two events. Humans care for their offspring, and ducks care for their ducklings: People can abstract from these facts a simplified statement about maternal care. But how important are the details that were lost? Can people make conclusions about human caregiving by studying ducks with their ducklings? In examining claims about child development, people need to notice whether supportive material comes from studies of another species and decide whether a claim is acceptable. Our tendency to pursue abstraction can make this difficult to do.

A second seductive idea discussed by Kagan is one of enormous importance for the study of child development: *infant determinism*, which is the assumption that experiences in the first few years of life are of overwhelming importance and cannot easily have their impact altered or corrected by later events. It is possible that this idea is true, but it is presently a seductive idea rather than a well-supported principle. Again, examination of claims about development should check for the presence of the assumption of infant determinism and consider that conclusions drawn directly from this assumption may not have a solid basis in fact.

Adults may also find their thinking "seduced" by the assumption of *adultomorphism*, a made-up word based on *anthropomorphism*, or the assumption that animals think and feel as humans do. *Adultomorphism* is the assumption that infants, children, and adolescents share the motives and abilities of adults. Adults holding this assumption feel they are able to understand child development issues on the basis of their own experiences, without examining the facts of child development. At best, adultomorphism confuses students; at worst, of course, it can lead to child abuse by adults who assume that a child is able to obey any adult command and refuses to do so only out of malicious opposition. Professional research reports rarely involve adultomorphic thinking, but claims made by nonprofessional life coaches and parent educators may be based on adultomorphism.

Why Is It All So Complicated?

Intuitively, people expect young children's lives to be explained by simple factors and uncomplicated connections and expect only a bit more complexity for adolescents. (At the same time, adults think their own lives are so full of complications that no one can appreciate them.) This expectation is a mistake, of course. If anything, children's lives are governed by more complex rules than those of adults because the rapid physical and mental changes of childhood are factors in themselves, beyond the experiences and hereditary factors that are more obvious. In this section, I comment on some other issues that contribute to the complexity of child development and can slow students' understanding.

Values and Political Goals

An important complicating problem in the understanding of child development is that some of our beliefs are guided by *values* and others by *political goals*. As is the case in many areas of life, our thoughts about child development are affected as much by how we want things to be as by what they actually are.

The values connected with child development issues are powerful. They include the status and obligations of men and women, the importance of obedience and independence, and the relative values of the immediate family and the community. The duties and entitlements of boys versus those of girls, as well as the duties and entitlements assigned to minority versus majority populations, are part of our value system. With respect to infants and sick or injured older children, important values include the importance of quality of life versus life itself. Unfortunately, in the universal situation of limited resources, the needs of children are often compared to the needs of the elderly, and values help people determine which group is given more. Further, beliefs about how life should be—equity as a measure of fairness, for instance—may help to determine expectations about similarities or differences between groups of people (boys and girls, perhaps). An individual's commitment to any of these values helps to determine the questions he or she asks and the answers he or she accepts about aspects of development.

Although values play a strong role in guiding individual thoughts, it is important to remember that groups of people share values that help determine their political goals, which in turn help to determine the group's actions regarding children, such as a vote on school funding. Values also make it likely that the group will emphasize beliefs about children that are congruent with their goals. Political organizations may feel little need to present all relevant information when making a decision affecting children but instead may choose to work with myths, misunderstandings, or partial truths that predispose others to agree with them. The existence of political goals can influence discussion of research evidence, as was seen some years ago in the books *The Bell Curve* (Herrnstein & Murray, 1994) and *The Myth of the First Three Years* (Bruer, 2002). These popular books discussed the effects of genetics versus early childhood experience on children's school performance and contributed to arguments about the appropriateness of funding for early childhood and other school programs.

The study of child development has probably never been a "pure" science. For example, developmentalists may be interested in certain issues because the issues are related to programs to improve children's physical and mental health. In fact, value-based decisions are a major way of deciding what is an improvement and what is not. A recent book, *Science in the Service of Children* (Smuts, 2006), describes how the developmental sciences came out of a combination of ideals, scientific and otherwise. Does this mean that the study of child development is vague and subjective in nature? Is it an immature science or one with inadequate methods (Cahan, 2007)? No, but the role played by values in the study of child development is so strong that one must be careful to evaluate what is really so and what is simply how people think things should be.

Variations on the Developmental Theme

Individual Differences

The complexity that must be faced before one understands child development is only partly a matter of values and politics. The facts about development are complicated. The common term *average child* is confusing shorthand that means that any group of children will contain individuals who are quite different from each other. People can accurately say they know a child whose measurable characteristics are equivalent to the mathematical average of the measurements of all children in a group, but in fact we can only average numbers, not children. Paradoxically, a group may not include any child whose measured characteristics are exactly the same as the average child, that hypothetical person who has measurements equivalent to the average taken from every child's measurements.

In child development, perhaps even more than in adult life, individual differences are key, and understanding the extent of those differences is vital in understanding how development progresses. The term that describes the extent of individual differences is *variability*. (This word applies to other kinds of difference, too, but those are discussed later.) Without getting too deeply into statistics, there are quantitative measures of variability, such as standard deviation or variance. These statistics are ways of stating the amount of variability in a group, just as the average or mean is a way of stating the number that best describes the whole group.

Information about children often states the average measurement (e.g., IQ) in a group, but less frequently gives a measurement of variability. However, knowledge of variability provides greater insight into the nature of a group and helps in making good decisions. Take, for example, a decision about giving resources to two groups of needy babies, if you can give money to one group only. The average weight of both groups is 6 pounds, which is within the normal range. But what if one group had very low variability in weight, with all of the babies weighing about the same? And what if the other group had very high variability, with half of the babies weighing only 3 pounds and the other half weighing about 9 pounds? When you have this information about variability, it's easy to see that the group with the very small babies needs more help, even though both groups have the same average weight.

Individual differences may be brought about by different events in the environment, by hereditary factors, or by a combination of the two. In the highly variable group of babies described previously, the small babies may have had small parents, they may have been born prematurely, or a combination of factors, such as a small mother receiving poor nutrition during pregnancy, may have affected the birth weights. The description of individual differences only identifies the variation, not why it occurs, although the "why" is also an important issue.

The existence of a great deal of variability and individual differences in children's development is one of the reasons our casual observations cannot give us a very good idea of what children are all about. Especially in today's small families, people have limited opportunities to observe anyone's development except their own. As it happens, a small sample of people chosen out of a large population (all children in the world) may not resemble the large population at all closely. In fact, in choosing a small sample, we may accidentally come up with a group of people who are dramatically different from others. Our own observations may be helpful in providing us with vivid stories and examples, but they will not necessarily help us avoid myths and other mistakes.

Population Differences and Diversity

The issue of diversity is another aspect of variability. The term *diversity* means variation, really, but today the term is used primarily to refer to the importance of considering ethnic differences. Discussion of diversity often focuses on the consideration of everyone's needs and tolerance and encouragement of ethnic differences, such as those of speech, dress, or religious practice. In terms of the study of child development, however, the concept of diversity should also mean that people base their understanding on information from many different types of human beings, rather than assuming that one group can represent the world's total population. Although it may seem to some students politically incorrect to suggest that developmental events can be different for different ethnic groups, this is the case, and to ignore the fact is to risk unfair and inappropriate treatment of some groups of children. Diversity and its implications involve a form of variability based on population (group) differences, not on individual differences. Such variability may be based on genetic differences between groups or on experiential factors, such as diet or health care, or, in some cases, on a combination of both. Once again, describing variations does not immediately explain them.

Age Differences

The concept of variability is a useful way to think about the most-studied aspect of childhood: developmental change. Whether considering physical growth, sexual maturation, cognitive advancement, or emotional change, when talking about development, people are talking about variation among age groups. Older children as a group are taller than younger children, and younger children as a group are more emotional than older children. We designate a course as a child development, developmental psychology, or developmental science course because its basic focus is on variations that go along with age. Developmental change may be caused by genetic factors, by experience, or by a combination of the two, but it accompanies changes in chronological age. Note that this last sentence does not say development is *caused* by age; age cannot cause anything except perhaps permission to get a driver's license. Factors such as experience and maturation (the result of genetic commands) cause developmental change. Because these factors accompany age changes, it is easy to forget that they are separate from chronological age.

Examining the Evidence: Recognizing That a Belief May Be Mistaken

Most questions about child development involve one of the forms of variability just discussed and may include considerations about why variability occurs and the form it takes. These questions may be answered by references to myths, misunderstandings, or seductive ideas, or the answers may be derived from systematic research. The assumption of this book is that a better understanding of child development comes from systematic investigations of the facts rather than myths or unexamined ways of thinking. But how do we examine beliefs about child development? How can we decide whether a statement about development deserves our confidence or not? Myths and misunderstandings do not come neatly labeled and, where these beliefs are widespread, the situation may be very confusing.

Defining Terms

Of all of the steps necessary to examine a statement about child development, the first is probably the simple matter of defining terms. Many terms used in discussing development lead people to say, "I can't define it, but I know it when I see it." Unfortunately, this is not good enough because vague definitions or guesses make it impossible for people to use words to communicate information. In addition, many words used to describe children's characteristics, such as *aggression, autism,* or *independence,* carry their own value messages that may be interpreted differently by different listeners. The meaning assigned to some terms may be influenced by movies or other media presentations—an example is the movie *The Rain Man,* which has a near monopoly on most people's definition of *autism.* Words with strong value and emotional implications, such as *bonding* and *attachment,* are not often used with their technical definitions in general conversation or in media presentations.

Care in using words about child development is essential to communication and has significance for practical decision making. A jury that makes a decision about *attachment* should know what the word means or their deliberations may not be at all to the point. Children and families can be affected for good or ill by accurate or inaccurate use of words. As stated in one discussion of this issue, "If our careless, underspecified choice of words inadvertently does damage to future generations of children, we cannot turn with innocent outrage to the judge and say, 'But your honor, I didn't realize the word was loaded'" (Elman et al., 1998, p. 391).

One way to examine a statement about child development is to check the definitions of the words used. Do the stated or implied definitions match the way other sources define the terms? Do the authors at least discuss the issue, perhaps saying that they intend to use a term with a slightly different meaning than is common? If there is no discussion, and if the meanings do not seem to jibe with the technical definitions typically used in professional materials, it would be wise to question the reasoning involved. Particular caution should be used when a condition or characteristic is frequently referred to by an abbreviation, such as ADHD (attention deficit hyperactivity disorder) or RAD (reactive attachment disorder). Using these abbreviated forms saves time, but it can also lead both speaker and listener to assign to the condition some qualities that the condition is not usually considered to have. This *criterion creep*, or slow change in definitions, results in conclusions that are not necessarily justified by the evidence.

Developmentally Appropriate Practice

The term *developmentally appropriate practice* refers primarily to the use of procedures that are beneficial to a particular age group of children. For example, caregivers should frequently pick up and carry infants. A 6-year-old, on the other hand, does not need this type of care and would probably be very annoyed if subjected to it. For our purposes in this book, the concept of *developmentally appropriate practice* is a reminder that information collected from one age group may or may not explain anything about the characteristics of other age groups. A belief formed from information about adolescents and generalized to preschoolers, or vice versa, may be legitimate, but caution should be used. One must examine the information carefully and decide, on a case-by-case basis, the appropriateness of the generalization. For example, people often speak of dementia in the elderly as a "second childhood," but in reality the cognitive losses of dementia do not cause the individual to think as a young child does. Such comparisons and confusions may lead to inappropriate conclusions, as when a frustrated and distressed school-age child is regarded as "a big baby."

Where Did the Information Come From?

Definitions and developmental concepts can be clues to mistaken conclusions about child development, but the most significant question relates to the way information was collected and analyzed—the research design. Systematic investigations of child development can lead to reliable information and permit valid conclusions. What conclusions are permitted depends on the research design, so examination of a claim needs to include examination of the sources of the information. The lengthy, detailed research reports one finds in professional journals are lengthy and detailed for precisely this reason: They allow readers to examine the background of the information that led to a conclusion.

Understanding how a study was carried out is essential for most questions about child development, but in no case is it more important than for studies of *interventions*, which are defined as any procedure or treatment used to assist or improve development. Interventions for children may include psychotherapy; educational programs, such as specialized reading approaches; dietary improvements, such as the sale of fruit instead of candy in school lunchrooms; or sex education programs, whether abstinence focused or otherwise. Conclusions about the effectiveness of interventions have enormous practical significance, both in terms of the children helped and in terms of the allocation of resources to programs or localities. Understanding the systematic research used to test an intervention is an essential step toward concluding whether the intervention is, or is not, effective. Concern about the evidentiary basis of treatments is of great importance in clinical psychology today, and authors commenting about clinical issues have provided important ways to think about various childhood interventions.

Anecdotes and Testimonials

Statements about child development that are based on personal experience should be taken for exactly what they are—a description of a single experience—and should not be generalized to other children. A story about a specific child is interesting and valuable as a story about an individual. However, it is impossible to determine how typical the child is of children in general—or to judge the uniqueness of the child compared with other children—from reading an anecdote or a testimonial. Unfortunately, readers can be easily distracted by the vivid details of a personal story and assume that there is more meaning in the anecdote than there is in "dry" statistics, but the truth is the opposite (Stanovich, 2003). Stories can be valuable ways for students to imagine some flesh on the bare bones of academic description, but conclusions drawn from them must be examined with care.

Testimonials are a special type of anecdote. A testimonial is a statement given by a person who has received an intervention and feels that he or she has benefited from the treatment or program. (You will notice that testimonials never say the person thought the treatment was a waste of time.) Again, even if one assumes that the testimonial is an accurate description, it is not appropriate to conclude that everyone would have the same response to the treatment. In fact, dozens of other people may not have been helped or even may have been harmed by the intervention. Testimonials should never be taken as reliable evidence for a statement about child development, and if they are offered, other aspects of the claim should be examined carefully. The ethics codes of some professions, such as clinical social work, prohibit professionals from asking for testimonials.

What if the testimonial is your own? Is your own experience to be weighed more heavily than data gathered from a large number of other people? Are you unique, so it's not surprising if research does not seem to apply to you? Or do your contradictory experiences (if any) invalidate reports of research on other people? These are all difficult questions because there is no doubt that people intuitively feel their own experiences are the most important of all sources of information. Looking at the matter objectively and honestly, however, people need to be aware that, if a testimonial about another individual is untrustworthy, so are one's own personal stories. Like every other individual, you have much in common with the average person's experience, but you also share in the variability of the group and are thus different from the average. Research reports based on participants who are like you speak to some aspects of yourself but do not reflect every detail of individual difference. Unusual individual characteristics or experiences deserve careful study but do not usually mean that information based on a large group can be dismissed as wrong.

Systematic Investigations

Anecdotes and testimonials are based on information collected without any particular plan or design. Acceptable statements about child development need to be supported by investigating ideas systematically, following established rules, and drawing conclusions on the basis of those rules. However, there is more than one kind of systematic investigation into child development, and more than one kind of conclusion that can be drawn. An important step in examining a statement about child development is to examine the type of investigation performed and the appropriateness of the suggested conclusion.

Experimental research and randomized designs. In considering experimental designs, one needs to begin with the definition issue. Although in everyday speech people often use the word *experiment* interchangeably with *research* or *study* or *investigation*, the term *experiment* is a technical term with a specific meaning. In an experiment, a researcher can determine whether participants have one set of experiences or another and thus can compare people who have had one treatment to those who have had a different treatment, but who are similar in all other ways. (*Treatment* in this case could mean an intervention, a learning condition, a book to read, a food to eat, or any other experience.)

The researcher assigns participants *randomly* to one treatment or another. This does not mean that the researcher assigns participants on impulse; rather, random assignment involves a repeatable randomization procedure, perhaps using a random number list, and assignment to a treatment without consideration of participant characteristics or the whim of the researcher. The assumption is that there will be nothing about a participant that will make him or her more likely to get one treatment or the other, so any differences in outcome are the result of the treatments, not of preexisting characteristics of the participants. Studies of interventions that follow this pattern are sometimes called randomized controlled trials (RCTs).

Randomized designs are considered the gold standard for investigation. Because existing characteristics of participants are randomly distributed across the two groups, any differences in results (e.g., children perform better with one reading program than another) may be said to have been *caused* by the treatment, provided that the statistical differences in results are big enough. If a statement about a child development issue claims that a treatment has caused the outcome, but the design is not randomized, the reader should seriously question the conclusion. A number of the essays later in this book address this issue.

Randomized designs sound like a desirable approach to investigation, and they are—when they can be carried out. But studies of child development cannot always employ randomized designs, for several reasons. For one, some of the treatments or conditions under study are of interest precisely because they are potentially harmful. Ethical considerations prevent intentional exposure of children to harmful situations, so no matter how useful it would be to know about certain outcomes, researchers cannot find out about them in an experimental way. Second, many of the factors researchers would like to study are not under their control, and thus children cannot be randomly assigned to one group or another. For example, researchers would like to know about the effects of gender or ethnicity on a number of developmental outcomes, but boys cannot be transformed into girls or children of one ethnicity changed to another ethnicity. And, of course, the central question about child development relates to change with age, and researchers can only wait for a child's age to change, not control what age a child is.

Even where a randomized design is possible, it may not be very clear what to randomize. For example, a burning issue in schools involves bullying: Is it possible to establish effective antibullying programs? How do we find out whether or not a program is effective? Assigning individuals to treatments does not make much sense because this would mean that different children in a classroom receive different treatments, but the children affect each other, so researchers cannot know for sure whether one treatment or another was effective. What if researchers assign classrooms randomly to different treatments? These children still meet on the playground or in the neighborhood, and the treatment one group received can indirectly affect the others. What if researchers randomly assigned entire schools to treatments? This would be better in terms of conclusions but would require a large number of schools and children. The simple term *randomized design* does not seem so simple when considering specific applications. Examining these issues is essential as one tries to assess claims about child development.

Why is there such emphasis on control groups—perhaps better termed *comparison groups?* Why not just see how a group of children is doing at the beginning of the school year, make sure they receive an important educational program, and then test them again at the end of the year? This can be a reasonable approach for adults, but it is not acceptable for children, and researchers who take this approach should be questioned about their conclusions. Children continue to develop in all ways even though their experiences are limited. The process of *maturation,* or change with age caused by genetic factors, is always operating, even in severely handicapped children. Children change in the course of a school year, whether they are in a wonderful or a mediocre school, whether they spend their time herding goats, or whether they are bedridden for serious medical treatment. The question is not whether children change during a treatment; children do change. The question one should ask is *how much* of the change is caused by the treatment and how much by maturation. The more rapidly change occurs at a particular point in development, the more important it is that a comparison group's progress be charted and compared to the development of a group receiving a treatment. Without such a comparison, it is all too easy to assume that any change was caused by the treatment, and without a comparison, one cannot know whether a treatment actually did harm rather than good.

Nonrandomized designs. When investigating aspects of child development, researchers can easily find themselves dealing with factors that cannot be randomized, or problems where it is not clear how to do the job of randomization. In these cases, researchers turn to *nonrandomized* approaches in which there is much less control over the many factors that can influence an outcome. This is perfectly acceptable—there is little choice in the matter, in fact—but it means that readers must be especially alert in their assessment of conclusions from the investigation.

When a randomized design is used, it is assumed that characteristics of the children are similarly organized in the two groups being compared. These characteristics (called *variables* because they can vary from person to person or over time) are not exactly the same for all participants, but one expects randomization to mean, for instance, that redheads or hockey fans are equally likely to be in either group. The only consistent difference between the groups is initially the *treatment variable*, or the condition they experience. (This is a variable because it varies from one group to the other.) If the two groups are different on the *outcome variable*, the characteristic measured (e.g., school success), and there were no other consistent differences between the groups that could have caused their outcomes to be different, then one can say that the treatment caused the outcome.

In a nonrandomized design, however, one cannot be sure that the treatments are the only differences between the groups. Therefore, it is not possible to draw a clear conclusion that a treatment caused an outcome. To make this assessment, one needs to decide whether the design was randomized or non-randomized. If the design was nonrandomized, caution in drawing conclusions is essential. Many of the essays in this book repeat this caution.

One common nonrandomized design is a *quasi-experiment*. This term is misleading, causing some students to assume that a quasi-experiment is a type of experiment. It is not, by definition, because experiments always involve a type of randomization or a similar approach that ensures that treatment variables are not mixed with other variables. Quasi-experiments are studies in which a researcher compares outcomes for people who were nonrandomly assigned to groups. This nonrandomized assignment might mean that people assigned themselves, for instance by seeking out a certain kind of psychotherapy. Or participants may have been placed into a group by another person. For example, a mother might have decided that her shy child would benefit from camp or karate lessons, or a teacher may have wanted all the bullies in her class to be in the program she personally believed in. These are situations where characteristics of the child had an effect on the treatment received.

When a child's characteristics contribute to the choice of treatment, there is no way to know whether the outcome resulted from the treatment or from something directly related to the children. The two treatment groups are different on more than one variable, but there is little information about anything but the treatment variable. A poorly understood characteristic of each child is accompanying the child's treatment, and the variables cannot be separated from each other. When two variables go together in this way, they are said to be confounded, although *confused* and *confusing* might be better words. *Confounded variables* make it difficult to draw a clear conclusion, as many of the essays in this book attest.

Studies of Age Differences

Nonrandomized studies are used to investigate age differences because, of course, researchers cannot assign children to ages or make them older or younger than they actually are. As children age, they have varied experiences to learn from, different diets or disease exposures to affect their development, and so on. Children of different age groups are different in ways that are associated with their chronological ages but are not necessarily caused by the genetic factors that guided their maturation. This means that comparison of age groups can be confounded with accidental differences between the groups.

Although some complex designs have been brought to bear on the investigation of age differences, two fairly simple types of design are common and need to be understood. One is a *longitudinal* design, in which one group of children is tested or measured repeatedly over a period of time to discover changes that occur with age. When the data are analyzed, each child is compared to him- or herself at different ages, rather than to other children. In this way, individual experiences, such as cultural differences, are ruled out of the discussion, and the focus is on the basic changes over time. This approach is in many ways ideal, but it can take a long time (depending on the period of life being studied) and requires a lot of clerical work to keep track of participants. If families move away or lose interest, the work already done on those children may be lost.

A second fairly simple design for studying age differences is the *cross-sectional* approach, which studies groups of children of different ages but tests each child once. The results from each age group are then compared to the other age groups. This seems like a short, sweet, sensible way to do things, but there is a problem: What if there were something unusual about one of the groups? For instance, what if an epidemic during the gestation of one group caused a developmental problem that was not obvious? The development of members of that group could be slowed, causing the researchers to assume that development was slow during a certain age period, then sped up rapidly (this would appear to be the case when looking at the normally developing, slightly older group). If the groups are close together in age, medical problems would probably be the primary source of confusion, but if younger and much older children were compared, social changes such as new methods of teaching reading or reductions in school athletic activity could become confused with age differences.

Correlation: A different nonrandomized approach. Another type of nonrandomized design involves a *correlational study.* In this type of design, there is no comparison of groups or treatments. Instead, each member of a large group of children is examined on two or more measurable characteristics. For example, a researcher might look at skeletal age (the development of the bones toward their mature form) and at measures of reproductive maturity, such as breast development. For each child tested, two measures would be labeled so that researchers would know which skeletal age measure went with which breast assessment. All of these paired measures would be analyzed by means of a statistical test for correlation, and the results would tell whether one measure predicted the other—that is, do children with less-mature skeletal development also have less-developed breasts, and do those with more advanced development in one area also show advancement in the other area? If the numbers are related in the way just described, skeletal age and breast development would be said to be positively correlated.

Correlational studies can be very informative and good guides to further work on a topic. However, conclusions drawn from correlations must be carefully stated. Correlational studies are not good enough to support the claim that one factor *causes* the other. Both may be caused by one or many other variables. Unfortunately, writers of headlines and speakers of television sound bites regularly ignore this fact and confidently declare correlations to be evidence of causality. Many studies of child development use a correlational approach, especially if they are dealing with an important issue where variables cannot easily be controlled, such as education, delinquent behavior, or adolescent sexual activity. Caution is needed when claims are made about causality based on the outcomes of correlational studies.

Sources of Information: Safe or Sorry?

So far, our discussion of ways to examine child development claims and beliefs has focused on assumptions and ways of investigating issues. Consideration of these points is indeed the best way to examine claims and reject myths or mistakes. Some claims are perfectly adequate in these ways but nevertheless should be rejected or given limited acceptance. These claims fail to take into account other existing evidence, either because the author missed its existence or failed to understand it completely. (Isn't there enough trouble for students without this? Yes, published authors can and do make mistakes.) Unfortunately, some authors practice cherry-picking and include only material that supports their own conclusion; this is an unethical practice and not likely to be found in work published in professional journals, but it has been known to occur.

How can you find further evidence about a claim or belief about child development? Often students become frustrated by electronic searches and cannot figure out a suitable keyword. It may be easier and more effective to start with the publication in which the claim was made. Whether reading a book, a professional publication, or a popular magazine, you will find a bibliography or reading list at the end of the article or book that provides a good starting place for your search—and in many cases will be all you need. Reading the listed materials provides an idea of whether the author of the original publication was correct in citing those sources as supporting his or her conclusion. Don't forget that each listed reference is also likely to have its own bibliography, and if you follow up on those lists you will soon have a great deal of information to examine.

Textbooks also are an important source. Although textbooks may not have much to say on a particular topic, the textbook's bibliography provides relevant references. Follow these leads for further information.

Two outstanding professional journals provide excellent research reports on child development issues: *Child Development* and *Developmental Psychology*. Unfortunately, the growth of child development studies and the shortage of journal space have made some articles in these publications so concise and complex that they can be quite difficult for beginning students to follow. Even so, if a given article is overwhelming, reading the abstract, introduction, and discussion sections can be very informative.

Parenting magazines and similar popular publications can provide articles with useful overviews, but generally these articles do not provide references to background material, making it difficult to follow up on the evidence or ratio-nale for claims. If you want to follow up on an unusual topic in such a maga-zine, searching for other work by the same author may provide helpful background. Magazine materials intended for life coaches or parent educators should be considered with caution; they may be excellent, or they may simply repeat common myths and mistakes. Internet sources on child development range from brilliant to dangerously deceptive. A Google search can be a won-derful way to find statements of common beliefs that may be myths or mis-takes. A keyword search using *child discipline* can bring up thousands of Web sites for advocacy organizations, support groups, and concerned individuals, providing a picture of popular positions on this topic. Such a search shows whether a mistaken claim is just an unusual error or whether it is part of a pop-ular belief system. Inspection of these Web sites reveals whether proponents of a position refer to serious systematic evidence for their stance or whether they operate at the level of anecdotes or testimonials. Inspection can also reveal whether the site is run by a commercial organization with a primary interest in sales of products and services rather than in the sharing of information.

In some cases, a Google search can show research evidence itself, but this depends on whether authors have posted published material on Web sites. Many professional journals place an embargo on publications for some months after they are issued, and of course many authors do not choose to put mater-ial on the Internet when it is available in print. But searching the Internet for specific research material is worthwhile. Students should keep in mind that a publication that appears only online may not be as well managed or edited as one that has a print version, although some online publications are excellent. When an Internet search yields references to journal articles that must be paid for, students should be sure to check their own college or university library to see whether the publication is available there in print or electronic form.

Some excellent Web sites specialize in guiding readers to reliable child development material. One of these, www.cfw.tufts.edu, has existed for some years and provides links to other Web sites that provide good information about children and families. Links on this site are presented by topic and by age group, so it is easy to use. The Society for Research in Child Development (SRCD), the organization that publishes *Child Development*, has an informative Web site that includes material about children of all ages. For information about the infant and preschool periods, a very helpful Web site is that of the organization Zero to Three.

The study of child development has an important characteristic that makes it different from, for instance, the study of psychological testing. Child development studies involve a *multidisciplinary* approach. Children develop in an environment shaped by family, school, community, national, and world events, all of which can affect developmental change. Information relevant to child development can come from psychology, social work, nursing, pediatrics, public health, epidemiology, psychiatry, occupational therapy, physical therapy, education, and many other sources. Students who are searching for supporting and challenging information related to a claim should remember this and look to more than one discipline for evidence.

The Work Ahead

The main part of this book involves a series of essays on child development claims that may be myths, mistakes, or misunderstandings. These essays are marked according to age group and topic, so they can be used in conjunction with textbooks that are organized either chronologically or topically. The essays discuss the claims and consider them with respect to appropriate issues of research design, internal logic, and supporting or opposing evidence from other sources. Because the goal of this book is to encourage critical thinking and thorough consideration of claims about child development, each essay is followed by a short reading list and a set of questions for active student involvement. Referring to this introductory section may be helpful if you have trouble answering a question.

The ability to analyze and evaluate claims comes only with practice. No amount of reading or instruction can provide you with assessment skills that must be honed through active involvement with relevant questions and answers. Such active involvement can be fun but can also be a painful struggle at times when your favored mantra is "just tell me the answer." Unsupported claims do just tell the answer, which is why they are so attractive to readers. But unsupported claims, accepted when they should not be, can cause problems for children, families, communities, and schools, if no one attempts to evaluate them. In the long run, adults who are able to evaluate child development claims can provide the best environment for children and the best future for all of us.

Side Arguments

What will happen when you master ways of assessing claims about child development? Will you be able to win arguments at holiday dinners and in bars? Regrettably, no such short-term benefit can be predicted. It's more likely that your dissection of a mistaken claim will get the response, "Well, I believe it, anyway." Just like children, adults are more likely to depend on the statements of sources they trust than to try to examine evidence. Where values are concerned (as is the case with child development), this tendency is even stronger (Bloom & Weisberg, 2007). But even though you will still lose arguments, the task of evaluating evidence is well worth doing, for yourself and for others, and once you have mastered these skills you will know that you have learned something important.

References

Bloom, P., & Weisberg, D. S. (2007). Childhood origins of adult resistance to science. *Science, 316*, 996–997.

Bruer, J. T. (2002). *The myth of the first three years*. New York: Free Press.

Cahan, E. D. (2007). The child as scientific object. *Science, 316*, 835.

DYG, Inc. (2000). *What grown-ups understand about child development: A national benchmark study*. Washington, DC: Zero to Three.

Elman, J. L., Bates, E. A., Johnson, M. H., Karmiloff-Smith, A., Parisi, D., & Plunkett, K. (1998). *Rethinking innateness*. Cambridge, MA: MIT Press.

Herrnstein, R., & Murray, C. (1994). *The bell curve: Intelligence and class structure in American life*. New York: Free Press.

Kagan, J. (1998). *Three seductive ideas*. Cambridge, MA: Harvard University Press.

Smuts, A.B. (2006). *Science in the service of children, 1893–1935*. New Haven, CT: Yale University Press.

Stanovich, K. (2003). *How to think straight about psychology*. New York: Allyn & Bacon.

Waber, D. P., de Moor, C., Forbes, P., Almli, C. R., Botteron, K., Leonard, G., et al. (2007). The NIH MRI study of normal brain development performance of a population based sample of healthy children aged 6 to 18 years on a neurophysiological battery. *Journal of the International Neuropsychological Society, 13*, 1–18.

PART I

Genetics and Prenatal Life

Claim 1

Genetic factors play such a strong role in human development that genes alone can determine certain human behavioral characteristics.

Susan likes coffee a lot and often has some when out with friends. But she'd rather have it at home because there it's easier to fix it the way she wants. Susan likes to put the cream in the cup and then add the coffee to it rather than the other way around. "That's weird," say her friends. "How come you do it like that?" "I don't know," replies Susan. "My dad does the same thing, and so does Grandma. I guess it must be genetic. People say I smile just like the two of them, too. But, you know, my adopted sister fixes her coffee the way I do."

Could Susan's coffee habits be genetic in origin?

The connection between genetic factors and behavior is sometimes obvious in animals. For example, some dog breeds tend to be very calm and friendly, and others are quite aggressive. Some cattle are much less aggressive than others, which is important because no matter how much milk a cow can give, if you can't get close to her, you won't get milk. Other animal behaviors may be affected by both genetic factors and experience—for instance, some dogs have the potential to become excellent retrievers, but unless they have a chance to be trained in this skill they will not master the retrieving task.

Some human characteristics are strongly determined by genetic factors, and a specific genetic difference may govern many aspects of development (Kaplan, Wang, & Francke, 2001). On the other hand, some developmental changes appear not to be genetically governed but instead are influenced by experience only (Roisman & Fraley, 2006).

It is often quite difficult to figure out the connection between human genetics and behavior. Human beings select their own mates; they are not deliberately bred for certain behaviors as dogs may be. The belief that genes are directly responsible for a person's habits and actions is probably based on dramatic claims derived from some studies of twins. Popular reports about twins who were separated at birth and later reunited contain startling similarities. Some twin pairs who were raised apart from each other are reported to have given their dogs the same name and to have displayed identical idiosyncratic behaviors, such as flushing a toilet both before and after using it.

Can such reports provide strong evidence about the connection between genes and specific behaviors? A number of problems arise when making too much of this kind of evidence. One problem has to do with possible differences between volunteers and people who are reluctant to participate in research. Studies of reunited twins depend on twins to respond to advertised studies or to seek out ongoing research programs. In these cases, the reports may represent only the twin pairs who discover, to their surprise, that they resemble each other greatly, rather than those who discover that they are not at all alike. And of course twin pairs who were not reunited—or twins who never even knew they had a twin sibling—would not be included in this study. It's possible that twins who resemble each other are more likely to go to the same places, do the same things, and discover each other than are twins who are quite different.

Another issue has to do with the small number of separated and reunited twins compared with the large numbers of nontwin siblings or twins who were never separated. Twinning is unusual in humans, and situations where the babies would be separated are even less likely. Counterintuitive though it may be, small rather than large samples are more likely to provide extreme results because extreme measures have more of a chance to average out when large samples are used. The effect of extreme results in small groups is exaggerated when the news media report on only a small group of cases where there is a surprising resemblance between twins and not on others where there are small and undramatic resemblances.

Studies of reunited twins may show genetic effects on intelligence or health but are not very good evidence that specific behaviors can be "in the DNA." However, other sources of information support the idea that genetic factors are powerful. People with an unusual genetic makeup sometimes display uncommon behaviors, such as hand-wringing. Babies of different ethnic backgrounds may show different behaviors shortly after birth, when it seems there has been too short a time for differences to be learned.

More often, though, it appears that an individual's *phenotype*, or developed physical and behavioral characteristics, is determined by genetic factors and environment working together in complicated ways (Plomin, 2000). For example, children share their parents' genetic material, but the children's development is also shaped by experiences their parents choose for them, such as music lessons, low-fat meals, or severe physical punishment. The parents' choices for their children may be the result of the parents' own genetic makeup, their childhood experiences (either repeating them or rejecting them), or a combination of the two as well as many other factors. In some degree, parents' genetic makeup plays a role in their children's experiences as well as in their children's genetic characteristics.

Genetically determined characteristics of a child's appearance or behavior can also cause others to treat the child in predictable ways. A small, thin child may be treated with more care than a large, robust child who is rarely sick and does not seem to mind minor pains and injuries. The experiences of both the thin and the robust child are not random events but are indirectly related to each child's genetic makeup so that the long-term effect of the genetic material is potentially much greater than the individual's physical characteristics alone.

As children become older, they are increasingly free to choose their own experiences and thus to shape their own development. Some of their choices may be determined by past experiences, and some by genetic components. But certainly some choices in later childhood and adolescence come about because of genetic material as well as body type, activity preferences, or emotional tendencies that result from the biological inheritance.

Directly or indirectly, genetic factors can have a powerful effect on behavior, and in recent years developmental psychologists have placed much stress on this fact. However, it seems that, as is so often the case in psychology, the way the question is asked helps determine the answer. For instance, what would happen if you were to ask one group of parents to rate the similarities between their monozygotic (identical) twins and another group of parents to rate the similarities between their dizygotic (fraternal) twins? The ratings would be very different: The parents would report the similarities between the monozygotic twin pairs as very strong and the similarities between the dizygotic twin pairs as quite small. Ask trained observers to rate the twin pairs, however, and you'll get a different outcome. The monozygotic pairs would still be rated as more similar, and the dizygotic pairs as less similar, but the differences between the two would be a good deal less than the differences the parents reported. Parents seem to exaggerate the similarities between monozygotic twins and the differences between dizygotic twins (Roisman & Fraley, 2006). When questions about causes of behavior take these factors into account, genetic characteristics seem to play a smaller role in development, and shared environmental factors, such as parenting, seem to play a larger role. Perhaps some of the existing beliefs about genetic effects have given those factors more weight than they should have.

A curious issue about genetic effects involves the question of when in life a genetic factor is likely to come into play. We would expect genetic factors to play their strongest role early in life, before much learning has occurred, and environmental factors to have a greater effect as more learning takes place. But one study found higher correlations between intelligence test scores of elderly twins than between those of younger twins (McClearn et al., 1997). It seems that there may be genetic influences that exist but whose effects cannot be observed in children and adolescents.

Conclusion

It is possible for specific human behaviors to result from specific genetic makeups, but in most cases behaviors are the result of various combinations of heredity and experience. It's hard to see how a complex behavior like Susan's coffee drinking could be determined by genetic factors, and the possibility that the behavior was learned is suggested by the actions of her sister, who is not biologically related but behaves in the same way.

CRITICAL THINKING

1. Use a child development textbook to define the term *passive genetic-environmental correlation*. Describe a scenario that shows this kind of connection between genes, experience, and developmental outcome.

2. Use a child development textbook to define the term *evocative genetic environmental correlation*. Describe a relevant scenario that is an example of this type of correlation.

3. Use a child development textbook to define the term *active genetic-environmental correlation*. Describe a relevant scenario that is an example of this type of correlation.

4. In studies of separated twins, how would similarities in a twin pair make the twin siblings more likely to reunite?

5. One of the studies described earlier (Roisman & Fraley, 2006) involved ratings of twins by parents and by unrelated observers. Using this study for information, describe the differences in the ratings. Would you expect the parents to rate opposite-sex dizygotic twins as more different from each other (i.e., with lower correlations of ratings), or would you expect the parents' ratings of same-sex dizygotic twins to have a lower correlation? Explain your answer.

References

Kaplan, P., Wang, P. P., & Francke, U. (2001). Williams (Williams Beuren) syndrome: A distinct neurobehavioral disorder. *Journal of Child Neurology, 16*, 177–190.

McClearn, G. E., Johansson, B., Berg, S., Pedersen, N. L., Ahern, F., Petrill, S. A., & Plomin, R. (1997). Substantial genetic influence on cognitive abilities in twins 80 or more years old. *Science, 276*, 1560–1563.

Plomin, R. (2000). Behavioural genetics in the 21st century. *International Journal of Behavioral Development, 24*, 30–34.

Roisman, G. I., & Fraley, R. C. (2006). The limits of genetic influence: A behavior-genetic analysis of infant-caregiver relationship quality and temperament. *Child Development, 77*, 1656–1667.

Claim 2

There is no harm in putting off childbearing until the mother's career is established.

Jeff and Marina postponed having children until they were in their early 40s. They both earned law degrees and wanted to get their practices established before starting a family. They were so busy that they did not think very much about pregnancy. Now Marina has discovered she is pregnant, and she is so excited that she tells everyone she meets. Most people congratulate her, but a few look uncertain and ask her how old she is. Someone even tells her, "I hate to say this, but you might have waited too long. My grandmother had my uncle when she was 45, and he was never really healthy, though nobody ever found what was wrong with him."

Of course Marina is frightened and concerned about this comment and is not sure what to think. Should she anticipate having a sickly baby just because of her age?

In the distant past, most women did not live long enough to have babies as "older mothers"—defined not so long ago as mothers 35 years and older. Even after the development of effective contraception, many women began their childbearing life in their early 20s and gave birth to all of their children before 30. As recently as the 1960s, women who became mothers after 35 years of age were referred to as "elderly." But later childbearing has become more common, a shift which has created anxiety about the effects of later births on both mother and baby because social changes and improved contraception have caused more women to delay childbearing into their late 30s or even their 40s.

This change has not caused an epidemic of sickly babies; in fact, healthy older mothers are not much more likely than younger women to have babies with problems—except for one serious birth defect, Down syndrome.

Down syndrome is a problem of development that involves a combination of disturbed physical and mental features. (A *syndrome* is a combination of symptoms that occur together.) The characteristics of Down syndrome include shortened thigh bones, a flattened skull and nose, eyelids of an unusual shape, and a large tongue. Some level of mental retardation is part of Down syndrome, and many people with Down syndrome have heart and intestinal problems that may be serious and even fatal. Many fetuses with Down syndrome die before birth, and the death rate of people with Down syndrome is higher than normal at all ages. To add to the severe disadvantages of this condition, people with Down syndrome who live into adulthood are likely to experience a very early onset of Alzheimer's disease—the loss of mental functioning usually not seen until much later in life. However, the development of people with Down syndrome may be strongly affected by their social and educational environments (Van Dyke & Lin-Dyken, 1993; Van Hooste & Maes, 2003), which can influence their social and emotional development and lead to positive relationships (Hodapp, Ly, Fidler, & Ricci, 2001).

Down syndrome is caused by changes in chromosomes within the ovum. (Experts have not established whether chromosomes from the sperm ever contribute to Down syndrome.) Although chromosomes, which work in pairs, normally separate from their partners and duplicate when a cell divides into two, in Down syndrome, this process has not proceeded correctly. Instead, in the usual case, the separation of a set of paired chromosomes has not occurred, and the resulting chromosome contains both members of the pair when it should contain only one of the partner chromosomes (Sherman, Allen, Bean, & Freeman, 2007). As a result, at fertilization, when the ovum takes in all of the sperm's chromosomes, the resulting organism has one more chromosome than normal for a human, a situation called "trisomy" because there are three chromosomes where there should be a pair. As the fertilized ovum begins to divide and produce the cells of the new organism, each of the new cells has the same unfortunate extra chromosome.

The additional chromosome, with the characteristic group of genes it carries, has a pervasive effect on development. Rather than a single changed characteristic, such as nose shape, shoe size, or eye color, the person with Down syndrome suffers changes in many parts of the body, including the brain and its related mental functions and visual ability.

Down syndrome is fairly easy to recognize, although not every affected individual has all of the symptoms. Why, then, is there a popular belief that general weakness and poor development are the lot of children of older mothers, rather than the occurrence of Down syndrome? Perhaps this belief goes back to the period, not so many years ago, before the chromosomal cause of Down syndrome was first identified. At that time, people may have had difficulty telling with certainty the difference between some children with Down syndrome, some with other genetic problems, and some whose disorders were caused by infection or dietary deficiencies. Such a belief in general developmental problems, if it already existed, might actually be intensified by suggestions that pregnant women older than 35 years should undergo prenatal testing. Such testing is usually most concerned with Down syndrome but may detect other genetic problems as well, perhaps leading some people to think that many problems are associated with later childbearing.

The task of connecting Down syndrome with a mother's age was not an easy one, so it is only recently that experts have clearly understood that children of healthy older mothers have specific rather than general risks. Variables confounded with maternal age are many. For example, older women are almost always married to older men, and although only a very small proportion of Down syndrome cases have been shown to result from chromosomal problems in the sperm, this fact cannot simply be assumed (deMichelena, Burstein, Lama, & Vasquez, 1993). Also, older mothers may have had more pregnancies and births than younger mothers, and perhaps the repeated pregnancies affect the reproductive system and increase the probability of a chromosomal error. Thus, both the father's age and the number of previous pregnancies confound with the mother's age, and only careful analysis of chromosomal makeup can clarify the cause of Down syndrome.

Researchers have studied these confounding variables. Investigators compared the number of Down syndrome conceptions among women of different age groups who were matched on possible confounding variables, such as number of previous births and father's age. This work yielded the rate (*proportion*, or number of Down syndrome conceptions for a certain number of women) for mothers of different ages and showed a much higher rate for 45-year-old mothers than for 30-year-olds.

Establishing the facts about maternal age and Down syndrome took meticulous work but could not be perfectly accurate because not all fetuses with Down syndrome survive to be born. Genetic problems like Down syndrome cause miscarriages, and some of these losses are so early in a pregnancy that the women do not realize they were pregnant. In other cases of loss during the first couple of months, medical staff may not test the pregnancy tissues to determine whether Down syndrome was present. And, of course, older mothers might choose to terminate pregnancies because they already had all of the children they wanted or because health problems were threats to both mother and baby. In those cases, it's likely that no testing for Down syndrome would take place.

Chromosomal abnormalities other than Down syndrome do not show similar relationships to the mother's age. Of course, older women may have developed illnesses that can have an impact on the baby's development. For example, diabetes is more common among older than among younger women. Older women may also be more likely to have heart and blood pressure problems that endanger the pregnancy. Assuming that the mother is healthy, however, there are only infrequent genetic problems other than Down syndrome to be anticipated for her baby.

Conclusion

As long as an older mother's general health is good, her baby has an excellent chance of good development and good health, with one exception: the increased probability of Down syndrome, a serious birth defect. Marina's health is good, but she will certainly be advised to get prenatal testing for Down syndrome.

CRITICAL THINKING

1. What are three or four other variables that may be confounded with maternal age? For example, would you expect an older mother to have more or less education than a younger mother? Explain your answer. You may want to refer to one of the resources in the reference list for further information.

2. Using a child development textbook for information, identify the time in a mother's life when the original chromosomal error that causes Down syndrome might occur. Describe the events involved in the chromosomal error that caused a case of Down syndrome. Keep in mind that the timetable for development of an ovum is very different from that for a sperm.

3. Does the placenta in a Down syndrome pregnancy also contain cells with an extra chromosome? Explain your answer.

(Continued)

(Continued)

4. Using a child development textbook, read about evocative genetic-environmental correlation. How does this idea relate to Down syndrome and how might it affect a child's degree of mental retardation?

5. A 45-year-old woman recently terminated a pregnancy that had been diagnosed as involving Down syndrome. What is the probability that her subsequent pregnancies will involve a Down syndrome diagnosis? Explain your answer. (You may want to review appropriate material in a statistics textbook as you consider this problem.)

References

deMichelena, M., Burstein, E., Lama, J., & Vasquez, J. (1993). Paternal age as a risk factor for Down syndrome. *American Journal of Medical Genetics, 45*, 679–682.

Hodapp, R. M., Ly, T.V., Fidler, D.J., & Ricci, L. A. (2001). Less stress, more rewarding: Parenting children with Down syndrome. *Parenting: Science and Practice, 1*, 317–337.

Sherman, S. L., Allen, E. G., Bean, L. H., & Freeman, S. B. (2007). Epidemiology of Down syndrome. *Mental Retardation and Developmental Disabilities Research Reviews, 13*, 221–227.

Van Dyke, D., & Lin-Dyken, D. (1993). The new genetics, developmental disabilities, and early intervention. *Infants and Young Children, 5*(4), 8–19.

Van Hooste, A., & Maes, B. (2003). Family factors in the early development of children with Down Syndrome. *Journal of Early Intervention, 25*, 296–309.

Claim 3

If a child's problem is genetically caused, the problem will be present at birth and will stay the same throughout life.

Tom and Cara McDonald have been worried that their children may be at risk for genetic problems. Cara McDonald's grandmother had several miscarriages, and several of her other babies died in infancy. Cara's own mother had no problems, but an aunt had a child who died young. When little Jack McDonald is born in blooming health, the McDonalds relax and forget about their earlier worries.

Are genetic problems present at birth and in the same form throughout a person's lifetime? Or can a genetic problem show up later?

People frequently assume that any genetically caused problem is present at birth and will persist in much the same form throughout a person's life. Conversely, people think that a problem that becomes apparent later in life is caused by an experience with the environment. For instance, the idea that autism has a genetic cause is often rejected by families, who are often heard to make remarks such as this: "The child was perfectly normal at birth and for months afterward. Then he had an immunization or was sick with the flu or had some other experience, and he changed completely. There was no genetic problem because nobody else in our family is autistic—it was the experience that caused the trouble."

Of course, you can't rule out the possibility that an experience caused a child's autism or any other problem, such as cerebral palsy or mental illness, that may not have been diagnosed at birth. But neither can you rule out the possibility that a sudden change is at least partly determined by a genetic component. Even well-understood genetically caused problems do not necessarily have the same symptoms at different stages in development. Rett syndrome is an example of a cognitive and behavioral disturbance that is clearly caused by a genetic problem—in this case, a mutation in a specific gene on the X chromosome. Boys who have this mutation usually die very young, but girls survive. Initially, the girls develop normally, but in late infancy they begin to lose developmental ground. Girls with Rett syndrome display the basic steps in a number of developmental processes, with the beginnings of hand control, mastery of a few words, and walking. But these achievements do not last long. The girls lose the abilities they had developed, begin to wring their hands in a stereotyped way rather than make voluntary movements, and tend to become anxious and irritable as they regress behaviorally (Miller, 2006; Neul & Zoghbi, 2004).

Another good example of the different effects of genes at different ages is Williams syndrome, a condition that develops when certain areas of a chromosome are lost during a stage in the early development of a sperm or ovum. Williams syndrome is not fatal or terribly debilitating, so the ongoing development of affected individuals provides a display of changing genetic effects. Adults with Williams syndrome have some cognitive problems, especially in dealing with quantities. However, they have wonderful language abilities and are at the same time highly sociable and obviously lacking in some kinds of social skills. People with Williams syndrome do not have much social anxiety; thus they do not feel awkward in social situations and do not pay attention to social signals. These social signals provide people with much better social abilities, even though they may feel uncomfortable as a result of social anxiety.

What would you guess about the characteristics of people with Williams syndrome, who are talkative and fluent as adults? Do they learn to talk early? No, in fact they have quite different characteristics as children than as adults. As infants and toddlers, people with Williams syndrome commonly go through several behavioral stages, each different from what you would expect of genetically typical children of the same ages. In the early months, babies with Williams syndrome are intensely colicky, crying frantically and unable to be soothed. Although many other babies experience the apparent stomach pain, distress, and crying referred to as colic, most babies have less severe cases that are resolved earlier than in cases of Williams syndrome.

When children with Williams syndrome emerge from their colicky period, they make contact with other people through their intent stares and a voracious search for eye contact. Genetically typical infants are interested in eye contact, too, and use it for communication with others by the end of the first year, but they quickly move on to use speech as communication—an achievement that is delayed for another year or so in infants with Williams syndrome. When they do start talking, children with Williams syndrome quickly become charming and chatty conversationalists (Dobbs, 2007).

It is easy to tell the difference between the early nontalking stage shown by children with Williams syndrome and their later talkative stage. Although these children have the same genetic makeup from birth, they switch from being unusually silent to being unusually garrulous. Are there any other such reversals in Williams syndrome behavior as children age? One group of researchers looked at the poor number skills of school-age children with Williams syndrome and wondered how they had compared to typical children earlier in their lives. Of course, infants and toddlers cannot do arithmetic, but they can show by preferential looking whether they are paying attention to the number of objects in a group shown to them or simply to the kind of objects they see. When the researchers set up their experiment and compared babies with Williams syndrome to babies with Down syndrome and to genetically typical infants, the babies with Williams syndrome performed better than the others on detecting number differences—again, the opposite of the characteristics seen in their later lives (Paterson, Brown, Gsödl, Johnson, & Karmiloff-Smith, 1999).

If Rett and Williams characteristics are genetically caused, how can they come and go like this? Don't people have the same genetic makeup all of their lives? One possibility has to do with genes turning on or off, functioning or not functioning, a phenomenon that depends on many factors. A gene's activity can be affected by maturational changes, events such as dietary changes or sickness, or other experiences. When a gene is turned on, it helps the cell make a protein, which in turn assists with chemical processes, such as the cell's use of oxygen, and it may do this differently in some cells than in others. When a gene is turned off and the protein is not made, the cell's chemical processes are different than they are when the gene is turned on. Considering that behavioral characteristics result from the functioning of a group of cells, it appears that a change in genetic functioning has the potential to cause a reversal of behavioral characteristics.

However, most human characteristics, behavioral and physical, are caused by the complex effects of multiple genes interacting with complicated environmental events. Although the behaviors of people with Rett and Williams syndromes seem to be based on aspects of single genes, one must keep in mind that the determination of the Rett or Williams phenotype may depend on the influence on other genes when the most significant genes do not operate as they should. It is possible that changes with age in people with Rett and Williams syndromes and, yes, people with autism, may occur because of a combination of events, both genetic and environmental. For example, high levels of stress hormones found in the bodies of girls with Rett syndrome (and measured in their urine) can possibly have a negative effect on brain development. Slowing or alteration of brain development can in turn influence the girls' ability to deal with numbers. More information about these factors may someday enable experts to develop helpful treatments for genetically caused behavior problems. In fact, there have already been efforts to use psychotherapy to help the obsessive-compulsive behavior associated with Williams syndrome (Klein-Tasman & Albano, 2007).

Conclusion

Genetic material does not necessarily function in the same way throughout a lifetime, so even a condition that appears to have come on very suddenly may be due to changes in genetic factors and not to the effects of either pleasant or unpleasant experiences. It is to be hoped that the McDonald baby has no genetic problems, but what can be seen at birth is not necessarily the only effect of genetic material.

CRITICAL THINKING

1. Using a child development textbook, find two disorders that have genetic components but that are not detectable until adulthood. Explain your choices.

2. Why would boys with Rett syndrome die early, whereas girls with the disorder survive with disabilities? Use a child development textbook to find another disorder in which boys are more seriously harmed than girls. What do the two disorders have in common?

3. What role would you expect the intense stare of children with Williams syndrome to play in evoking adult reactions? How might the adults' reactions affect the child's later language development and use?

4. Using a child development textbook, find information about attachment behavior and the friendliness of toddlers with Williams syndrome, as described in the Dobbs (2007) article referenced in this section. What differences do you find between the social behaviors of Williams toddlers and genetically typical toddlers?

5. Is it possible for a boy to have Turner syndrome? Using a child development textbook, find information about genetic control of the development of the reproductive system to explain your answer.

References

Dobbs, D. (2007, July 8). The gregarious brain. *New York Times Magazine*, pp. 43–47.

Klein-Tasman, B. P., & Albano, A. M. (2007). Intensive, short-term cognitive-behavioral treatment of OCD-like behavior with a young adult with Williams Syndrome. *Clinical Case Studies, 6*, 483–492.

Miller, G. (2006). Getting a read on Rett syndrome. *Science, 314*, 1536–1537.

Neul, J. L., & Zoghbi, H. Y. (2004). Rett syndrome: A prototypical neurodevelopmental disorder. *Neuroscientist, 10*, 118–128.

Paterson, S. J., Brown, J. H., Gsödl, M. K., Johnson, M. H., & Karmiloff-Smith, A. (1999). Cognitive modularity and genetic disorders. *Science, 286*, 2355–2358.

Claim 4

Unborn babies are not influenced much by the environment outside the mother's body.

Malinda is pregnant with twins and is getting very big and clumsy. She needs to rest a lot and has time to think about the babies. "Do they listen when I play music?" she wonders. "Sometimes I think they kick in rhythm to it. And what if people talk loudly? I had a fight with my husband the other day, and we called each other some nasty names. We made up later, but I wonder if the babies heard the argument and remember it. My grandmother used to say a baby could get a strawberry mark if a mother ate too many strawberries. I'm sure that's not true, but I wonder about these other things."

How much do Malinda's soon-to-be-born babies actually experience?

Can unborn babies figure out anything that is happening around them? Do they learn from and remember events that occurred during gestation? Or do they start absolutely from scratch with their first experiences on the day they are born?

The unborn human being is in a peculiar position, both literally (upside down, at least toward the end of gestation) and figuratively. Surrounded by protective membranes and cushioning amniotic fluid, the fetus is defended from all but the most direct blows. Even during the early embryonic period, before the membranes and fluid are present, the developing organism is thoroughly protected from impact by the tissues of the mother's body. If a normal pregnancy could be easily damaged by external physical forces, many babies would be lost to injury and abortion clinics would not exist.

On the other hand, an unborn child can be seriously damaged by infectious agents and toxic substances that cross the placenta, which filters out most but not all potentially harmful materials. Harm can thus come to the fetus from some aspects of the environment that penetrate the mother's body, and if this harm includes damage to the brain, later cognitive development may be compromised. The developing individual can even be predisposed to diseases that will not appear until adulthood (Phillips, 2006).

But what about the harmless aspects of the environment? Not every effect of the outside world is a dangerous one. Can the fetus be influenced by external events, either directly or indirectly? Harmful effects are defined by the damage to the physical development of a fetus or by the creation of long-term behavioral or intellectual problems. Are other harmless effects shown in behavioral changes, either temporary or lasting? The abilities of prematurely born babies to see, hear, taste, and smell certainly suggest that a fetus past a certain age of gestation has the sensory capacity to respond to stimulation. Of course, for stimulation to occur, the stimulus must reach the unborn through the tissues of the mother's body, the membranes, and the fluid that surrounds the fetus and fills his or her mouth, nose, and ear canals. Sounds, tastes, and the physical pressures of touch can all do this. Animal studies and some work on human beings have shown that flavorful foods eaten by the mother transfer in taste and smell to the amniotic fluid, as they do later to mother's milk. If a pregnant mother eats garlic, lemon, coffee, or chocolate-flavored foods, the unborn baby experiences those flavors as they pass over the tongue in the amniotic fluid. Rat pups prefer to drink milk flavored with particular tastes that were given to their mother during her pregnancy, and some researchers have speculated that humans like the flavors they experienced prenatally when certain foods were part of their mothers' diets. The taste of the amniotic fluid acts as a "flavor bridge" that encourages a preference for foods frequently served at a family's table (Mennella, 1995; Mennella & Beauchamp, 1993).

Taste experiences are delivered through the amniotic fluid. The flavors' sources are actually inside the mother's body because the mother consumed them. But what about the influence of events that remain external to the mother? Can the fetus hear what is going on in the outside world?

Sound waves can travel through a mother's body and through the amniotic fluid—in fact, they travel faster through solids and liquids than they do through the air. The sounds of a mother's heartbeat are known to penetrate the uterus, and, rather less romantically, the sounds of her stomach and intestines must do so also. Sounds that come from outside the body are also carried into the uterus, but they are muffled by the mother's tissues and partially masked by other simultaneous sounds, such as the maternal heartbeat.

The fetus is not in the ideal situation for listening to details of sounds, especially if the mother has high blood pressure, which changes the transmission of sound to the fetus (Lee, Brown, Hains, & Kisilevsky, 2007).

Because sound, however muffled, can penetrate to the unborn baby and because many hearing functions develop months before birth, it is possible for a baby to "listen" to external sound events, such as people speaking or music. But showing whether the fetus is actually affected by what he or she hears is still unclear. To prove such an effect, the unborn baby's behavior needs to change in a measurable way, either immediately or in a way that can be detected after birth.

Some years ago, a remarkable study concluded that babies can learn from speech sounds heard before birth—not what words mean but rather some information about the sounds and rhythms of language. In their complicated and careful study, DeCasper and Spence (1986) prepared two stories: the familiar *Cat in the Hat* and an alternative version called *Dog in the Fog*. (A third story they used is left out of this discussion for purposes of brevity.) Women who were about 7.5 months pregnant were asked to record the two stories. After they had done so, the women were assigned one of the stories to read aloud twice each day until childbirth. The reading was to be done in a quiet place and at a time when the fetus was "awake" and moving around. These precautions were to ensure that the fetus could hear as clearly as possible and that he or she was as likely as possible to be "listening" to the stories.

About 2 days after the babies were born, the babies were tested for reactions to their mother's recordings of *Cat in the Hat* and *Dog in the Fog*. Each baby was given a nipple with a switch inside it, and by sucking faster or slower the baby could activate the switch and turn on one or the other of the recordings. The researchers wanted to find out whether the babies would change their sucking rate more readily if the change let them hear the familiar story that had been read before they were born or if they would respond more to a chance to hear the unfamiliar story. Their responses were also compared to those of babies who had not heard the stories before they were born. The babies whose mothers had read aloud before they were born changed their behavior more rapidly when the action let them hear the familiar story than when the change turned on the unfamiliar story. Whether the story was *Cat in the Hat* or *Dog in the Fog* did not matter. The babies worked to hear the story that had been read aloud before they were born, suggesting that they had learned from what they heard.

The idea that mothers can "bond" with their unborn babies by talking to them or tapping or rubbing their pregnant bellies is discussed in popular books (Stoppard, 2008), but no research evidence exists to support the idea of intentional maternal–infant communication before birth.

Conclusion

Before birth, babies can experience tastes and sounds and may learn from experiences in ways that can affect their later behavior. It's possible that Malinda's twins will learn a preference for the music she plays before they are born, or for some speech sounds, but they do not understand the words themselves when they hear people speaking.

CRITICAL THINKING

1. If unborn babies learned from sounds, as DeCasper and Spence (1986) concluded, the same should be true of prematurely born babies of the same gestational ages as the read-to fetuses in the DeCasper and Spence study. Describe how you would carry out a similar study to test the effects of hearing a story on prematurely born babies. Use a child development textbook to identify problems of premature babies that your study might need to consider.

2. Use a child development textbook to find information about habituation. Do the facts about habituation suggest that newborn babies would prefer the familiar story or an unfamiliar one? A familiar taste or an unfamiliar one? Explain your answer.

3. In the DeCasper and Spence study, the researchers gave about half of the babies a chance to listen to the familiar story first and the novel story second. For the other half of the group, they reversed the order. What was the point of doing this?

4. Why did DeCasper and Spence assign each mother a story to read aloud only *after* she had recorded both stories? Explain your answer.

5. Some of the studies on prenatal taste experiences were performed on unborn animals. Using the bibliography of a child development textbook, look up the titles of studies cited as relevant to prenatal and newborn development. What proportion appear to have involved human subjects and what proportion involved animals? Are there problems or advantages to this situation? Keep in mind that the goal of studying child development is the understanding of events in human life.

References

DeCasper, A. J., & Spence, M. J. (1986). Prenatal maternal speech influences newborns' perception of speech. *Infant Behavior and Development, 9,* 133–150.

Lee, C. T., Brown, C. A., Hains, S. M. J., & Kisilevsky, B. S. (2007). Fetal development: Voice processing in normotensive and hypertensive pregnancies. *Biological Research for Nursing, 8,* 272–282.

Mennella, J. A. (1995). Mother's milk: A medium for early flavor experiences. *Journal of Human Lactation, 11,* 39–45.

Mennella, J., & Beauchamp, G. (1993). Early flavor experiences: When do they start? *Zero to Three, 14*(2), 1–7.

Phillips, D. I. W. (2006). External influences on the fetus and their long-term consequences. *Lupus, 15,* 794–800.

Stoppard, M. (2008). *Bonding before birth.* New York: DK Publishing.

Claim 5

As a mother-to-be gets closer to the date when her child will be born, she needs to be more careful about alcohol and drugs, because the risk of birth defects increases throughout pregnancy.

Twenty-year-old Jennifer did not plan to become pregnant, but she decided to go forward with the pregnancy that surprised her and her boyfriend. While considering what to do about the pregnancy, Jennifer continued her usual life and did not tell too many people what was happening. Now, at about 5 months into her pregnancy, her clothes are getting tight, and even the people she has not told are beginning to get the picture. When she goes out to a bar one night, a friend tells her, "Hey, you better taper off. Your baby is getting big, so you shouldn't be drinking."

Is Jennifer's friend right about this?

The idea that an unborn baby becomes more vulnerable as it progresses toward birth and life as a "real person" is one that strikes people as intuitively correct. Most people know that in sufficient quantities drugs and alcohol can do real harm to adults; thus, people assume that as an unborn child begins to resemble an adult more closely, its needs and vulnerabilities become more like those of adults, too.

The idea that a baby is more vulnerable to harm as it nears birth also matches the subjective experience of pregnant women. In the early weeks and even early months of pregnancy, women usually do not "feel pregnant." They have no real sense of a developing organism inside their bodies. Instead, they feel like their ordinary nonpregnant selves, but selves who are a little sick, queasy, or extra tired, as if coming down with the flu. Some pregnant women find it hard to believe that anything they do can affect a growing child, whose existence is not even obvious. In the second trimester (4th–6th month of pregnancy), most women experience *fetal embodiment*— a sense of the unborn child as within and a part of the mother's body—and an accompanying sense of worry about possible harm to the baby. In the last trimester of pregnancy, the baby's growth and movement capture a lot of the mother's attention and she usually begins to think about the baby as a separate person from herself, potentially threatened by dangers, such as the events of birth. Many mothers are aware of what an unborn baby does, whether it is awake, kicking and moving, or quiet. If the baby is quiet for too long, the mother may become anxious and seek help and assurance that her unborn child is still alive.

Unfortunately, the actual vulnerability of an unborn baby follows quite a different pattern from the mother's feelings about it (Meyer, Yee, & Feldon, 2007). The possibility that birth defects will be caused by drugs, alcohol, or disease is by far the greatest in the *early* part of the pregnancy, from about Day 18 to Day 56 after conception. Day 18 is only a few days after the mother misses her first menstrual period. By the time the mother feels worried about injury to the fetus, much less danger to development is possible.

To understand this situation, examine the events in early development. As the fertilized ovum moves into the uterus, it divides into a clump of cells that are much like each other; though there is some differentiation, the cells are *equipotential*—they have the possibility of developing into any of the various cells that will make up the body. After implantation in the wall of the uterus, during about Day 14 to Day 18 after conception, the cells begin to divide and differentiate so that new cells that are produced are not necessarily identical to the cells that gave rise to them. During the *embryonic* period of development, all of the types of cells that will be needed are produced, and the foundations for all of the body's organs are established—if an organ system is missing at this time, it will not develop later. After Day 56, when the *fetal* period begins, much less differentiation occurs.

Major birth defects, such as the absence of a limb, the development of the heart or intestines outside of the chest, or a cleft palate can occur because of an environmental effect that interrupts differentiation and prevents the formation of a needed cell type. Such environmental events may be avoidable (e.g., alcohol or drug use) or not so avoidable (e.g., exposure to a contagious disease or a food toxin). In all cases, the event stops a part of cell differentiation, and as a result a body part never develops as it should (Shonkoff & Phillips, 2000).

Although many women are not certain that they are pregnant during this especially vulnerable time, they may experience a form of protection that is outside their control and often unpleasant: *morning sickness* or *pregnancy sickness*—an unaccustomed queasiness or even vomiting that can occur at any time of day, not just in the morning. Pregnancy sickness often includes sensitivity to unusual flavors and strong smells, especially smells of food. Perhaps this increased sensitivity prevents women in early pregnancy from consuming foods that may be partly spoiled or contaminated. A slightly deteriorated food may be eaten by a nonpregnant person, who notes that it's a bit "off" but not too bad; a woman in early pregnancy may find the taste so disgusting that she refuses to eat it. Unfortunately, people cannot depend on smells and flavors to provide complete protection, as some dangerous food contaminants do not change the taste.

Why doesn't differentiation start again after the contaminated food, or drug or toxin, has passed through the mother's body? This would be an excellent way to prevent birth defects if it could be managed, but it is not the way early development works. Genetic information encoded in the cells defines *what* differentiation will happen and *when* it will occur. The schedule of differentiation is built into the species and cannot be changed. If a process is interrupted, there is no time in the schedule to repeat or correct it; instead, that process—the differentiation of a type of cell—is bypassed, and as a consequence the foundation of a body part fails to be built, resulting in a birth defect.

One part of an unborn baby's development continues to be vulnerable into the period when the mother becomes most concerned, the last trimester— brain development. The complex human brain results from other complicated processes in addition to differentiation of new cell types. Brain cells move from place to place to form elaborate patterns, such as the six cell layers of the cortex. The brain cells also form multiple connections with each other, enabling them to send messages from one part of the brain to another. These developmental processes can also be disrupted by environmental events (e.g., contagious disease), but the result of the disruption is a functional problem—as in the case of mental retardation, for example—not an obvious physical defect, such as a shortened limb.

Of course, normal development depends on the presence of needed factors, not just the absence of harmful ones. A mother's diet plays an important role in supporting developmental change as well as simple growth in size (Ricciotti, 2008). But again, as is the case for alcohol and drugs, the timing of dietary and other effects on development helps to determine the outcome (Brodsky & Christou, 2004).

In addition to the effects of drugs and alcohol on the still-developing brain during the fetal period, drinking and drug use during late pregnancy are likely to continue after childbirth. Although a baby's physical development is no longer directly affected by the mother's intake of toxins (unless the mother is breastfeeding), it is clear that drug and alcohol use indirectly interfere with the sensitivity and responsiveness of caregivers and therefore have a real impact on later child development.

Do pregnant women take these facts into consideration? One study of women in Denmark concluded that almost 90% reduced their alcohol intake when they became pregnant—but 40% of them still had one alcohol binge during the pregnancy (Kesmodel, Kesmodel, Larsen, & Secher, 2003). Although this is not the best outcome, it does show that education about drinking in pregnancy is having an effect.

Conclusion

The most vulnerable period of prenatal development actually occurs very early, before many women are even aware that they are pregnant. At this time, environmental events are most likely to cause major birth defects. If any harm was to come to Jennifer's baby as a result of prenatal alcohol exposure, much of it has probably already happened, although problems of brain development are still possible. However, even if her present drinking does no harm, Jennifer would do well to develop drinking habits that allow for the baby's need for sensitive, consistent care.

CRITICAL THINKING

1. Using a child development textbook for information, define the term *teratogen*. Are all birth defects caused by teratogens? Explain your answer.

2. Would you expect a specific type of birth defect, such as cleft palate, to occur because of the *kind* of teratogen encountered or because of the *timing* of the encounter? Use the book *From Neurons to Neighborhoods* (Shonkoff & Phillips, 2000) to find information about this issue. Explain.

3. Would you expect teenage mothers or older mothers to have more trouble understanding prevention of birth defects? Using a child development textbook, find information about adolescent physical and cognitive development and use your findings to formulate your answer.

4. Could you use the information in this section to determine the cause of a particular child's birth defect? Explain your answer.

5. What confounded variables might make it difficult to investigate whether birth defects are caused by alcohol or drugs? (Remember, confounding variables are factors that commonly accompany the events under study—in this case, alcohol and drug use. Confounding variables make it difficult to know which of many possible events actually caused an outcome.) You should use a child development textbook to find information about the role of genetics in habitual alcohol use.

References

Brodsky, D., & Christou, H. (2004). Current concepts in intrauterine growth restriction. *Journal of Intensive Care Medicine, 19,* 307–319.

Kesmodel, U., Kesmodel, P. S., Larsen, A., & Secher, N. J. (2003). Use of alcohol and illicit drugs among pregnant Danish women, 1998. *Scandinavian Journal of Public Health, 31,* 5–11.

Meyer, U., Yee, B. K., & Feldon, J. (2007). The neurodevelopmental impact of prenatal infections at different times of pregnancy: The earlier the worse? *The Neuroscientist, 13,* 241–256.

Ricciotti, H. A. (2008). Nutrition and lifestyle for a healthy pregnancy. *American Journal of Lifestyle Medicine, 2,* 151–158.

Shonkoff, J., & Phillips, D. A. (Eds.). (2000). *From neurons to neighborhoods: The science of early childhood development.* Washington, DC: National Academy Press.

Claim 6

If a woman who is taking antidepressant medication becomes pregnant, she should stop taking the drugs because they may cause birth defects in her baby.

Melody is in her late 30s and is planning to marry soon. She has had a long history of depression and was anorexic in her early 20s. She is doing well now but has been taking antidepressants for a couple of years. Melody and her fiancé would like to have children and are worried about her ability to conceive because it is already late in her reproductive life. They are also very concerned that her antidepressants will cause problems in a baby's prenatal development.

Should Melody stop taking her medication now to provide the best possible prenatal environment when she does become pregnant?

Depression is more common among women of childbearing age than among other groups of people. This is one reason for concern about the effects of antidepressant medications on early development—the people who are most likely to need the medications are also the ones who may become pregnant. In addition, pregnancy is normally a time of some emotional turmoil rather than a uniformly calm, cheerful period. Given these facts, one can conclude that a number of newly pregnant women may be experiencing emotional distress at a level that needs treatment.

Antidepressant drugs can be very effective, but of course any medication during pregnancy needs to be investigated for *teratogenic risk*—the probability of causing birth defects. Drugs that affect the mother's central nervous system (and probably the unborn baby's) are of special concern. Although the time of greatest risk of birth defects is in the earlier part of a pregnancy, continuing brain development can be disturbed by medications taken later in pregnancy as well.

Does this mean that women with a history of depression should avoid the use of medication if they become pregnant? And what about those whose first pregnancies are accompanied by a first-time depression? The question seems simple, but the answer is not (Niebyl, 2005). Any answer must balance the risk of birth defects caused by antidepressant medication against other possible causes of birth defects as well as the effect of depression on the mother's later ability to care for the infant.

One difficulty with answering this question is the presence of many confounded variables. For example, a real problem is that untreated, depressed mothers-to-be may self-medicate with alcohol, tobacco, and over-the-counter or street drugs to escape tormenting emotions. Serious depression involves more than a few hours of crankiness or depressed mood; the disorder lasts for days or months and subjects sufferers to an inescapable sense of sadness, dread, and self-blame. Without antidepressant medication to blunt these painful feelings, depressed women may seek out other means of escape, which may have more serious teratogenic potential than the small risks that have been documented for many modern antidepressant drugs. Avoiding antidepressants for fear of birth defects makes little sense if the mother-to-be turns for comfort to other teratogens. These may include "alternative" or "natural" medications whose effects have not been thoroughly studied (Woodward, 2005).

Other potential effects of depression also complicate the issue. Depression during and following pregnancy—often known as *perinatal mood disorder*—can seriously affect a mother's ability to care for herself during her pregnancy and for her infant after birth. If the child of the current pregnancy is not the mother's first, care for and relationships with older children in the home may also be negatively affected. Ill effects of depression on relationships with a spouse, friends, parents, and siblings may deprive the new mother of social networks when she most needs support to help her meet the demands of infant care.

Most women (50% to 70%) with new babies experience a bout of the *baby blues*: A new mother may cry easily, feel overwhelmed and incompetent, and fear that she will never get "back to normal." These experiences are uncomfortable but do not last more than a couple of weeks and do not need substantial treatment, especially if the mother has never been depressed before. A bout of the baby blues does not prevent a mother from taking good care of her baby.

A smaller number of women, about 10%, suffer from serious depression beginning about 6 weeks after the baby's birth. Many of these women also experienced depression during their pregnancy. They feel sad and tired but have trouble sleeping, may feel anxious and guilty, and may be disturbed by involuntary thoughts about harming themselves or their babies.

These mothers do not in fact directly harm their babies, but their depressed feelings and thoughts make them less sensitive and responsive to their baby's needs than is desirable. The early months of infants' lives are normally a time when mothers learn how to comfort their babies and talk to them in ways that help babies begin to pay more attention to language. Nondepressed mothers normally speak in a cheerful tone, have a responsive face, and employ a special energetic way of talking to babies that attracts the babies to social interactions that are mutually fun. These social interactions help both mother and child begin an affectionate relationship. This goal is much more difficult for depressed mothers. Maternal depression saps a mother's energy and interest in her baby. She may perform basic child care chores, but they provide little of the enrichment that encourages good early development (Brennan et al., 2000). In addition, the mother's depression may damage her relationship with the baby's father, possibly causing the marriage to break up and deprive the baby of contact with his or her father.

A very small proportion, far less than 1%, of new mothers have such serious emotional disturbance that they become psychotic and, if untreated, may harm their children. Some of the women who become so seriously disturbed have shown depression during pregnancy and following the births of previous children. Psychosis following childbirth is far from common, but a discussion of treatment during pregnancy needs to take into account this possible outcome of untreated emotional disturbance (Spinelli, 2004).

Of course, substances other than antidepressant medication may lead to more risk of birth defects, and some of these are more likely to be experienced by women of childbearing age rather than by other groups. For example, some research has suggested that prenatal exposure to chemicals used by manicurists may cause long-term cognitive, language, and behavior problems as well as physical effects in children (Greenhouse, 2007).

Conclusion

Although medication for depression during pregnancy has a slight chance of causing birth defects, on balance it appears that a baby's development is subject to more harmful influences if the mother is not treated rather than if she is. Melody's previous history of depression suggests that it would be wise for her to continue her antidepressant medicine both now as she is considering pregnancy and after she is pregnant. She needs to consult carefully with the professionals who provide her medical and psychological care.

CRITICAL THINKING

1. Can a woman who avoids antidepressants during pregnancy be sure that her baby will be born without birth defects? Use a child development textbook as a reference when explaining your answer.

2. In the article by Brennan et al. (2000), the authors investigated children's vocabulary development as well as their behavior. Why would the mothers' depression be expected to affect their child's vocabulary?

3. Other than the occurrence of birth defects caused by medication, how would you think effective treatment of depression during pregnancy would affect both a mother's health and that of her baby in the first year after birth?

4. Read about the Andrea Yates case in the article by Spinelli (2004). How did Yates's case differ from more common cases of maternal depression?

5. Use a child development textbook to find information about children's relationships with their fathers. Comment on how a child's development might be affected if the father rather than the mother experienced serious depression.

References

Brennan, P. A., Hammen, C., Andersen, M. J., Bor, W., Najman, J. M., & Williams, G. M. (2000). Chronicity, severity, and timing of maternal depressive symptoms: Relationships with child outcomes at age 5. *Developmental Psychology, 36*, 759–765.

Greenhouse, S. (2007, August 19). Studies highlight hazards of manicurists' chemicals. *New York Times*, 26.

Niebyl, J. R. (2005). Antidepressant drug use in pregnancy. *Journal of the Society for Gynecologic Investigation, 12*, 297.

Spinelli, M. G. (2004). Maternal infanticide associated with mental illness: Prevention and the promise of saved lives. *American Journal of Psychiatry, 161*, 1548–1557.

Woodward, K. N. (2005). The potential impact of the use of homeopathic and herbal remedies on monitoring the safety of prescription products. *Human and Experimental Toxicology, 24*, 219–233.

Claim 7

Mothers care for their babies well because they have a maternal instinct.

Joan's mother was worried when Joan became pregnant with her first child. "She's never even played with baby dolls. She doesn't take any interest in her brother's new baby. How is she going to take care of this child when it comes?"

"Don't worry," replied her friend. "Joan has a maternal instinct like anybody else. As soon as the baby is born, she'll know what to do."

Was the friend right, or should Joan's mother be concerned?

Our first step in analyzing this claim is to deal with definitions. The word *instinct* is one whose technical meaning has shifted over the years, as well as one that is only loosely defined by most of its users. *Maternal instinct* is even more uncertainly defined. Partly as a result of these problems of definition, little research focuses directly on the question of human maternal instinct. Thus, our discussion of maternal instinct must consider research on related topics and on logical connections between observations. These approaches require reasoning by analogy, a form of logic that can be abused by overgeneralization or by unjustified leaps of reasoning.

In addition to these logical difficulties, a very wide range of caregiving behaviors of human mothers (and fathers too) must be considered: from devoted care to severe neglect to even murder of children as well as the modern, puzzling phenomenon of surrogate motherhood, in which a child is conceived and borne by one woman and given to other people for parenting (Baslington, 2002).

What are the possible definitions of *maternal instinct*? Most people who say that actions are *instinctive* mean that people do not need to learn certain things from experience; instead, they are "born knowing how," even though they may not display what they know until they are older or until they are in the right circumstances, such as that of caring for a baby. Saying that something is instinctive may also mean that it is automatic—the individual does not have to think about what to do but immediately starts to do the right thing as soon as the opportunity presents itself. *Maternal instincts* by definition occur only in mothers and involve behaviors that mothers need to do to ensure their babies' survival. In other words, according to these definitions, maternal instincts in human beings closely resemble the tendencies of nonhuman animals to care for their babies without instruction or previous experience.

The implication of this definition of human maternal instincts is that human mothers do not have to learn how to take care of their babies because they have inborn skills and knowledge as animals do. In other words, the existence of a maternal instinct, as defined previously, means that both animal and human females are immediately able to address their infants' needs and are also willing and even eager to care for their young.

Let's start our consideration of this belief by thinking about the comparison of human mothers with animal mothers implied in this statement about "instincts." It is obviously true that animals do not read Dr. Spock's writings or consult the Internet, and much of their caregiving seems to occur without specific learning having occurred. However, some important additional points need to be made about animal behaviors. First, most newborn animals are far more competent than human babies are; animal young can creep to the mother's body to stay warm and to nurse or, like baby birds, can signal for food just by opening their mouths wide. These babies can do without the complicated care that human infants need for optimal development: The jobs of animal mothers are not usually as complicated as the jobs of human mothers. Second, good care of animal young is by no means universal among animal mothers, who may abandon or even kill their young. Sows of some breeds are famous for lying down on their piglets and crushing them if the farmer has not carefully removed each as it is born. Nervous, high-strung racehorse mares may be frightened of their own foals and attack them. Rats and mice eat their placentas and any dead or dying pups and occasionally consume the rest of the litter while they are at it. Maternal behavior among animals is not necessarily what we want to see in human mothers, so reasoning from animal to human maternal behavior may involve a mistaken analogy.

What's more, many questions about the "instinctive" nature of animal mothering exist. People who use *instinctive* to mean that a female animal performs her caregiving the same way despite her previous experiences are quite wrong. In fact, experimental work with animals shows that experiences during pregnancy can make it less likely that an animal mother will do her job properly. For example, a female rat normally goes to work licking clean all of her pups after birth, removing fluids and bits of membrane that make it impossible for the young to breathe. However, if during the pregnancy the mother is prevented from licking her own body, she is less likely to do the cleanup, and the pups may die. Another aspect of the animal mother's experience involves monitoring the young. One of a mother rat's big jobs is to retrieve pups that have climbed out of the nest and cannot find their way back, thus leaving them vulnerable to cold, hunger, or danger. A virgin female rat that is placed with some pups does not do a very good job of retrieval, but after a few days of experience she improves and even begins to secrete hormones that resemble those of a mother rat with pups.

These examples show that animal maternal instincts are not inborn, at least not in their complete form. Another important aspect of animal mothering is that the mother cares best for young that are active, healthy, and demanding. Animal mothers are much more likely to neglect or even kill and eat babies that are quiet and inactive, which of course are the ones most likely to be sick or injured at birth.

In examining the claim that there is a human maternal instinct, one needs to consider first what it would mean to claim that human mothers follow the same behavior patterns as animal mothers, and for the same reasons. Animals display many forms of poor mothering, including infanticide, as well as many examples of devoted caregiving. To claim an instinctual basis for mothering is thus not the same as explaining how and why good mothering occurs. Human mothers do not carry out common animal mothering tasks, such as licking fluid, membranes, and feces off their babies, so their specific actions are not comparable to those of animals. However, humans, like animals, show a mixed record of good and bad caregiving. The existence of cruel or careless actions of mothers toward their babies would thus not argue against human maternal instincts.

When considering animal mothers, one can see that mothering activities are just about the same for every member of a given species. Mother goats act in ways that are like other mother goats, mother sheep resemble other mother sheep, and so on. These similarities among species members are one of the reasons why people think of animal mothers' behaviors as instinctive. No such statement is true about human beings, however. When considering the issue of maternal instinct from an entirely human perspective, one needs to consider the most common and essential child care routines, such as feeding and cleaning.

Observations show that infant care varies considerably from culture to culture. Mothers learn from instruction or observation the "right" ways—as defined by their society—to hold, feed, clean, and play with their babies. There appears to be no "natural" form of mothering, unaffected by learning. What and how infants should be fed, whether they should sleep alone or with their parents—these basic care questions are answered very differently in different cultural groups, suggesting that human mothers learn at least some of their ways of rearing babies. It might be thought that the process of breastfeeding is instinctive, but in fact mothers in different cultures follow somewhat different breastfeeding patterns, and a new mother who has never seen a baby breastfed may need a lot of help to do a successful job.

In considering animal mothering, people should note that circumstances such as the health of the young have a strong influence on a mother's caregiving. For humans, too, much evidence exists showing that circumstances have serious effects on maternal care, whether for good or for ill. The baby's health, responsiveness, and appearance all influence the mother and encourage or discourage her care activities. Poverty and emotional trauma make it less likely that a mother will be eager to care for her child. In the slums of Brazil, as elsewhere, poor mothers have been reported to feel that some babies "don't want to live" and therefore should not be fed (Scheper-Hughes, 1992).

The circumstances that determine how well a mother cares for her baby may be related to the mother's attitudes and emotions that were present even before pregnancy. Some authors have suggested that caregiving is influenced by the mother's beliefs about her own mothering abilities and that those beliefs in turn may emerge from the mother's feelings about her own vulnerability and her faith that other people will help her (Farrow & Blissett, 2007). However, these ideas about a mother's attitudes remain substantially untested.

One interesting point to consider about human maternal instincts is that human mothers are not the only people to care for young children. Fathers frequently do at least some part of the caregiving. In the United States today, grandparents, brothers or sisters, and babysitters or day care providers do part of the caregiving of children, and in other parts of the world the "child nurse" tradition puts little girls to work minding younger children. To define behavior as instinctive when it can be carried out by people of different ages, genders, and relationships with the baby seems to make the term meaningless.

As is the case for many myths and misunderstandings, the issue of human maternal instinct has a practical as well as an abstract side. The belief that mothers instinctively care for babies can be a dangerous one. People who share this belief are less likely than others to see the importance of support and education intended to prevent child abuse and neglect. The belief in human maternal instinct also increases the chances that the public will punish and reject abusive mothers as inhuman—lacking in the normal instinctive makeup shared by other human beings (Barnett, 2006). Realizing the effect of circumstances in determining how well mothering is performed can encourage us to work toward social changes that protect children and prevent abusive treatment.

Conclusion

Human mothers do not automatically know how to care for their babies, and women without caregiving experience can benefit from guidance and instruction. Joan's mother cannot make Joan learn more about the needs of a baby, but she might want to gently assist Joan to have more experiences with young children before her own baby is born. Maternal instinct cannot be counted on to guarantee good caregiving.

CRITICAL THINKING

1. Are there terms other than *instinct* that you would need to define before analyzing the claim discussed in this section? (Keep in mind that human babies are not always cared for by their biological mothers.)

2. Develop operational definitions for two important terms in this essay, other than *mother*, *child*, and *maternal*.

3. What kinds of information would be helpful in a discussion about maternal instinct? List three sources of information and state their relevance to the claim. Would these sources include personal experiences or anecdotes? Why or why not? The Farrow and Blissett article (2007) provides helpful information to answer this question.

4. Can a researcher compare two cultural groups to find out whether one has better child care patterns than the other? What confounding variables would make it difficult to know whether one child care pattern is better?

5. What aspects of a baby's appearance and behavior may cause adults to care for him or her? If a baby causes adults to provide care, would you say that the situation fits your definition of *instinct*? Explain your answer. Scheper-Hughes (1992) provides some relevant information.

References

Barnett, B. (2006). Medea in the media: Narrative and myth in newspaper coverage of women who kill their children. *Journalism, 7*, 411–432.

Baslington, H. (2002). The social organization of surrogacy: Relinquishing a baby and the role of payment in the psychological detachment process. *Journal of Health Psychology, 7*, 57–71.

Farrow, C., & Blissett, J. (2007). The development of maternal self-esteem. *Infant Mental Health Journal, 28*(5), 517–535.

Scheper-Hughes, N. (1992). *Death without weeping.* Berkeley: University of California Press.

Claim 8

Babies work hard to be born.

Marcus heard two people in his office talking about a New Age treatment called rebirthing, and he asked them to explain the concept. "You wrap a person up in a blanket, and then they wiggle and kick to get out of it, just like they did when they were born. It's like starting all over again as a new person." Marcus wasn't sure whether wiggling out of a blanket would make anyone start anew, but he thought a baby might have to fight to be born, so he could see that this method was like being born all over again. But as he thought it over, he wondered how a baby could wiggle to be born but couldn't crawl until 5 or 6 months of age.

Was Marcus right to question the notion of a struggle to be born?

Do babies wiggle and kick their way out of the birth canal? People often assign intentions to unborn infants (e.g., "I guess he'll get born when he decides to"), and the idea that a baby achieves birth through his or her own efforts may be a way people have of thinking of babies as competent and independent even before birth. The belief that a baby is in charge of birth also shows up in some fringe psychotherapies, such as rebirthing, in which a child or an adult pushes through a narrow passage in an imitation of the birth process, sometimes while helpers push rhythmically against the "baby" as if mimicking the contractions of the uterus. The goal of this ceremony seems to be a symbolic new beginning, thus leaving behind the problems of earlier life.

In reality, the baby during birth is passively subjected to the physical forces of the uterus and eventually to the pressures of the mother's voluntary pushing. The first step in the process is one that no infant could accomplish voluntarily: the gradual enlargement of the cervical opening. As the baby lies head down (typically) in the uterus, contractions of the powerful uterine muscles repeatedly force the baby's head downward against the ring of muscle that has held the bag-shaped uterus closed. Slowly, the repeated pressure of the head stretches the cervix to a width that the head can pass through. Because the head is the largest and least flexible part of the fetus, the rest of the body can follow the head through the same opening.

As the head moves down into the vagina, the process becomes more complicated, but the baby remains passive—acted upon rather than acting. The head and body need to pass through a channel that is solidly backed by the mother's pelvic bones. Whereas the cervix was able to stretch to let the baby be moved out of the uterus, the bony structure of the pelvis prevents the tissues of the vagina from yielding as much under pressure. Instead, the baby's head has to yield and the body to shift position for the birth to be successful.

The baby's skull is not a solid bony structure of the kind seen in adult skeletons but instead is a series of bony plates, each incompletely developed and quite soft compared to adult bones. These plates are placed under considerable pressure as the uterus continues to contract, push the baby's body down, and thus press the baby's head against the bony structures behind the tissues of the birth canal. The skull yields under these pressures and is gradually molded into a longer, narrower shape that is able to pass through the narrow outlet between the mother's pelvic bones. (In most cases, the "deformed" skull returns to its rounder shape in a few days without any help.)

At this point in the birth process, the baby's physical makeup and position become especially important, but the baby does not contribute any intentional movements. There is turning and twisting to be done, but these movements occur mechanically because of physical pressures, not because of the baby's efforts.

The oval shape of the human female pelvic outlet makes it easier for the head to pass through when the baby "looks" toward the mother's back. But if the baby's head were straight on the shoulders, this position would mean that the shoulders would be cross-wise in the narrow part of the pelvic outlet. For the shoulders to line up with the long axis of the pelvic outlet—and pass through—the baby needs to be in essence looking over its shoulder, with its face toward the mother's back. This position is typically produced gradually as the baby's body is slowly moved into the right position by the repeated pressure of contractions. The baby must have a normally flexible neck, or the repositioning will not be possible.

What is the baby doing all this time if not trying to be born? The baby is actually being the greatest help to the birth process by inhibiting movements and going along with the mechanical pressures exerted on his or her body. Unlike newly born or older babies, who respond to stress by fighting and yelling, babies during birth display the paralysis reflex. Babies in the birth canal move very little and use no more oxygen than usual—almost as if they have gone to sleep in the midst of the pushing and pressure (Lagerkrantz & Slotkin, 1986).

Before and during birth, babies are very unlikely to fight or make an effort to be born. They have a limited amount of oxygen, which they receive from the mother's lungs via her bloodstream and the umbilical cord. Babies outside the womb breathe and can take in oxygen faster when it is needed for a vigorous effort. Conversely, if an unborn baby tries to increase activity beyond a certain point, the baby will start to asphyxiate as the need for oxygen surpasses the supply. The fetus cannot make his or her mother breathe faster or use any source of oxygen other than the mother's lungs to increase the oxygen supply. Therefore, the unborn baby's environment in the uterus limits it to a quiet, passive response to strong stimulation like that of birth.

Although young humans tend to be resilient and able to recover from harmful influences, it is a mistake to think of babies as "in charge" of their development and birth. On the contrary, fetuses and newborn infants are passive recipients of a wide variety of factors that affect birth and health outcomes, including ethnicity and other genetic factors and the mothers' use of drugs and alcohol, her diet, and her level of prenatal care (Shiao, Andrews, & Helmreich, 2005). Preterm births due to infection or other pregnancy complications are among the most serious problems for infants, and it would be quite unreasonable to imagine that a weak, thin, premature baby would be able to struggle to be born.

Conclusion

Babies do not work to be born but instead become quiet and passive during the process, a strategy that aids birth much more effectively than any effort or movement could do. Marcus's officemates misunderstood how babies behave during birth, and their misunderstanding made them accept a practice that is probably not helpful and is potentially harmful.

CRITICAL THINKING

1. How might an apparently minor problem in a baby, such as a stiff neck, affect a birth? How would a baby's position in the uterus head up or head down affect what happens during birth? Explain.

2. Because adults dislike stress and physical pressure, they may think that birth is painful and unpleasant for a baby. Using a child development textbook, find information about birth by Cesarean section. Do the difference between Cesarean and vaginally born babies suggest that the latter have suffered during the birth process? (Don't forget about the baby's production of stress hormones, which is discussed in Lagerkrantz & Slotkin, 1986.) Explain your answer.

3. How is a baby's brain protected when the skull is pressed and molded during the birth process? Does birth entail dangers to a baby's brain other than physical pressure?

4. Find out how long different parts of labor and delivery last. What is the period of time when pressure on a baby's head is most intense? Consult a child development textbook to provide evidence for your answer.

5. Consider the source of oxygen for a fetus before and during birth. What does this situation imply for becoming passive under the stress of birth, rather than crying and struggling? How do matters change when the baby cries for the first time?

References

Lagerkrantz, H., & Slotkin, T. H. (1986). The "stress" of being born. *Scientific American, 254,* 100–107.

Shiao, S.-Y. P. K., Andrews, C. M., & Helmreich, R. J. (2005). Maternal race/ethnicity and predictors of pregnancy and infant outcomes. *Biological Research for Nursing, 7,* 55–66.

Claim 9

"Crack babies" can't be cured and will always have serious problems.

Maria and Ric's children had grown up and were on their own, and the couple began to think about becoming foster parents. They were aware that many children had parents who could not take care of them but did not want them to be adopted. Social service workers told Maria and Ric about a baby whose mother was in prison on drug charges but hoped to get her family back together when she was released. Maria and Ric were enthusiastic, but then Ric thought of something. "What kinds of drugs did the mother do?" he asked. "Is this a crack baby? If it is, we won't take it. They have too many problems. I saw in the paper that they never have normal intelligence or behavior no matter what you do."

Was Ric's attitude justified by the facts about crack-exposed children?

Publicity about increased use of crack cocaine in the 1990s culminated in the term *crack baby*, used to describe a child who had been prenatally exposed to this form of cocaine. Newspaper and television reports emphasized the idea that prenatal crack exposure essentially broke the baby, who could never recover from such an experience (Thomas, 2000).

Teratogenic birth defects are certainly one possible outcome of prenatal exposure to drugs, some of which can cross the placenta and disrupt events of early development. However, not all street drugs seem to cause birth defects. Heroin, for example, is not associated with specific birth defects, such as cleft palate or learning impairment. Neither is cocaine—and, in fact, crack babies do not have obvious specific birth defects at a higher rate than non–drug-exposed babies do. When crack babies do have birth defects, they are generally associated with the time during gestation when the babies were exposed to cocaine, not to the cocaine effects alone.

It does seem surprising that cocaine-exposed babies do not have more obvious physical problems. The level of drugs that the unborn baby experiences is much higher than the level in the mother's bloodstream, and the developing brain would be expected to be quite vulnerable to the drug's effects. Because it seems so likely that an unborn baby would be affected by cocaine exposure, researchers have searched for subtle problems that might result from changes in brain development, including sensory problems, such as visual or auditory impairment; cognitive problems of memory or problem solving; emotional difficulties, such as impulsiveness; and motor problems caused by inappropriate messages sent from the brain to the muscles (Bono, Sheinberg, Scott, & Claussen, 2007).

The major problem related to cocaine exposure seems to be physical stiffness. Increased or decreased muscle tension in different parts of the body can be due to differences in motor messages sent from the central nervous system and can produce stiffness or floppiness in a baby's body. Crack babies tend to extend their limbs (move them away from the trunk) more readily than to flex them (move them toward the trunk), and as a result they have trouble with actions such as sitting, which involve flexion. This may seem to be a very minor problem, but the sitting position is an important part of experience, allowing babies to use their hands to reach, grasp, and bring things to their mouth, thus practicing hand-mouth and then hand-eye coordination. Stiff babies who are placed in a sitting position tend to fall backward as they extend their arms and legs, so it is difficult for them to practice using their hands for looking and reaching. Fortunately, like adults who suffer from sore, stiff muscles, crack-exposed babies benefit from stretching exercises and practice with flexing and can achieve the changes that allow them to sit, reach, and grasp in a normal way. Of course, a baby cannot be instructed to perform stretches alone; he or she needs a caregiver who will work intensively, and with sensitivity, to develop the physical abilities the baby needs.

Specific birth defects are obviously a matter of serious concern, but evidence of the rarity of specific defects does not establish crack as a safe prenatal experience. Drugs can cause worrisome outcomes other than physical deformities. For example, cocaine ingestion can decrease blood flow to the mother's uterus, reducing the amount of oxygen and nutrients delivered to the fetus. Such reduction in blood and oxygen can alter the fetus's own blood circulation and result in prenatal stroke—the bursting of blood vessels in the brain—with consequent severe damage to brain cells. These events can cause serious problems, but they are not problems specific to cocaine because other drugs or events can have similar effects.

Like other women who use drugs or large amounts of alcohol, crack users often have extremely poor diets and lack appropriate medical care. Poor maternal nutrition during pregnancy affects both the mother's health and that of her unborn baby and may cause low birth weight as well as dangerous nutritional deficiencies. The absence of medical care may result in other poor health practices and in a failure to treat diseases such as syphilis and gonorrhea, which may affect a fetus's health and development. Again, however, these are general effects, not specifically caused by crack, and may be found in babies whose mothers never used crack but have had poor health practices and diet for other reasons.

Premature birth is more common among crack users than among nonusers. The contraction of blood vessels characteristic of cocaine's effects can cause an abrupt beginning of labor and the delivery of a premature infant who has all of the many problems associated with premature birth. Once again, although prematurity may be caused by crack use, premature birth is unfortunately far from uncommon, and its effects are similar, no matter what caused the early birth.

Newborns who have been exposed to heroin or to barbiturate drugs are likely to show withdrawal symptoms similar to those of adult addicts who are deprived of their usual drug intake. This withdrawal syndrome does not seem to occur with crack-exposed babies, or at least it has been difficult to tell such problems from the ones caused by prematurity or other factors. Of course, it is very possible that a baby who has been exposed to crack has also been exposed prenatally to other drugs, and those may cause withdrawal symptoms. A "crack baby" may well be a "heroin baby" or a "meth baby" at the same time.

When thinking about outcomes for crack-exposed babies, it is important to consider the effects of being cared for by crack-using parents (Smith, Johnson, Pears, Fisher, & DeGarmo, 2007). Like other drugs, crack distracts adults' attention from the baby and decreases the sensitivity and responsiveness that encourage good early development. Crack has been reported to have a particularly powerful effect on the user's attention; unlike heroin, crack cocaine is not used in a scheduled way that allows for some of the normal behavior essential to infant care. In addition, if crack is smoked in the home, an infant can inhale secondary smoke, just as with cigarette smoking. Although the mother's use of crack is the primary factor before the baby's birth, the father's use of the drug becomes equally important after birth. Although prenatal crack exposure does not necessarily mean that a child will suffer abuse, it may be a good indication that social services are needed by the family (Doris, Meguid, Thomas, Blatt, & Eckenrode, 2006).

Each of the problems described here is to some extent treatable and surmountable, but as the risk factors multiply, the chance of normal development for crack-exposed babies is reduced. Risk factors can operate to produce other subsequent risk factors. For example, drug-exposed children often have language delays that may be due both to the prenatal drug use and to the social environment they experience after birth. Language delays can lead to other developmental problems, such as aggressive social behavior and disobedience, and can delay literacy, causing school failure and frustration. Early intervention has been reported to help correct these problems (Bono et al., 2005).

Conclusion

Although prenatal crack exposure is not associated with specific birth defects, other factors, such as poor maternal diet and health care, premature birth, and poor infant care, may combine to create serious long-term problems of development that are difficult to cure. Ric's concerns are at least partially justified, but the problems he worries about are caused by multiple factors, not by crack alone.

CRITICAL THINKING

1. Using a child development textbook, find information to cite in a discussion about the influence of genetics on the problems described in this essay. Would you expect the effects of crack exposure to be the same for all infants? Explain your answer.

2. Discuss how timing of crack use influences the problems described in this section. Use evidence from a child development textbook to support your answer.

3. What assumptions did Thomas (2000) make about crack effects? Consider effects both on individuals and on schools.

4. When a pregnant woman uses crack, what other likely characteristics of her lifestyle can affect her child, either before or after birth? Use the articles by Bono, Bolzani Dinehart, et al. (2005) and Bono, Sheinberg, et al. (2007) for more information.

5. Assuming that an exposed infant stays in its mother's care, and she continues to use crack, what effect on the child's language development would you anticipate by the time he or she reaches school age? Explain your answer.

References

Bono, K. E., Bolzani Dinehart, L. H., Claussen, A. H., Scott, K. G., Mundy, P. C., & Katz, L. F. (2005). Early intervention with children prenatally exposed to cocaine: Expansion with multiple cohorts. *Journal of Early Intervention*, 27, 268–284.

Bono, K. E., Sheinberg, N., Scott, K. G., & Claussen, A. H. (2007). Early intervention for children prenatally exposed to cocaine. *Infants and Young Children*, 20(1), 26–37.

Doris, J. L., Meguid, V., Thomas, M., Blatt, S., & Eckenrode, J. (2006). Prenatal cocaine exposure and child welfare outcomes. *Child Maltreatment*, 11, 326–337.

Smith, D. K., Johnson, A. B., Pears, K. C., Fisher, P. A., & DeGarmo, D. S. (2007). Child maltreatment and foster care: Unpacking the effects of prenatal and post-natal parental substance abuse. *Child Maltreatment*, 12, 150–160.

Thomas, J. Y. (2000). Falling through the cracks: Crack-exposed children in the U.S. public schools: An educational policy issue. *Journal of Educational Policy*, 15, 575–583.

PART II

Infants and Toddlers

Claim 10

Parents need to have contact with their babies right after birth, so they can bond with them.

When Eric and Tina's little girl, Emma, was born, there were some minor problems for both mother and baby. Emma was taken away to be watched and cared for in a special nursery, and her parents did not get to hold her until the next day. Now Emma is a happy, healthy, lively 2-year-old. When Eric was asked how she was doing, he replied, "Oh, very well, especially considering that we never got a chance to bond with her."

Does a parent's relationship with a child really depend on immediate contact after the child is born?

Many of the beliefs discussed in this book date back centuries, but the claim that parents require early contact to bond with their babies began in the 1970s. It had its origin in a much-publicized research project carried out by M. H. Klaus and J. H. Kennell (1982; Klaus, Kennell, & Klaus, 2001). Although these researchers later noted some errors of analysis and interpretation and tried to soften the impact of their report, the public continues to favor a simplified version of the story.

To understand the issues involved requires a good definition of bonding. Bonding is one of those things that few can define, but everybody thinks they "know it when they see it." The researchers (Klaus & Kennell, 1982) who originally used the term later tried to clarify that they were not comparing human relationships to chemical glues. Bonding, they later said, was not necessarily instantaneous nor was it a process that made each member of a pair equally concerned and involved with the other. Instead, *bonding* is an emotional development in which an adult begins to have powerful, positive feelings toward an infant, to be preoccupied with, concerned with, and prepared to make any sacrifice for that baby. Although most parents develop these strong positive feelings, some do not (Sluckin, 1998).

Bonding may begin in anticipation of a birth or an adoption, but it progresses through contact with the baby who is the object of the bonding. Bonding may involve very quick development of strong feelings, like falling in love at first sight, or it may take weeks or months to develop. In either case, however, the issue is an emotional change in the adult, not in the infant, although the baby's later emotional development is influenced by the care of a devoted—or an indifferent—caregiver.

Unfortunately for researchers' understanding of bonding, the adult's emotional change is not signaled by some simple observable event. There is no litmus test for bonding, although many attempts have been made to assess the nature of maternal–infant interaction and the way this interaction reflects the mother's emotions (Horowitz, Logsdon, & Anderson, 2005). Emotional changes often lead to behavior changes, so one can look for behaviors that might indicate bonding. Generally, bonding is associated with increased attention to the baby, such as looking, talking, and touching. But these actions are very much affected by individual personality and cultural factors. For example, a naturally quiet or depressed mother may not talk much compared with a more outgoing person or one in better mental health. Without a measure of the mother's behavior before birth, there is no way to know which behavior is the effect of bonding and which is the effect of other factors in the mother's life.

Cultural factors and social expectations also play a part in bonding. A middle-class American woman (who has heard all about bonding) may look at and talk to her baby as frequently as she thinks makes her a good mother, but women from some traditional societies may avoid too much looking and talking, wishing as they do to avoid attracting the attention of harmful spirits to their babies. For these traditional women, avoiding looking too much at their baby may indicate their deep emotional involvement, whereas looking freely might indicate that they are indifferent.

Because it is so hard to measure some bonding-related behaviors, and much harder to measure bonding itself, early research on this topic looked at other factors that could be measured easily, such as the timing of a mother's first contact with her infant after birth and aspects of the baby's development. Researchers speculated that bonding might only be possible when infants are extremely young. However, in the United States at that time, customary practice gave most mothers only a glimpse of their babies shortly after birth. According to hospital routine, babies were taken to a nursery, where the staff pediatrician, who usually came in only once a day for this purpose, examined the infant before the child had more contact with the mother. (During this time in history, fathers were not significantly involved at this point of newborn care.) Such practices would be less than ideal if it were true that early contact was needed for bonding purposes.

As the issue of timing of mother–infant contact received more attention, researchers became interested in comparing how mothers and babies would react in two different situations—an arrangement by which mother and baby spent time together in the first few hours after birth versus the then-customary delayed contact. A change in hospital policy in one city made it possible to carry out a study that was close to the ideal of a randomized comparison. As the hospital switched from a delayed-contact to an early-contact policy, researchers were able to compare mothers and babies with births in the last days of the old policy to those with births in the first days of the new policy. It seemed reasonable to think that chance alone determined whether a baby was born during one week or during the next week, so any differences between the groups of mothers and babies ought to be related to their experiences with early or delayed contact. In fact, the early contact babies were later reported to perform better on several measures, including language development at age 5 years, and the mothers were judged to be more attentive and affectionate.

Discussion of this research focused on the idea that the mothers had responded to early contact with their babies by better bonding, that bonding had led to improved relationships and more attentive and sensitive baby care, and that improved care had resulted in improved child development. But should you conclude that all of this is correct—that early contact causes bonding, bonding causes good child care and development, and therefore all families need to have early contact with their babies? No, there are several problems with those conclusions. Very few mothers and babies were in the study, causing statistical problems. (Most statistical tests are intended for use with large numbers of participants and have problems with the biases that may be associated with small groups.) It was difficult to know how to interpret certain measures, such as the length of breastfeeding time. And all of the mothers were very young and poor and experiencing practical problems, such as where to live and how to care for their babies. Problems like these are not characteristic of older, more educated, more affluent mothers, who may not respond in the same way to early contact as the younger mothers did. Mothers' care of infants and infant development are probably affected by many factors working together, rather than simply by early contact and the events referred to as bonding. For example, the mothers' own childhood experiences may affect the ways they think about and respond to their children (Jefferis & Oliver, 2006).

However, parents usually receive a lot of pleasure from holding their baby very soon after birth, and this is a good enough reason to allow and encourage early contact with healthy babies.

Conclusion

It is hard to measure how parents "fall in love" with their babies, and existing research does not make it very clear that early contact is necessary for good relationships and development. Emma was developing very well, and obviously her parents were doing the right things for her. Eric and Tina might have been saved some worry if they had not believed that early contact could make such a big difference in their daughter's progress.

CRITICAL THINKING

1. Using a child development textbook for information, comment on the importance of a mother's age, education, and socioeconomic status for her baby's development. How might these factors be related to bonding?

2. Describe the differences between attachment and bonding. Use evidence from a child development textbook in your description.

3. Use the Internet to access four or five commercial Web sites offering information about infant and child care and parenting. How do the sites define bonding and attachment?

4. With respect to the research discussed in this section, should you be concerned about confounding variables and generalizability? Explain your answer.

5. Using information from a child development textbook and this section, argue for or against the idea that studies of animals can be useful in understanding how human parents react to their babies. Be sure to consider relevant research discussed in textbooks, such as Harry Harlow's studies of infant monkeys that were raised in isolation and their later reactions to their own infants.

References

Horowitz, J. A., Logsdon, M. C., & Anderson, J. K. (2005). Measurement of maternal-infant interaction. *Journal of the American Psychiatric Nurses Association, 11,* 164–172.

Jefferis, P. G., & Oliver, C. (2006). Associations between maternal childrearing cognitions and conduct problems in young children. *Clinical Child Psychology and Psychiatry, 11,* 83–102.

Klaus, M. H., & Kennell, J. H. (1982). *Parent-infant bonding.* St. Louis, MO: C.V. Mosby.

Klaus, M. H., Kennell, J. H., & Klaus, P. (2001). *Bonding: Building the foundations of secure attachment and independence.* New York: Perseus.

Sluckin, A. (1998). Bonding failure: "I don't know this baby, she's nothing to do with me." *Clinical Child Psychology and Psychiatry, 3,* 11–24.

Claim 11

Babies are born with emotional attachments to their mothers and can recognize their mothers at once.

Linda was very excited about her first baby, soon to be born. "I've carried her all this time, and I just can't wait to get a look at her! It will be so wonderful when she sees me and knows I'm her mommy! We'll just look and look at each other."

Linda's excitement is a very positive sign, but will she be disappointed with her baby's response to her? Will the baby know her? How might you tell?

Attachment and recognition are not the same thing, although of course a baby would have to recognize a person in some way before he or she could show attachment. Because recognition has to come first, examination of this claim must begin with the baby's relevant experiences and abilities for recognition. Can a newborn baby recognize his or her mother—by sight or in any other way?

Recognizing a person involves remembering a previous experience with him or her, either a visual experience of the face or some other detail, such as posture or movement. Memory for another person can also be based on recognition of the voice or a characteristic smell or taste (e.g., the taste of the mother's milk). Or memory and recognition can be based on touch sensations, such as skin texture, warmth, or pressure exerted in holding. After a few weeks of life, a baby has had many opportunities to learn about sensory experiences with parents and other caregivers, but at the time of birth a baby has had no opportunities for the experiences of touch, sight, or smell and only limited experiences for taste (through the amniotic fluid) and hearing (sound waves passing through the mother's body). Newborns can perform some complex perceptual tasks (e.g., noticing that an object they see has changed in both shape and movement; Laplante, Orr, Vorkapich, & Neville, 2000), but this does not necessarily mean that they can deal with all the characteristics that make up a human face or voice, even if they had seen or heard the person before.

It is possible that newborns can recognize their mother's voice. Babies' hearing is much better developed than their vision, and they have already experienced hearing the sound waves that travel through their mother's body into the uterus—even though their mother's voice must sound a lot different after it passes through skin, muscle, and fluid than when it is heard through air. There does seem to be evidence that newborns can recognize their own mother's voice. Infants will work (by sucking on a nipple) to hear their mother's voice rather than that of other women (DeCasper & Fifer, 1980). However, it is impossible to know whether the baby's response shows simply the recognition of a voice the baby has heard before or whether the baby recognizes his or her mother as a person who has a special role in the baby's life. Because babies tested weeks after birth do not seem to respond with very different emotions to their mothers than to other people, it seems most unlikely that newborns have such a complex set of feelings and thoughts as those associated with emotional attachment.

Within days after birth, infants recognize the smell of their mother's milk and turn toward it, if they have been breastfed. (Bottle-fed babies do not do this.) Breastfed infants possibly learned the smell after birth, although some evidence suggests that unborn babies learn the smells and tastes of their mother's food through their experiences with the amniotic fluid inside the uterus (Mennella & Beauchamp, 1993).

As for recognizing the mother by sight, newborn infants have such limited vision that they would probably have difficulty recognizing an individual face, no matter how well known it is, for several reasons. For one, babies are only able to get a well-focused visual picture when objects are between 8 and 12 inches from their eyes. Anything too close or too distant is just a blur. The ideal looking distance is achieved when a caregiver holds a baby and bends his or her face toward the child's— and because well-cared-for infants frequently experience this type of contact, they have plenty of opportunities to become familiar with their mother's face or that of another frequent caregiver. Within a few weeks, babies can show that they remember their mother's face in one specific way; given several faces at which to look at different times, babies spend the most time looking at their own mother's face.

Infants also experience hearing their caregivers' voices, either talking or singing. Within a few months, babies may become interested or calmed in response to their mother's singing (Shenfield, Trehub, & Nakata, 2003), but it is not clear whether this response happens at birth.

What about attachment, though? Newborns seem to have some ways of recognizing familiar experiences with another person. Do these experiences have any emotional meaning for babies? Is a familiar person an important person, from a baby's viewpoint? Keep in mind how the baby feels, not how the mother feels. A mother would be distraught if she thought her baby had been kidnapped or was very sick. Does the baby feel any type of similar concern about separation from the mother, the father, or any other family member? *Attachment* is usually defined as a type of emotional connection where there is distress about separation and increased comfort when the attached person is reunited with the other.

Although there are standardized techniques for evaluating a 12-month-old's emotional attachment to an adult (Ainsworth, Blehar, Waters, & Wall, 1978), no such methods exist for newborns. Generally, emotional attachment is thought to be indicated when one person tries to stay near another or shows distress and grief when separated from another. Newborn babies have little ability to try to stay near someone because they cannot walk or even crawl. They can only maintain contact by crying and getting an older person to come to them. However, newborns seem to cry because of physical discomfort, not because someone leaves them. They will accept feeding and care from any adult, not just from their mother. If separated from their mother (e.g., by adoption), the youngest infants do not appear to grieve or to be distressed. Only after about 8 months of age are babies likely to show intense disturbance over abrupt, long-term separations. They cry, look sad, and have trouble sleeping and eating, unlike the youngest babies. These facts suggest that newborns have no emotional attachment to their mother but develop this important emotional response over a number of months of contact.

The evidence seems to show that newborns have no emotional attachment to the mother and only limited recognition of her. Yet many readers have observed that a baby's mother can calm a crying newborn when other adults are unsuccessful. Doesn't this mean that the baby knows and cares for his or her mother? In light of the previous evidence, this does not seem likely, and an alternative explanation must be considered: that the mother behaves in ways that other adults do not. The mother is genuinely concerned and highly motivated to comfort her baby and therefore persists in rocking, humming, and patting when others give up. In addition, the mother, who is often the primary caregiver, quickly develops experience with her baby and within a few days may be more aware than others of "what works" to soothe her baby.

The belief that newborns are emotionally attached to their mother has important implications for practical decisions about adoption, foster care, and infant day care. Babies in the first months of life are not likely to show distress when separated from their mother. This means that infant distress in a new situation means something about the situation itself—for example, a day care center may have too few or inexperienced caregivers, and a baby may protest against clumsy or even rough handling. A baby who complains in the first months of life generally has something specific to complain about. He or she is not anxious about separation, and certainly the infant of this age is not trying to control or manipulate adults.

New mothers who expect their babies to show strong attachment behaviors right away may be disappointed, withdraw from their baby, and start the new relationship on a rocky pathway. It is important for parents and other adults to understand that attachment is a gradual process. Mothers who experience depression during pregnancy or after their baby is born may be especially vulnerable to sad feelings about a baby who "doesn't love" them in the way the mothers believed would happen. Fortunately, newborns typically do enough to make parents feel that their baby cares about them. They look at adults' faces and eyes when nearby and often calm and relax in response to a parent's attempts to soothe them. These responses are good enough to start the parent-child relationship, and soon babies are so active and responsive that their parents are locked into their emotional connection. As the months go on, babies become attached and show the attachment in their behavior.

Conclusion

Newborn babies do not really recognize their mothers and do not show any emotional attachment to them. However, Linda's baby should behave sociably enough toward her, so she will probably not feel disappointed. Before long, the two will develop an affectionate relationship.

CRITICAL THINKING

1. Using a child development textbook as a source, create a definition of emotional attachment that works for the material discussed in this section. To work, your definition needs to apply to the relationship between adult caregivers and infants or young children, and it needs to focus on the feelings of the babies, not the adults.

2. Is your definition an operational definition? *Operational definitions* involve the ways an observer can measure whether an event or a phenomenon is present—for example, you might operationally define *anxiety* in a child in terms of the amount of time that a child spends crying and looking away from a person or an object. If your definition of attachment was not an operational definition, change your definition so it involves measurement of some kind.

3. Find and read the DeCasper and Fifer (1980) article. How did the authors choose the mothers and babies who participated in their study? If they had chosen differently, how might the outcome of the study have been affected?

4. Find and read any article that describes the Strange Situation, discussed by Ainsworth and her colleagues (1978) and most child development textbook authors. For which age group was this observational technique designed? Would you expect either younger or older children to behave in the same way as the group in the study? Citing information in your textbook or other sources, describe several reasons why you might expect children of other ages to behave differently.

5. Use information from a child development textbook to describe some ways in which you could test the vision of newborn babies. Remember that they cannot name letters of the alphabet as adults can, nor can they point to right or left as preschool children do during a vision test.

References

Ainsworth, M., Blehar, M., Waters, E., & Wall, S. (1978). *Patterns of attachment.* Hillside, NJ: Lawrence Erlbaum.

DeCasper, A., & Fifer, W. (1980). Of human bonding: Infants prefer their mothers' voices. *Science, 208,* 1174–1176.

Laplante, D. P., Orr, R. R., Vorkapich, L., & Neville, K. E. (2000). Multiple dimension processing by newborns. *International Journal of Behavioral Development, 24,* 231–240.

Menella, J., & Beauchamp, G. (1993). Early flavor experiences: When do they start? *Zero to Three, 14*(2), 1–7.

Shenfield, T., Trehub, S. E., & Nakata, T. (2003). Maternal singing modulates infant arousal. *Psychology of Music, 31,* 365–375.

Claim 12

Babies cannot see when they are first born.

Al and Janet were happy when Al's sister gave a baby shower for them, but Al thought it did not make much sense for someone to give them a mobile for the baby's crib. He thanked the donor, but later he said to his sister, "What's up with that, anyway? It's going to be months before this kid can see anything, even after his eyes are open. I wish she'd given us something we could use sooner."

Is the baby going to be able to see the mobile before many months pass? And how will anyone know if this happens?

A few people assume that human newborns cannot see—and that they have their eyes closed, like young kittens or puppies. Full-term newborns certainly have their eyes open, and very young preterm babies who might be born with sealed eyelids would be too immature to survive and develop normally. And, of course, newborns often have their eyes closed because they are sleepy, are avoiding a bright light, or are busy concentrating on something important, such as nursing.

Given that a new baby's eyelids are open, is it possible for him or her to see? To answer this question, researchers needed to figure out how to ask babies about their experience of vision. Of course, researchers needed to ask in some way other than speech, which is not yet possible for very young infants. Nonverbal methods of asking questions are a good deal different from the techniques eye doctors use to figure out the vision correction adults might need.

An example of a nonverbal way to question a baby would be a preferential looking method. This involves, for example, holding two cards with different sizes of stripes in front of a baby and measuring how much time the baby spends looking at each one. If the baby looks at both cards for the same amount of time, one can conclude that the baby cannot tell the difference between the cards and may not be able to see stripes that are too small (or, oddly enough, too large). Only if the baby looks at one card more than the other is it assumed that the baby can tell the difference and thus must be able to detect at least one set of stripes. (To get an accurate measurement, the baby must be tested a number of times, with each striped card sometimes on the left and sometimes on the right; otherwise, there may be confusion with a baby's simple preference for looking toward one side rather than the other.) The baby's vision may also be tested through *optokinetic nystagmus*, an automatic eye movement that occurs when an image moves past the eyes. If the stripes (or other pattern) are too small, the baby will not see them and his or her eyes will not move when the pattern moves.

Tests like these show that newborns have worse *acuity*, or vision for small details, than adults do. Months of development must pass before babies have a much-improved ability to see details. Testing also shows that newborns have very little ability to detect colors, and the pastels so popular for nurseries probably all look the same to new babies. Other research shows that babies also have poor depth perception in the early months and do not use their eyes in tandem the way older children and adults do.

Looking at the anatomy of the newborn eye, researchers found a couple of important structural and functional differences from the eyes of older humans. One difference is that the newborn eye does not have many *receptors*, or light-sensitive cells, which explains why babies cannot detect small details. The other important difference is that the lens inside a baby's eye is not capable of *accommodation*, the change in thickness of the structure inside the eyes that enables an older person to get equally clear pictures of near and distant objects. A baby's lens is "stuck" at the thickness needed for a particular distance—about 8 to 12 inches from the eye—and only objects at that distance look clear. Objects that are farther or nearer, such as mobiles, appear fuzzy.

Beyond the question of what newborns are actually able to see, what babies like to look at and what circumstances make them likely to look must be considered. There is no way to tell if a baby can see an object but simply lacks interest in it. From what has been discussed so far, it seems unlikely that newborns notice color differences or pay much attention to them. They do pay attention to complicated, moving patterns, especially those that are at the right distance from their eyes. A good example of an interesting object for a baby is a human face with bright eyes that moves its gaze from place to place. If the owner of that face held the baby upright with the baby's face about a foot away, the situation would be ideal for the baby to do some looking. And, rather surprisingly, it has been shown that newborns can actually imitate facial expressions of people who are facing them, by opening their mouths or sticking out their tongues (Meltzoff & Moore, 1983).

However little or much a baby may be able to see soon after birth, it is not possible for the infant to recognize the looks of either people or objects at first exposure. Prenatal life goes on in complete darkness and without any chance to see or learn about faces and other objects. Only after having some opportunities to see does the young infant get a chance to remember and recognize, and even that will be difficult for many months after birth. Having the ability for vision does not mean the baby has adult visual skills and all the thoughts and memories associated with vision. Preterm or sick newborns are sometimes given beds with pictures of their families on the sides, which really cannot have any direct benefit for the infant—but if it makes the parents feel better, there is probably some indirect advantage for the baby.

Even though a newborn's vision seems to be limited, visual ability may play a most important role even in early life. Human beings use their eyes to communicate and signal emotional reactions to each other. Parents find it thrilling when their baby makes "eye contact," and they work hard to get their baby to look at them. These sustained interactions may be a foundation for social and emotional relationships, and babies or parents with visual impairments may need help in finding other ways to communicate with each other (Dale & Salt, 2008).

Conclusion

Newborns have vision, but it is quite limited, and they would have a lot of trouble seeing an object as far over their heads as a hanging mobile above a crib. But Al's baby will show interest in a complicated, moving object (e.g., a human being) in weeks, not months, even though his vision will not be really good for some time.

CRITICAL THINKING

1. Using the information in this section, discuss the possible effect of a mobile on a newborn child. Keep in mind that mobiles vary in size, distance from the baby's eyes, and color. (Use a child development textbook to be sure that your definition of *newborn* is correct.) What kind of mobile would you design to elicit a response from a newborn?

(Continued)

(Continued)

2. The article by Meltzoff and Moore (1983) describes how a newborn can imitate the facial expressions of an adult. Read the article and explain how the researchers allowed for infants' visual weaknesses.

3. How does an adult face fit the pattern of things babies prefer to look at? Use a child development textbook to put together a list of patterns and other characteristics babies look at for long periods of time.

4. Use a child development textbook to find information about habituation. What effect would habituation have on the amount of time a baby looked at a pattern? Would this factor influence measurements of a baby's visual ability?

5. Use a child development textbook to find information about standard medical treatments performed immediately after birth that might temporarily affect a newborn's vision.

References

Dale, N., & Salt, A. (2008). Social identity, autism and visual impairment (VI) in the early years. *British Journal of Visual Impairment, 26,* 135–146.

Meltzoff, A. N., & Moore, K. M. (1983). Newborn infants imitate adult facial gestures. *Child Development, 54,* 702–709.

Claim 13

A baby's sleeping position can cause or prevent sudden infant death syndrome.

Angie's mother always told her that it was a good idea for her to keep her baby in bed with her at night. That way, she said, Angie could nurse the baby frequently and everybody could get some sleep. But when Angie took the baby to the pediatrician for her first checkup, she saw a lot of posters and pamphlets that said parents should not take a baby into their bed. To Angie's surprise, the resources also said not to put a baby to sleep facedown in a crib. The pamphlets warned that sleeping with parents or in a prone (facedown) sleeping position might result in SIDS—sudden infant death syndrome. Naturally, Angie was terrified at the idea that she might find her baby dead in her crib one morning. But when she tried to put her little daughter to sleep on her back, the baby cried and could not seem to relax.

What could she do? Is the facedown position really so risky? After all, Angie and all of her brothers and sisters had slept that way as infants and had developed well.

This claim is one that involves many variables, confused or confounded with each other in ways that make it quite difficult to conclude that a particular factor has caused an outcome. This is often the case when people try to understand the effects of practices that parents have chosen. Parents do not make their choices—of sleeping position or other caregiving techniques—at random but instead make decisions that are connected with their own personalities, cultures, education, and lifestyles. Each of those broader factors brings with it more variables that can influence an infant's life and health, so deciding on cause and effect can be almost impossible.

Sudden infant death syndrome is a term used to describe the unexpected death of an infant during sleep, without any serious signs or symptoms of illness even a few hours before death. Also called SIDS or crib death, this phenomenon most often occurs in babies between 2 and 4 months of age. The victims may have had slight colds, but otherwise they appeared healthy. Death by SIDS is rare, with a rate of 0.7 occurrences per 1,000 babies in the United States in 2000. (Figures on problems of this kind are surprisingly hard to get because they involve the time-consuming collection of information in counties and then in states and finally calculations that show the rate for the entire country.)

Though SIDS is rare, the possibility of SIDS is a source of anxiety for parents, who are deeply concerned about protecting their babies and fearful of finding them unresponsive in their crib. Parents' natural concerns are worsened by the knowledge that SIDS deaths have sometimes been followed by accusations that the death was due to neglect or even to murder. Because some such accusations have turned out to be true, the most innocent parents may be regarded with suspicion by friends and neighbors and may even suspect each other, adding serious anxieties to their grief for their lost infant.

In the early 1990s, reports from other countries, such as New Zealand, suggested that the prone (facedown) sleeping position might be a factor in SIDS and that the rate of SIDS deaths might be reduced by putting babies to sleep in the supine (faceup) position and making sure that no soft bedding could interfere with a baby's breathing. SIDS rates were reported to decrease when parents used a supine sleeping position for their babies in the first few months of life. (Babies eventually learn to turn over by themselves, so there is a limit to how long their sleeping position can be managed—but SIDS becomes much less likely after the 4th month of age, in any case.) Subsequently, pediatricians and government officials in the United States began to promulgate the Back to Sleep program, a parent-education program advocating the supine sleeping position. They argued that infants whose sleeping posture was supine were much less likely to die of SIDS. However, not all parents use the supine position, and not all physicians recommend it (Moon, Kington, Oden, Iglesias, & Hauck, 2007).

SIDS rates dropped after the Back to Sleep program began. Can this fact be interpreted to mean that supine sleeping caused the change in SIDS mortality? It is unusual for a single factor to be the cause of a developmental outcome—for example, a child's growth in height and the age when a child first walks have multiple causes—and it would be surprising if SIDS deaths had a single cause. But another issue is of importance here: that SIDS rates in the United States were already decreasing during the periods 1989–1991 and 1995–1998, before the Back to Sleep movement was well underway. Whatever factors were causing that decrease may have been responsible for the continuing reduction in SIDS rates in later years. Sleeping position may have been one among many factors—or it may not have been a causal factor at all.

Statistical analysis of data can explain many things, but it alone cannot tell whether one factor caused another. The only way to determine causality is through experimental work that can control for confounded variables. However, continuing analysis of data on SIDS shows that multiple factors seem to be connected with this type of infant mortality. For example, the presence of environmental tobacco smoke is associated with an increased SIDS rate. Surprisingly, babies are *less* likely to die of SIDS when they are sucking pacifiers.

Factors such as secondhand smoke, pacifiers, and sleeping position may directly affect the likelihood that a given baby will die of SIDS, or these factors may simply be associated and confused with other confounding variables. For example, more educated parents are less likely to smoke near their babies, so it is not possible to know whether the effect of environmental tobacco smoke on SIDS is a direct one or whether the parents' educational level makes them reluctant to smoke *and* causes them to behave differently in some other, unidentified way that is relevant to SIDS. For example, although researchers have concluded that bed sharing with adults is not actually an important risk factor for SIDS (Kattwinkel, Havek, Moon, Malloy, & Willinger, 2006), they do conclude that both breast-feeding (McVea, Turner, & Peppler, 2000) and the use of pacifiers (Schwartz & Guthrie, 2008) make SIDS less likely. These factors are also connected with educational level.

Other issues to consider are classification and reporting of infant deaths. Could the dropping SIDS rate indicate that infant deaths are being categorized in different ways than before, so the reported figures are changed even though there is no "real" change in the rate? Statistical analysis of possible causes of SIDS would certainly be affected by including or excluding particular deaths from the SIDS category. Deaths of infants that fit the rather general earlier description may or may not be classified as SIDS. In fact, at least two other classifications are possible when a sleeping infant is found dead and no obvious reason for the death is evident (there are actually three, if

murder is included). One such category is "accidental suffocation and stran-
gulation in bed" (ASSB); deaths in the second category are classed as "cause
unknown/unspecified." U.S. infant death statistics show that during the
1990s SIDS rates decreased and the rates of the other two categories did not
change; from 1999 to 2001, however, the continued decline in SIDS rates
was accompanied by an *increase* in rates of death from the other two
categories. The changed rates may thus have resulted from decreased classification and reporting of infant deaths as due to SIDS, and increased classification and reporting in the other categories, rather than a real change in
the hard-to-determine actual causes of death (Shapiro-Mendoza, Tomashek,
Anderson, & Wingo, 2006).

Conclusion

Although most parents want to follow all possible advice about protecting
their babies from SIDS, including using a supine sleeping position, it is by no
means certain that changes in sleeping position have caused changes in SIDS
rates in the United States. In fact, decreased SIDS rates may result primarily
from changes in classification and reporting of infant deaths. Angie may
decide that her baby's health and comfort—and her own—are better
achieved by a prone sleeping position, with a pacifier and without exposure
to tobacco smoke, and that the risk of SIDS is very small indeed.

CRITICAL THINKING

1. Describe three possible confounded variables that would confuse conclusions
   from your study if you compared families who offer their babies pacifiers
   with those who do not. Explain why these factors make it difficult to know
   whether pacifier use has any effect on SIDS.

2. About half of unexpected infant deaths occur while babies are sleeping with
   their parents. What characteristics or behaviors of babies might make the
   parents more likely to take a baby into their bed? What characteristics of
   the parents might make this more likely? How might such characteristics be
   related to infant death?

3. Using a child development textbook for information, discuss one or two
   other early childhood problems that might have their known rates affected
   by classification (diagnosis) and reporting. Explain your answers.

4. Babies sleeping with parents are most likely to die unexpectedly when the two are sleeping on a couch or in an armchair. What characteristics of parent or baby could cause this sleeping arrangement? What characteristics could cause infant death? Would some of those characteristics also be associated with infant death? Use a child development textbook to find information about factors such as temperament. The article by Kattwinkel et al. (2006) is also helpful.

5. Prone infant sleeping positions have been recommended and popular in the United States for the past 100 years. What differences might there be between caregivers who kept the "traditional" prone position and those who followed advice to use a supine position? How would these differences contribute to differences in SIDS rates? Use a child development textbook to explore health and child-rearing differences between demographic groups. Keep in mind that some groups are more likely than others to have grandparents caring for infants.

References

Kattwinkel, J., Havek, F. R., Moon, R. Y., Malloy, M., & Willinger, M. (2006). Bedsharing with unimpaired parents is not an important risk for sudden infant death syndrome: In reply. *Pediatrics, 117*(3), 994–996.

McVea, K. L. S. P., Turner, P. D., & Peppler, D. K. (2000). The role of breast-feeding in sudden infant death syndrome. *Journal of Human Lactation, 16,* 13–20.

Moon, R. Y., Kington, M., Oden, R., Iglesias, J., & Hauck, F. R. (2007). Physician recommendations regarding SIDS risk reduction: A national survey of pediatricians and family physicians. *Clinical Pediatrics, 46,* 791–800.

Schwartz, R. H., & Guthrie, K. L. (2008). Infant pacifiers: An overview. *Clinical Pediatrics, 47,* 327–331.

Shapiro-Mendoza, C. K., Tomashek, K. M., Anderson, R. N., & Wingo, J. (2006). Recent national trends in sudden, unexpected infant deaths: More evidence supporting a change in classification or reporting. *American Journal of Epidemiology, 163*(8), 762–769.

Claim 14

Development of the brain is caused by experience, so it's possible to cause quick cognitive or emotional changes by stimulating a child's brain in the right way.

Two-year-old Camillo had a terrifying experience with his family when their house caught fire. Although no one was badly hurt, they lost all their possessions, including their two dogs. Camillo's mother suffered from smoke inhalation and was treated at the scene, then taken to the hospital for a night of observation. The family was asleep when the fire broke out, so Camillo woke to screams, shouts, running feet, and breaking glass. Now he becomes frantic when his parents try to put him to bed and falls asleep on the floor, exhausted. His grandfather looked on the Internet for help and found a number of Web sites that offer to cure emotional trauma by methods ranging from neurofeedback to tapping on parts of the body.

Can these kinds of stimulation make Camillo's brain return to its normal patterns of sleeping and calm behavior?

The idea that brain development is caused by experience is far from completely true. It would be much more accurate to say that some of the development of some parts of the brain is guided by experience. Certainly, some parts of the brain show a good deal of *plasticity*—the capacity to develop in ways shaped by experience with the environment. Deliberate stimulation of the brain cannot cause cognitive or emotional changes unless the part of the brain in question is one that normally develops as a result of experiences.

The visual cortex, the area that receives and organizes information from the eyes, is probably the best example of plasticity. This part of the brain can only function well if it has developed in a way that lets people combine and coordinate pictures from the two eyes so that the world can be seen in three dimensions rather than two flat images, one from the right and one from the left. To do a good job, the visual cortex has to take into account the distance between the two eyes, which determines how similar or different the two pictures will be. But that distance changes as a baby's head grows, especially during the rapid growth period of the first year of life. The visual cortex must fine-tune its operations bit by bit until the distance between the eyes has reached the size it will have through childhood and adulthood.

Fine-tuning of the visual cortex is done through the brain cells' response to stimulation; those cells that are often activated are kept, and those that are rarely used are soon "pruned" (Barrett, Bradley, & McGraw, 2004). After the toddler period, the space between the eyes does not grow much, and the fine-tuning stops. Changes in visual experience (e.g., surgical correction of a "crossed" eye) no longer have much effect on the visual cortex after toddlerhood. Plasticity in this location becomes minimal, if it exists at all (Payne & Lomber, 2002).

Other parts of the brain and even other functions of the visual cortex, such as color perception, are much less plastic from the beginning. The environment does not mold the development of these areas and functions much, although of course a very poor environment, with much disease and a bad diet, can interfere with normal development. In areas of the brain with little plasticity, timing of experience is not as important as it is in the highly plastic areas of the visual cortex. If experience does make a difference to some of the less-plastic aspects of brain development, it probably does so gradually and subtly.

The cognitive and emotional areas of the brain are affected by experience as children learn information, attitudes, and the circumstances of emotional reactions. But these effects of the environment are relatively slow to develop and can happen in many different ways. Specific cognitive and emotional parts of the brain are not transformed suddenly by single events, although mood and behavior can be changed dramatically by intense traumatic experiences. Nor is it clear, in spite of much research, which cognitive or emotional experiences change which brain structures and whether such processes work differently at different ages. The connections between experience, brain development, and cognitive or emotional changes are not nearly as specific or as simple as the connections in the very plastic visual cortex (Willingham, 2006).

For the reasons just given, it is not very likely that a teaching method or a form of psychotherapy, neurofeedback, or any other intervention can transform a child's brain and quickly bring about cognitive or emotional change as a result. Schooling and emotional guidance continue to involve gradual changes. Age may also be a very significant factor. A dangerous event that occurs when a child is 2 months old will have quite a different effect on emotion and behavior than the same event occurring 2 years later. (However, because children develop at individual rates, one cannot use an exact chronological age to predict an effect, even if more information about the connection between age and outcome were known.)

It's never a good idea to try to jump logically from facts about one part of the brain to conclusions about others (Hirsh-Pasek & Bruer, 2007). Different parts of the brain follow different rules and develop at different speeds. Some brain areas even develop differently in boys than in girls. Even if transformation were possible, it would probably require different methods for different people.

An additional issue makes it difficult to move from what is known about brain development to teaching methods or therapy techniques that fit the brain perfectly: Much of what is known about brain development comes from studies of animals, not of human beings. Cats have been a popular subject for studies of the visual cortex because kittens are born with their eyes closed; therefore, their visual experience can be completely controlled. But whether research findings can be generalized from cat to human development is not clear because information about young humans is lacking. A thorough understanding of certain brain changes requires an autopsy, even in this day of rapid advances in imaging techniques. Elaborate brain autopsies are not usually performed on deceased children, although some such research was completed many years ago (and is still depended on today). Although imaging techniques show a good deal about adult brains, they are still difficult to use with young children, who do not care to stay still long enough to capture the images.

On the whole, does it make sense to generalize from animal studies to human beings? Sometimes this practice has been useful, but currently the similarity between developmental patterns of nonhuman species and those of human beings is uncertain. Nor can information from animals be used to create "brain-changing" instructional or psychotherapeutic techniques, which obviously cannot be tested on animals.

Not long ago, a group of early education specialists drafted a declaration (see www.jsmf.org/declaration) deploring the assumption that brain development was well-understood and could be put to work to help with parenting and teaching. Brain scientists have a long way to go before they can tell teachers and parents how to deal with the practical problems of child development.

Conclusion

Claims regarding techniques to alter the brain, and thus create desirable and rapid changes in cognition or emotion, are probably not based on good evidence. Camillo's grandfather and parents would do better to try to understand what he has been feeling and to work to restore his confidence and sense of security rather than try to find a quick fix for his distress. Conventional psychotherapy for the family and the child can be very helpful, even though it takes time and does not offer a magical cure.

CRITICAL THINKING

1. Use a child development textbook to create a definition of *plasticity*. Is there high plasticity in any aspect of development other than certain brain areas?

2. Create a definition of *experience-expectant* plasticity and describe an example of this phenomenon. Use a child development textbook for reference.

3. Create a definition of *experience-dependent* plasticity and describe an example, using a child development textbook for information.

4. Could later instruction or therapy change a characteristic that resulted from experience-expectant plasticity? Explain your answer.

5. Search the Internet for examples of the kinds of treatments Camillo's grandfather found. Describe two or three relevant Web sites and note the evidence they provide to support their methods. Do they discuss experience-expectant plasticity?

References

Barrett, B. T., Bradley, A., & McGraw, P. V. (2004). Understanding the neural basis of amblyopia. *The Neuroscientist, 10*, 106–117.

Hirsh-Pasek, K., & Bruer, J. T. (2007). The brain/education barrier. *Science, 317*, 1293.

Payne, B. R., & Lomber, S. G. (2002). Plasticity of the visual cortex after injury: What's different about the young brain? *The Neuroscientist, 8*, 174–185.

Willingham, D. T. (2006). Brain-based learning: More fiction than fact. *American Educator, 30*(3), 30–37.

Claim 15

Parents should not talk baby talk to their children, because this slows their language development.

Al became very annoyed with his mother-in-law when he heard her cooing to 3-month-old Carlie. "How is she ever going to learn to talk when she hears that baby-talk stuff all the time? Besides, it sounds so stupid. I'm embarrassed to hear you. Just talk normally when you're around the baby, okay?" Carlie's grandmother was offended, but to keep the peace she did not argue with Al. She thought to herself, "What in the world is wrong with him? Everybody talks to babies that way! Besides, I can tell that Carlie likes it because she gets quiet and looks and listens. But he's the father, so when he's around I won't talk like that—if I can help it."

Who was right? Does Al have good reason to think that his daughter's speech will be affected by what she hears now? Is baby talk a problem?

As is the case with many myths and misunderstandings, the accuracy of this claim depends on exactly what someone means by it. One interpretation of *baby talk* is the use of common childish mispronunciations of ordinary words, such as *basketty* for *spaghetti* or *muvver* for *mother*. It's obvious that if parents always say *basketty*, their child will not have many chances to hear the correct pronunciation of *spaghetti*, but most children will learn how to say this word before they ever take a date to an Italian restaurant. Baby talk can also mean family words for private functions, such as toileting. Children whose families use their own terms eventually learn the adult versions, but it is probably kindest to teach them what other people say before they go to preschool or visit a friend's house, where they may need to communicate their needs to adults.

Baby talk can also mean a specialized form of speech, probably found in all human groups, a form that follows different rules from the rules adults use to talk to other adults. This kind of baby talk is sometimes called *motherese* or infant-directed talk (IDT), and it is different in a number of ways from adult-directed talk (ADT). When speaking IDT, adults raise the overall pitch of their voice, produce changes in intonation by going from high to low pitches and back again, and speak sometimes loudly and sometimes softly. IDT conveys the maximum of emotional involvement but does not necessarily carry much other information.

People speaking in IDT also emphasize and repeat important words— "Where is the *doggie*? Do you see the *doggie*? What a nice *doggie*!" Sentences in IDT are shorter and simpler than they are in ADT, and, surprisingly, they are very grammatical, unlike the sloppily constructed and error-filled speech adults use when speaking to other adults. Adults who are speaking to babies also use dramatic and exaggerated hand gestures and facial expressions that parallel their speech patterns.

IDT can be annoying and even embarrassing to adults who overhear it. Listeners may feel that IDT has a silly quality that cannot be good for language development—certainly they would not want a baby to grow up to talk that way. If one adult spoke to another in the IDT pattern, offense would probably be taken and the speech interpreted as condescending or patronizing. These negative emotional reactions cause many adults to state their disapproval of baby talk.

To evaluate whether IDT is a good method for speaking to babies, however, one needs to observe how babies react to it, not just how adults feel about it. Babies typically respond to IDT with extreme interest and attention. Their eyes brighten and they smile and look at the speaker with interest and animation, whereas they react to ADT with a blank or serious expression and look elsewhere for entertainment (Bryant & Barrett, 2006).

A baby's interested expression has an important effect on adult caregivers— and on other children, too, although not as much (Rabain-Jamin, 2001). Caregivers like to talk to responsive babies and quickly give up the effort if a baby pays no attention. So, when using IDT and gaining a baby's interest, caregivers are likely to talk to the baby longer than they would otherwise do. Hearing lots of speech helps a baby's language abilities to develop, so there is a benign circle at work. Adults who use IDT capture a baby's attention, and the baby's attention stimulates the adult to keep talking. The more the adult talks during a baby's first year of life, the more the baby's understanding and use of spoken language will progress. In fact, the IDT type of baby talk encourages language development rather than slowing it (Barinaga, 1992).

For good language development, infants need to be able to hear the sounds of language and listen to the words—and listening will not last long if the baby does not find the speech *sounds* engaging and interesting. Among the first aspects of speech the baby must learn are the *phonemes*, or smallest meaningful sound units, of their parents' language. The very young baby listens (or fails to listen) equally to all kinds of voice sounds, but each language uses only some of those possible sounds. By listening to speech, the baby learns that an /s/ sound at the end of a word has a meaning, but a hiccup is not speech, even though the sound comes out of a person's mouth. Speech that attracts the baby's attention, such as IDT, helps infants figure out which mouth noises are part of language and which are not.

For young babies, the specific words an adult says and the topic of discussion are of very little importance. The youngest babies have no understanding of the words adults speak, and even older babies understand only a few words, such as their own names. If babies listen—and as a result eventually learn words and grammar—they do it because IDT sounds and behaviors attract their attention.

Of course, there are many individual differences in the experiences babies have with spoken language. Studies have shown that later born children are exposed to somewhat different kinds of speech than those heard by firstborn children (Oshima-Takane & Robbins, 2003). There is no single "speech diet" that is absolutely essential for language learning, but language that responds to infant interest does seem best, just as sensitivity and responsiveness in all areas seem to foster infant development.

As language development progresses and young children begin to understand words, they become more interested in what adults say and less interested in the way they say it. As children respond less to IDT, their adult caregivers modulate their speech to a less-exaggerated, less emotion-conveying form and begin to concentrate on new types of speech that attract the attention of toddlers and preschoolers. Children of these ages would rather hear an exciting story than have an adult speak in a high-pitched voice, and adults usually respond by giving the children what they want.

Conclusion

Babies' language development in the first year is actually helped by baby talk in the form of infant-directed talk, which attracts babies' attention and encourages them to listen and learn about their parents' language. Al would do better not to object to the way his mother-in-law talks to Carlie, and if he would look at Carlie's face while she listens, he would see that she is fascinated by infant-directed talk, however strange it may sound to an adult.

CRITICAL THINKING

1. Infants and toddlers often turn with interest toward television commercials, even when they have been ignoring the ordinary program just before the commercial. Using a child development textbook for information, describe what commercials and IDT have in common. Are there also some differences between IDT and commercial presentations? Explain your answer.

2. Bryant and Barrett (2006) studied responses to IDT in a number of different cultural and language communities. Why did the authors want to examine various language backgrounds? Why was it not sufficient to consider IDT among English-speaking families? Explain your answer.

3. Use a child development textbook to read about maternal depression. Would depression make a mother more or less likely to use IDT with a baby younger than 1 year old? What effect on a baby's language development would maternal depression likely have? Explain your answer.

4. What training should day care providers receive about IDT? Explain your answer.

5. Use a child development textbook to read about steps or stages in language development. At what age would you expect children to be more interested in a story and information rather than voice pitch and repetition? Explain your answer.

References

Barinaga, M. (1992). The brain remaps its own contours. *Science, 258,* 216–220.

Bryant, G., & Barrett, C. (2006). Infant preference for both male and female infant-directed talk. *Psychological Science, 18*(8), 740–745.

Oshima-Takane, Y., & Robbins, M. (2003). Linguistic environment of secondborn children. *First Language, 23,* 21–40.

Rabain-Jamin, J. (2001). Language use in mother-child and young sibling interactions in Senegal. *First Language, 21,* 357–385.

Claim 16

Breast-feeding makes babies more intelligent.

Mira was not happy about the idea of breast-feeding her first baby. She was only 20 years old and did not want to feel tied down. Also, she worried that nursing would spoil the shape of her breasts. Her mother pushed breast-feeding as the natural thing to do, but Mira wasn't convinced that it was for her. But then she read in a magazine that breast-feeding makes babies smarter. That seemed to Mira a good enough reason to put up with the inconveniences she anticipated.

Is there any truth to the claim that persuaded Mira?

Breast-feeding can be "sold" to some otherwise reluctant mothers and fathers when stress is placed on increased intellectual development, and breast-feeding support programs can sometimes be sold to the public with the same type of argument. It is true that comparisons of breast-fed and bottle-fed babies have shown advantages for the breast-fed baby. But what is the actual evidence that mental differences between groups of babies were *caused* by the feeding method, rather than by some other factor?

To answer this question, first one must consider exactly what is meant by "more intelligent." Depending on the time of life when measurement occurs, testing of intelligence can involve quite different abilities. Intelligence tests used to assess older children and adults are not useful for infants. Such tests are concerned with school-related skills, such as listening to speech and reading, skills that no infant has had time to develop. Appropriate intelligence tests for infants are developmental assessments that report the ages when babies perform certain tasks, such as sitting alone or reaching accurately. Infants who are unusually slow in developing physical abilities often show low scores on later school-related intelligence tests, but this is not necessarily the case, and some children who develop slowly because of physical problems later perform at normal or high intelligence on tests.

Developmental scores in babyhood are influenced by somewhat different factors than are later intelligence test results. An infant's developmental achievements are powerfully affected by general physical health, which in turn is determined by the occurrence of birth defects, by genetic factors, by diet, and by exposure to contagious disease. Although poor physical health may present a problem for later intellectual growth, tested intelligence in childhood is most affected by opportunities for experience and practice of complex skills, such as language. Even a child who enjoys robust physical health may show low intelligence scores if the child has had little experience with reading or even adult conversation. Similarly, a child with slow early development—perhaps because of a physical problem, such as cerebral palsy—may respond to good experiences with outstanding intellectual growth.

A second, and critical, issue in examining this myth involves understanding cause and effect. When two factors, such as breast-feeding and tested intelligence, seem to be related, people often assume that one causes the other, but this may not be so easy to demonstrate. The most direct way to show a cause-and-effect relationship would be to perform an experiment in which a group of babies is selected at random from a larger group and assigned to be breast-fed, and a group of other babies is assigned to be bottle-fed. Later, if researchers discover that the breast-fed babies are more (or less!) intelligent than the bottle-fed babies, it is reasonable to conclude that the feeding method brought about this outcome.

However, it is obvious that this fine research design is much easier to propose than to carry out. Mothers do not want to be ordered to feed their babies according to a researcher's wishes. And even if they were paid to cooperate, they might not do so. For that matter, cases exist where either the mother or the baby is not able to take part in the breast-feeding process (although this is less common than is sometimes thought). Those mother-baby pairs cannot be assigned at random to one group or another, so the research plan could break down even if all the mothers decided to cooperate.

The problems just discussed make it impossible to conduct a randomized study that assigns feeding methods to families and looks at the outcomes of types of feeding. Thus, researchers are left with the option of a nonrandomized, quasi-experimental approach, in which scientists compare two groups of babies whose mothers have decided either to breastfeed or bottle-feed. In reality, virtually all research on breast-feeding outcomes belongs to this type of research design.

Unfortunately, the mothers' decision makes it much harder to understand whether the feeding method *caused* any intellectual differences between groups of babies. Why did a mother make the decision she did? What characteristics does she have that affected her choice? Does the baby have some relevant characteristics? Mother and baby characteristics (Mortenson, Michaelson, Sanders, & Reinosch, 2002), which may also influence a baby's development in other ways, are *confounded* variables that confuse the issue of cause and effect. For example, highly educated mothers are more likely to breast-feed than are less educated mothers, their higher level of education and intelligence (Gomez-Sanchiz, Canete, Rodero, Baeza, & Avila, 2003; Gomez-Sanchiz, Canete, Rodero, Baeza, & Gonzalez, 2004) may encourage them to stimulate and foster their babies' mental growth, and they may pass on to their babies a genetic makeup that raises intelligence. Breast-feeding mothers are also likely to be of higher socioeconomic status (SES), and evidence shows that children of higher SES families hear many more words addressed to them in their preschool years than do lower SES children (Hart & Risley, 1995). Both of these confounded variables—SES and maternal education—have the potential to influence children's intelligence, and their association with breast-feeding makes it impossible to conclude with confidence that infant feeding method is the cause of intellectual differences.

Many reasons exist to question the claim that breast-feeding causes improved intelligence, but another important factor must be considered: Mothers who choose breast-feeding are not always able to carry out their choice. The process of breast-feeding demands more strength, coordination, and persistence from the baby than bottle-feeding does. Babies with birth defects such as cleft lip or cleft palate often cannot suck well enough to breast-feed. Premature or low birth weight babies, or those who are sick or injured, may have great difficulty in sucking; if a baby does not suck adequately, the mother's milk does not let down effectively, and she will not experience enough sucking stimulation to produce enough milk to feed the baby. For these reasons, babies who already have health problems are more likely to be bottle-fed than to be breast-fed and are also more likely to show slower development and possibly lower tested intelligence in the future.

One study examined many research reports on the advantages of breast-feeding and concluded that it is not known whether breast-feeding has the same effects on every child. The authors noted that premature babies seem to benefit cognitively from breast-feeding. Otherwise, no single, simple answer exists to questions about the effects of breast-feeding (Petryk, Harris, & Jonbloed, 2007).

One large study of feeding outcomes (Kramer et al., 2008) took an unusual approach and attempted a form of randomization of breast-feeding and formula feeding. Rather than attempting to randomize the actual feeding methods, however, these authors randomized programs for clinics that treat mothers and babies. Half of the clinics, chosen at random, were assigned a special program that was intended to encourage mothers to breast-feed, and the other half continued to use their old program. Mothers who attended the pro-breast-feeding programs were much more likely to breast-feed exclusively when their babies were 3 months old and continued to breast-feed. When the children were tested at the age of 6 years, those from the pro-breast-feeding clinics had small but significant superiority in intelligence scores compared with those from the other clinics. However, even when the babies were 3 months old, fewer than half of the mothers from the pro-breast-feeding clinics were nursing, so many formula-fed children were in that group. This research does not make it clear whether the feeding method or something else about the program was responsible for the higher intelligence; unfortunately, even a randomized design like this one may still have confounded variables at work, interfering with clear conclusions.

There are many reasons to question the statement that breast-feeding causes higher intelligence. This does not mean, of course, that bottle-feeding has demonstrated advantages, except when mothers are HIV-positive or have other contagious diseases. Nor should this discussion be taken as an argument *against* breast-feeding. Breast-feeding is a practice that has very positive effects for most infants' and mothers' physical health, especially in parts of the world where families lack access to modern medical care.

Conclusion

There are many good reasons for mothers to choose to breast-feed, but increasing a baby's intelligence has not been shown to be one of them. Mira made the right choice for the wrong reason.

CRITICAL THINKING

1. Choose one of the confounded variables mentioned in this discussion and state in a few sentences how it can influence the development of intelligence. Use material from a child development textbook in your argument. Material from Hart and Risley (1995) would also be helpful.

2. Using a textbook as a source, define the term *maternal depression* and state how this condition can influence both the choice of breast-feeding and the development of an infant's intelligence.

3. Search the Internet for the topic "breast-feeding." Choose 10 sources and note the reasons given in support of breast-feeding as well as against it (if any). Can you conclude that the myth discussed in this essay is a common one?

4. Read the articles by Mortenson et al. (2002) and Petryk et al. (2007). What confounding variables are discussed?

5. Describe another issue in child development that presents the same barriers to experimental research as breast-feeding does. Explain how the topics are similar.

References

Gomez-Sanchiz, M., Canete, R., Rodero, I., Baeza, J. E., & Avila, O. (2003). Influence of breast-feeding on mental and psychomotor development. *Clinical Pediatrics*, 42, 35–49.

Gomez-Sanchiz, M., Canete, R., Rodero, I., Baeza, J. E., & Gonzalez, J. A. (2004). Influence of breast-feeding and parental intelligence on cognitive development in the 24-month-old child. *Clinical Pediatrics*, 43, 753–761.

Hart, B., & Risley, T. R. (1995). *Meaningful differences in the everyday experience of young American children*. Baltimore: P.H. Brookes.

Kramer, M. S., Aboud, F., Mironova, E., Vanilovich, I., Platt, R. W., Matush, L., et al. (2008). Breast-feeding and child cognitive development. *Archives of General Psychiatry*, 65, 578–584.

Mortenson, E. L., Michaelson, K. F., Sanders, S. A., & Reinosch, J. M. (2002). The association between duration of breast-feeding and adult intelligence. *Journal of the American Medical Association*, 287(18), 2365–2371.

Petryk, A., Harris, S. R., & Jongbloed, L. (2007). Breast-feeding and neurodevelopment: A literature review. *Infants and Young Children*, 20, 120–134.

Claim 17

It is important for parents to work with babies and teach them how to walk.

Ron and Shawna were spending a lot of time with their little boy, Eli. Eli was just 11 months old and really wanted to use his legs. If held on an adult's lap, he stiffened his legs to stand up, and if put on the floor he would pull himself up by the furniture and "cruise" along sideways. He could walk a little way when holding an adult's hand but did a lot better when holding both hands of a person walking behind him. "This is breaking my back!" Shawna said. "I hope he walks by himself soon. But I know we have to teach him how to do it." Ron noticed other parents at the park encouraging their babies to toddle back and forth between them, and he looked forward to the time when Eli could do that.

Were Ron and Shawna right? Did Eli have to receive instruction and practice to be able to walk?

It's charming to see a baby who is just beginning to walk alone, staggering back and forth between Mom and Dad, sometimes with an older brother or sister getting into the act. Baby is proud and perhaps a bit surprised at this new skill; parents are pleased and a little anxious. They all smile at each other and get ready to deal with a fall—it's a nice picture of family life at its best. The baby's ability to move is also a good index of general development, and as such it was once much investigated and is regaining interest after a period of less research activity (Thelen, 2000).

Are parents teaching their baby to walk when they supervise, smile, and hold their baby's hands? How do these behaviors compare to other actions that we call teaching? If parents wanted to teach in the ways people often use with children, they might demonstrate how to walk and tell their baby, "Do it like this." They might reward their baby with a bite of cookie for every step taken and punish their baby when he or she crawled. These actions are usually considered to be connected with teaching. But do parents do these things and do them in the same manner, regardless of their culture (Solomons, 1978)? And would the baby not begin to walk if adults gave no instruction, rewards, or punishments?

In fact, babies can walk without having experienced much in the way of "teaching." Walking is a development that depends on maturation much more than instruction. Babies walk when certain physical changes have occurred to make walking possible: Their body proportions need to have altered from what they were at birth so that their lengthening legs and trunk counterbalance their large head, which makes it all too easy to fall over; their nervous systems need to have developed from the top down so that control over the lower as well as the upper body becomes possible; and their leg muscles need to have increased in strength to support their heavy upper body.

Like other new tasks, walking depends on a baby's motivation. Babies don't depend on adults to interest them in new skills; rather, they become interested on their own. Unlike older people, babies are interested in doing new things, even if those activities bring no specific reward, and they may even persist despite some discomfort or punishment. The term *mastery motivation* describes a baby's deep desire to perform difficult tasks and become more competent. Healthy babies are interested in walking when they are physically ready and will work very hard at it even if no one pays attention to them. Even babies with some physical handicaps strive to become mobile.

It seems, then, that healthy babies learn to walk without being taught. One might even say that they "mature" to walk rather than "learn" to walk. But does that mean that the doting parents of a new walker are completely useless in their baby's skill development? No. On the contrary, they teach some very important things.

The parents' smiles, attention, and readiness to help tell the young child that new abilities are important to loving caregivers, who share their child's joy in mastery and developmental progress. Pleasure in success and patience and tolerance about failure become shared parts of essential parent–child interactions. The foundations are laid for positive future relationships with teachers and others outside the family. Trying new things becomes associated with pride and pleasure, rather than with fear of failure and shame.

Parents' fascination with developments such as walking also teaches the parents to provide scaffolding for their children's other new achievements.

First-time parents, especially, may be unsure of how to assist their child's developmental progress while simultaneously allowing their child to feel independent. The development of walking provides an excellent example of this complex parental skill and lets parents practice smoothing the developmental process without intruding on the child's activity. One simple but important contribution a parent can make is to keep looking at the young walker, giving the child a face to look at and a constant focus that helps maintain balance. Just as figure skaters and dancers keep their gaze on an object while they twirl, young children who keep looking at one thing do a better job of keeping their balance—and, of course, a parent's smiling face is an easy thing to focus on. Parents also provide scaffolding by foreseeing and removing problems—for example, taking up rugs that a baby might trip on and checking to be sure that their baby's shoes and socks are big enough for fast-growing feet. As parents discover these ways to support walking skill, they also learn how to provide similar scaffolding for many later types of learning, whether in school, sports, or social environments.

A baby's body type makes a difference in walking ability: Slender babies place their feet in a more mature way than do chubbier babies. But most babies fall a lot. According to one study, 14-month-olds fell an average of 15 times in 1 hour of free play. Parents are generally sympathetic about these little falls, but they cannot do much about them except make sure their baby is walking on surfaces that will not do any harm. Some other more complicated aspects of walking take time to develop, too (Garciaguirre, Adolph, & Shrout, 2007). For example, many new walkers like to carry objects or toys, such as teddy bears, around with them, but they do not do a very good job of adjusting their balance, so they may need to be monitored carefully when walking outdoors or stepping onto a carpet.

What about children whose handicapping conditions make walking more difficult? Children with Down syndrome, for example, tend to have loose joints and weak muscles as well as a general slowness in development. Do they need to be "taught" to walk? Once again, encouragement and excitement from adults can help with the motivation to conquer difficult tasks and, especially, the ability to bounce back and try again after failure. But much of what is needed from adults is scaffolding of special tasks that toddlers with disabilities can gradually master. Children with Down syndrome may have poor vision that interferes with their ability to move, and corrective lenses can help with this. Special seats can help put children with disabilities into positions that encourage them to work toward independent movement (Williamson, 1988). Exercise on treadmill-type devices can strengthen leg muscles and help children with disabilities progress more rapidly toward mobility (Thelen & Ulrich, 1991). These methods support a child's development and learning, but they are not what is usually meant by "teaching."

Conclusion

Healthy children develop walking through a process of physical maturation and are not taught how to walk through their parents' efforts. However, efforts to help a child practice walking can encourage a child to try new things, and these experiences can help parents develop better approaches to use in support of later learning. Ron and Shawna are not actually teaching Eli how to walk, but they are teaching him (and themselves) some important things about learning and teaching.

CRITICAL THINKING

1. Using a child development textbook as a source, describe what the Russian psychologist Lev Vygotsky said about the role of adults in children's learning. How do Vygotsky's ideas contribute to practical understanding of toddlers' development of walking?

2. When toddlers first begin to walk, they may do well when an adult watches but fall soon after the adult looks away. How would you explain this fact, using ideas from this section?

3. Suppose an experimental study compared a group of toddlers who received walking instruction, rewards, and punishments to another group who received no special treatment. Given what you read in this section, would you expect the second group to walk earlier than, later than, or at the same average age as the first? Explain your answer.

4. Using material from Thelen (2000), describe the evidence that shows that increasing muscle strength is related to the ability to walk independently.

5. Using a child development textbook, define the term *scaffolding*. Choose a motor skill other than walking and provide an example of scaffolding an adult might use to help a child develop the skill. Williamson (1988) provides examples drawn from work with toddlers with disabilities.

References

Garciaguirre, J. S., Adolph, K. E., & Shrout, P. E. (2007). Baby carriage: Infants walking with loads. *Child Development, 78,* 664–680.

Solomons, H. C. (1978). The malleability of infant motor development. *Clinical Pediatrics, 17,* 836–840.

Thelen, E. (2000). Motor development as foundation and future of developmental psychology. *International Journal of Behavioral Development, 24,* 385–397.

Thelen, E., & Ulrich, B. (1991). Hidden skills: A dynamic systems analysis of treadmill stepping during the first year. *Monographs of the Society for Research in Child Development, 56*(1, Serial No. 223).

Williamson, G. (1988). Motor control as a resource for adaptive coping. *Zero to Three, 9*(1), 1–7.

Claim 18

Toddlers drop food on the floor because they want to make their parents mad.

Twelve-month-old Andrew had a way of infuriating his mother, Annie, at mealtimes. He would eat happily for a while, with Annie spoon-feeding soup or cereal that he couldn't handle by himself. Then he would eat pieces of cheese, cooked vegetables, dry cereal, or toast, polishing them off happily but messily. However, meals ended with a grand climax of throwing things. Whatever was left on the high-chair tray—including leftover spoons covered with applesauce—would go overboard. Andrew obviously did this on purpose, leaning over the side of the chair as he released each object and watching carefully as it bounced, crumbled, or splashed on the floor. Annie was angered by all the work this made for her, and she yelled at Andrew and occasionally even smacked him, but he kept doing it. What angered Annie even more was the thought that he knew she was angry but kept dropping things anyway.

Was Andrew dropping food with the intention of aggravating his mother?

Having to clean up a puddle of applesauce or pick green beans out of a shaggy rug would probably annoy most parents—especially if the mess occurred, as it usually does, at the end of a long day of work and family chores. However, parents' annoyance, predictable as it may seem to any adult, may have nothing to do with a young child's wishes or intentions. In fact, even preschoolers may have trouble recognizing emotional expressions (Russell & Widen, 2002).

Even adults do things that result in undesirable and unanticipated consequences. Because human beings of all ages experience unintended results of their actions, it would seem like a good idea to entertain some alternate hypotheses about why people do the things they do and whether certain results are unintentional. A toddler's eating habits may be maddening, but that may not be the toddler's plan. Adults should consider the possibility that young children have intentions when they drop or throw food, but those intentions may not include frustrating and irritating their caregivers. Why, then, would they do something that, to adult eyes at least, appears so silly and pointless?

One possible explanation was offered many years ago by the eminent Swiss developmentalist Jean Piaget. Piaget suggested that children in the first part of their second year of life are powerfully motivated to cause interesting events to occur. (These are, of course, events that are interesting to toddlers, not events that are particularly interesting to older people.) According to Piaget's theory of cognitive development, children do not understand that they can cause things to happen until they are about 1 year old. When they do catch on to this fact, they are intensely motivated to test it out repeatedly, just as, in Piaget's view, they have a strong need to practice and repeat any new achievement.

Having discovered their ability to initiate interesting events, young children find that they cannot do everything with equal ease. They are limited in what they can do by their own physical and motor development. A 1-year-old cannot build a machine with interlocking blocks, draw a recognizable picture, or turn on a computer. If restrained in a high chair at mealtime, the toddler cannot run around in circles, pull off shoes and socks, or try to brush the dog's teeth. Most of the things a high-chair-bound child can do involve dropping or throwing of available objects—food and eating utensils. Dropping or throwing objects is interesting and yields some important new information about the physical world: For example, liquids like soup or milk, if dropped, make little noise and redistribute in novel patterns across the floor; a spoon, on the other hand, makes a noise but does not change in size and may show only a slight alteration in shape.

The desire to learn new and intriguing information about the world provides a strong alternative motivation, one that explains why toddlers drop food without intending to anger adults. But other aspects of this claim should be considered by comparing the child's feelings to those of an adult. Why might it be that an adult would want to make someone else mad and is it possible for a toddler to share the beliefs and social skills that this vengeful adult has? Working to make someone else mad actually involves a quite complicated understanding of others' thoughts and emo-tions. An adult who can successfully and intentionally act to make others mad must be able to conceptualize how the other people would feel in a given situation, even though the feeling might not be the same one that the person would experience. In addition, if the would-be annoying person has any sense, his or her intention will be to produce feelings of anger and frus-tration but not of sufficient intensity to provoke retaliation. People do not usually want to make other people so mad that they respond with a punch; instead, people who inflict vengeance want their victims to simmer in help-less, uncomfortable rage, unable to do anything about it. To manage this requires careful and skillful anticipation of the degree of anger created and the likelihood that victims will fight back.

Such complex assessment of others' responses is only possible for people with a well-developed theory of mind—those who can predict with some accuracy how another person will think and feel (Fonagy, Gergely, Jurist, & Target, 2002). Toddlers have taken the first steps in developing theory of mind. However, they have little understanding of the meaning of applesauce on the floor and a tired and frustrated parent. Toddlers would not plan to throw food or anticipate the anger as a result of food throwing and the pun-ishment as a result of anger, even if the action has sometimes had that effect in the past. In fact, toddlers still rely heavily on their parents' sensitivity to communications to help establish the understanding of others' thoughts that will help in later conflicts (McElwain & Volling, 2004).

Curiously, early steps in theory of mind include a stage in which children assume that what any person does is what they want to do (rather than something that happens by accident or through lack of knowledge). This *desire psychology* stage is exactly parallel to adults' assumption that a baby who makes them mad has wanted to make them mad. Although adults have probably developed much further and can show advanced theory of mind in ideal circumstances, fatigue, frustration, and anger sometimes combine to limit adults to a much more childish view of other people.

As a final point in this section, consider toddlers' responses to angry parents. When children think that angry behavior is a joke, they may laugh, but on the whole they do not seem either pleased or amused when their parents are angry. It seems unlikely that they would intentionally provoke anger if they do not enjoy it. Angry shouting or physical punishment causes crying and emotional upset, of course. But children show distressed reac-tions even to adults who are suppressing anger, clenching their teeth, not looking at the child, or not speaking. Most young children respond to this confusing and threatening behavior by trying to approach the parent and by crying or becoming withdrawn if rebuffed. Young children do not seem to enjoy any aspect of angry parents, so it seems unlikely that they would make intentional efforts to annoy. However, a child might be defiant without having the intention of causing anger, and a certain amount of this behavior may actually indicate good development. According to some research, toddlers who are actively resistant are also likely to behave positively toward their mothers, and children of depressed mothers are less likely to show resistant behavior (Dix, Stewart, Gershoff, & Day, 2007).

Conclusion

Although toddlers sometimes make their parents mad by throwing food, the children probably have a very different intention resulting from their level of cognitive development. Toddlers' development of theory of mind is not sufficiently advanced to allow the performance of deliberately annoying behavior, although well-developed toddlers may display resistance to what parents want. Annie would still be tired and frustrated with thrown food, but she might feel better if she understood that Andrew is not trying to make her life difficult.

CRITICAL THINKING

1. Read more about Piaget's theory in a child development textbook. Would Piaget have said that babies younger than 12 months of age have no knowledge of cause and effect? Explain the steps of development as babies come to understand how they cause changes in other people's moods or behavior. (This is not a question about development of theory of mind. Concentrate on the general idea of causing change, not the idea of knowing what the moods or beliefs are.)

2. Do you think parents who believe in this claim (that toddlers behave in intentionally annoying ways) are more or less likely to punish their child than those who do not accept this belief? What about parents who take the point of view described in the article by Dix et al. (2007)?

3. Use a child development textbook or one of the references in this section to find a description of the development of theory of mind. At what stage of theory of mind are adults who believe that a child who makes them mad actually wants to make them mad? Considering that adults can think about minds at the same level as children do, what do you conclude about development?

(Continued)

(Continued)

4. What observable behavior would cause you to conclude that a child intends to annoy an adult? You may want to consider first which adult behaviors make you think that another adult wants to annoy you, but don't forget to consider the child's probable level of theory of mind. Explain your answer.

5. Do the points discussed in this essay imply that parents should simply clean up children's messes and allow them to drop food as long as they want to? What are possible alternatives that would meet the needs of both parents and children? Keep in mind that children need to practice steps in cognitive and motor development. You may want to review these developmental steps with the help of a child development textbook.

References

Dix, T., Stewart, A., Gershoff, E. T., & Day, W. H. (2007). Autonomy and children's reactions to being controlled: Evidence that both compliance and defiance may be positive markers in early development. *Child Development, 78,* 1204–1221.

Fonagy, P., Gergely, G., Jurist, E. L., & Target, M. (2002). *Affect regulation, mentalization, and the theory of the self.* New York: Other Press.

McElwain, N. L., & Volling, B. L. (2004). Attachment security and parental sensitivity during infancy: Associations with friendship quality and false-belief understanding at age 4. *Journal of Social and Personal Relationships, 21,* 639–667.

Russell, J. A., & Widen, S. C. (2002). Words versus faces in evoking preschool children's knowledge of the causes of emotions. *International Journal of Behavioral Development, 26,* 97–103.

Claim 19

It is a good thing for an infant or a toddler to have experience with many caregivers, not just one or two.

Twelve-month-old Emma's mother, Holly, was telling her friend about Emma's child care center, which Emma had recently started attending when her mother went back to work full-time. Holly said how much she approved of the center's policies. "They have lots of different people taking care of the kids, and different ones on different days. I think that's a great way to make Emma independent and friendly. Anyway, I wouldn't want her to get attached to a caregiver and not want to be with me so much. She cries a lot when I leave her there, and when I look in the window she's in a corner by herself, looking sad, but I'm sure she'll get used to it soon. Some of the other kids are really friendly and want me to pick them up as soon as I go in."

Is Holly right in her approval of the child care center's policies?

Many of today's parents of young children attended day care or preschool when they were children, but of course they cannot clearly remember the experience. When they think about group care for their infants and toddlers, they may simply take their memories of kindergarten or first grade and apply them to younger children as a way of imagining proper child care for the very young. American parents tend to be concerned about their children's education, so it is not surprising that they take school as a model for infant and toddler care. One of the rules about school is that children should obey and respond to all the adults there—their own teacher, other teachers, the principal—so the idea of accepting many caregivers may be an important one in parents' thinking. Many parents reason that there should be similarities between their very young children's experiences and those the parents remember of their own experience, but professional groups such as the National Association for the Education of Young Children (NAEYC; 2005), do not agree.

The number of caregivers working with infants and toddlers has a special significance because of the connection with the children's development of attachment and healthy understanding of social relationships. Infants and toddlers who have a small number of consistent caregivers usually form a secure attachment to those adults, and after the age of about 8 months are much slower to accept unfamiliar people than they used to be. When young children are surrounded by a large, unpredictable group of caregivers, they may be less likely to develop secure attachment and may not show the same emotional changes that are characteristic of children with a few, consistent caregivers.

Although child development professionals feel that the emotional change to preference for familiar people is healthy and desirable, parents may perceive it as a matter of concern. Some young parents think their children will remain as friendly and outgoing as they were at 4 or 5 months of age. They are surprised and worried when an older baby begins to avoid strangers and fear that this behavior will be a permanent personality trait. Other parents need to use child care services, but they want their young children to have emotional attachments only to the parents—not to their other caregivers. Such parents may want infants and toddlers to have many different caregivers so that they do not have a chance to become attached to anyone else. Some parents may simply consider attachment behavior to be a nuisance, associated as it is with intense emotional reactions to separation or to the approach of strangers. Parents with this concern may believe that having many caregivers makes a child friendly, outgoing, independent, and adventurous—all characteristics that are preferred by many American parents. Young parents may consider a child who has strong attachments to a small number of caregivers to be unfriendly, clingy, shy, and overly dependent—characteristics they do not favor. (Behavior may be different among children in cultures where it is customary to have many caregivers, however; Whaley, Sigman, Beckwith, Cohen, & Espinosa, 2002.)

It is not easy to carry out research to clarify which child care situation best encourages good early development. The big question is, do infants and toddlers benefit from having many caregivers, as some parents believe, or do they do best with a smaller number of adults caring for them? This question is not likely to be answered through difficult experimental procedures that randomly assign some children to experiences with many caregivers and others to a care situation with a few consistent care providers. Such studies are simply not very practical. It is much easier to compare children from day care centers where each child interacts with many adults to those from settings where each child has only one or two caregivers who provide predictable care. However, with this kind of comparison, many other confounding variables are likely to affect the children in the two child care settings, so it is difficult to draw clear conclusions from these simple comparisons. Most often, information about the effects of multiple caregivers is based on generalizations from clinical work and from past child care arrangements, such as those in England during World War II, neither of which may actually be typical of modern child care experiences (Freud & Burlingham, 1973). But the sources available suggest that toddlers are calmer and happier and learn more effectively when they have had a chance to develop secure relationships by frequent interactions with small numbers of adults. These sources of information do not indicate that children with many caregivers are independent or friendly as a result of their care.

To further complicate the research issue, information from the sources mentioned earlier has been applied by organizations such as the NAEYC to establish guidelines advocating a small number of consistent caregivers for young children. Child care programs accredited by NAEYC (National Association for Education of Young Children, 2005) must follow those guidelines and as a result have characteristics that certainly affect the types of children enrolled and that may affect the children's development. Such high-quality, accredited programs are usually more expensive and more selective of both children and teachers than many other programs. If children in these accredited programs show excellent cognitive and social development, caution should be taken when making the assumption that the small number of caregivers caused good development. It is possible that the programs accept few children with developmental problems, increasing the number of good outcomes; it is also possible that parents who can afford high-quality programs are also able to foster their children's development in other ways. In fact, it may be that being a well-developed child from a well-functioning family is the cause of the good experience with the program, rather than the other way around. It would be a mistake to think that research has clearly answered questions on this topic.

So far, I have discussed the possible direct effect of multiple (or few) caregivers on children's social and cognitive development. But what about less direct effects? An example of a less direct effect involves the result of a caregiver's familiarity with a child's characteristics, familiarity that would increase with amount of time spent in interactions with the child and decrease if many caregivers shared that time. Although adults and infants make many mistakes as they try to communicate, they are more persistent in their efforts if they know each other well. Adults are not as likely to give up on understanding a particular baby when they have the confidence that comes from many successful communications in the past. If a caregiver has too many infants to care for, or if the caregiver has no time to get to know them, or if staff turnover means that all the caregivers are new to all the babies, chances are that the adult will not have the energy or interest to work toward communication about physical or emotional needs. Other factors, such as physical crowding, can also affect children's responses and make them more difficult to care for (Legendre, 2003).

Conclusion

Young children probably benefit from better individual care and chances to form secure attachments when they have a small number of caregivers. However, the difficulties of research in this area make it hard to present clear evidence for this claim. There is no good evidence that having multiple caregivers is advantageous, so it is probably wisest for parents to seek child care that exposes children to small numbers of adults whom children can get to know. Holly's assumption that toddlers are "friendly" when they approach a stranger is a misunderstanding of early development and not a good reason to choose this child care center for Emma.

CRITICAL THINKING

1. Using a child development textbook for information, describe the kinds of experiences that seem to foster attachment. Why would these experiences be less likely to occur with multiple caregivers?

2. A parent education pamphlet says that children who are securely attached will not cry when left at the child care center. Comment on the accuracy of this statement, using a child development textbook to support your position. What role does temperament play in this behavior? How about age?

3. Read an account of group child care during World War II (e.g., Freud & Burlingham, 1973) What are three ways in which the experiences of those infants and toddlers were different from those of children in modern child care centers?

4. Find information about early language development in a child development textbook. Explain the benefits of infant caregivers' persistence in efforts to communicate. Use the concepts of communicative or interactive mismatch and repair. Keep in mind that successful communication can mean understanding infants' signals as well as sending messages to infants.

5. Discuss the confounded variables that make it difficult to compare programs with many children per caregiver to those with few children for each caregiver. Consider matters such as staff training and salary as well as parents' characteristics that might cause them to choose one program rather than another.

References

Freud, A., & Burlingham, D. T. (1973). *Infants without families and reports on the Hampshire Nurseries, 1939–1945.* New York: International Universities Press. (Note: If this book is not available, similar reports can be found in *Psychoanalytic Study of the Child*, volumes dated late 1940s–1950s. This publication is owned by many college and university libraries.)

Legendre, A. (2003). Environmental features influencing toddlers' bioemotional reactions in day care centers. *Environment and Behavior, 35,* 523–549.

National Association for the Education of Young Children. (2005). *NAEYC early childhood program standards and accreditation: The mark of quality in early childhood education.* Washington, DC: Author.

Whaley, S. E., Sigman, M., Beckwith, L., Cohen, S. E., & Espinosa, M. P. (2002). Infant-caregiver interaction in Kenya and the United States: The importance of multiple caregivers and adequate comparison samples. *Journal of Cross-Cultural Psychology, 33,* 236–247.

Claim 20

Some children would starve to death if their parents did not coax them to eat.

Five-year-old Ellis was thin but healthy and well within the normal weight range. He did not like to eat, and every family meal was unpleasant as Ellis whined, gagged, and bargained over each bite of food, even things he had accepted on other occasions. If Ellis said he wanted pancakes, his father, Rob, would jump up from his own meal and mix some batter to cook for Ellis, who would then eat only if plenty of syrup were on the pancakes. Their neighbor asked Rob why in the world he was encouraging Ellis to be so picky and allowing Ellis to limit himself to food that was not very nutritious. Rob was embarrassed at this question but finally confided that he honestly believed that Ellis could starve to death if not given what he wanted. Rob admitted that Ellis's little sister, Beth, ate normally, but he still maintained that Ellis needed special treatment.

Was Rob right in thinking that Ellis would be endangered if treated differently?

It is true that a small proportion of children need special care in their feeding, but this number is probably not nearly as many as some parents believe, nor is the special care necessarily a matter of coaxing. Parents' concerns for infants are sometimes reflected in playing "airplane" with the feeding spoon, and their worries about older children may be shown in their willingness to provide a special menu for a child who is able to eat most family food. When children are actually at risk for nutritional problems, however, these kinds of care usually are not what they need.

Reluctance to eat certain foods—or, it sometimes appears, to eat at all—can be a characteristic of certain periods in development, a part of a personality pattern, or an indication of physical conditions that require serious treatment. The appropriate parental response depends on which of these causes is at work and on the age of the child.

The period of infancy is normally one of strong appetite for food and little concern with food preference. Infants readily consume most of what comes their way, including some items that are not food but are within reach. Older infants may find some solid foods difficult to eat and may gag on foods with lumps until they learn to handle them in their mouths, but infants are rarely picky eaters. Infants who seem to have poor appetites or difficulties with particular foods may have medical problems that need treatment. Coaxing them to eat is probably not the answer to what might be a serious problem. Neither does coaxing help children who were tube-fed as infants because of medical problems and who are now reluctant to eat; however, treatment programs can help correct this problem by allowing children to make their own eating decisions. Children with emotional or pervasive developmental problems, such as autism, may also need special feeding care (Ledford & Gast, 2006).

The toddler period, which begins at about 1 year of age and lasts about 2 years, is the time when parents often notice that their children are reluctant to eat or are beginning to have strong food preferences. As younger infants, these children grew very rapidly and needed a high-calorie intake of food. With few teeth, infants received most of their calories from milk, and because of their small stomachs, they needed a considerable volume of milk, consumed frequently, to support their quick growth. By the toddler stage, however, children's growth rate slows, and even though their body is larger, the urgency of appetite is not as great as in infancy. With more teeth and better eating skills, toddlers can consume more calorie-dense foods than an infant can and therefore do not need to eat as frequently. Unfortunately, even young children may have the ability to persuade parents to provide calorie-dense foods, such as candy, which provide few nutrients but reduce children's appetite for more appropriate foods (Blinkhorn, Roberts, & Duxbury, 2003).

At the same time that toddlers are going through these physical changes, they are characteristically becoming neophobic in their behavior and emotions—suspicious of new experiences, including unfamiliar foods or food cooked and presented in different ways. To maintain an adequate and varied diet, toddlers need to adjust to new foods, but their neophobia makes them quite reluctant. Parents usually can help encourage acceptance simply by putting a new item on their child's plate without showing concern about whether the child eats the food. Eventually, after some days or weeks, the food becomes familiar and the child tries it and then eats it. Begging, coaxing, bribing, or punishing in these situations usually creates the opposite effect from what is desired.

Some children have a temperamental pattern that includes avoidance of new experiences, including foods. This avoidance pattern is evident from birth and becomes more apparent as the child gets older. Temperamentally avoidant children sometimes gradually limit their food intake to a few items—hamburger and peas, for example. They may respond with intense distress to the foods they avoid, as well as to situations they perceive as disconcerting. These children are the classic picky eaters, who may be getting an adequate diet but are certainly not getting any fun out of their food (or allowing their parents to enjoy meals). Again, threats and bribes are counterproductive. Coaxing and offers of substitute meals are likely to encourage these children to limit their diet even more. Temperamentally avoidant children won't starve, but they may not take in a healthy variety of foods or develop eating habits that will serve them well as they get older, so they do need help. These children do best in a quiet, pleasant, and orderly setting, where they are offered small amounts of attractively prepared foods or are allowed to help themselves to the food that is offered. Avoidant children can benefit from their parents' patient support, with respect both to eating and to other activities, such as playing with other children.

Although most childhood eating problems are a matter of developmental stage or temperament, not all are this benign. Poor eating and slow growth in infants may indicate inadequate care, for example, the inability of a depressed mother to respond to her child's cries. They may also be symptoms of underlying medical problems. Rett syndrome, a disorder that resembles autism in certain ways, includes poor eating and growth failure among its symptoms. Children with Rett syndrome cannot be cured by improved nutrition, but attention to their eating is needed so that their health can be maintained as well as possible (Deidrick, Percey, Schanen, Mamounas, & Maria, 2005).

Children who have been deprived of food by abusive caregivers may be anxious about any delay in feeding and may hoard food, but they may also become indifferent to food, and it may be difficult to return them to a healthy level of food consumption. Experiences of near-starvation can have long-term effects that seem paradoxical—for example, an individual who might be expected to be ravenous actually has little interest in food.

Anorexia nervosa in adolescents is, of course, a potentially life-threatening disease. Anorexic teenagers—usually girls, though occasionally boys—do not respond well to persuasion, threats, or bribes, and they need appropriate medical care. An extended period of anorexia can cause physical changes that interfere further with food intake and needed weight gain. As patients begin to take in more food, they are likely to experience uncomfortable bloating and constipation. Alterations in blood and other fluids can contribute to heart damage, especially if well-meaning caregivers provide high-carbohydrate foods, such as candies and ice cream, in an effort to encourage weight gain (Mehler & Crews, 2001).

Conclusion

Healthy children who limit their food intake are unlikely to starve, but they need help and support in increasing their choices of foods. Efforts to persuade them to eat are likely to backfire. Some medical and psychological problems do cause life-threatening food limitation, but professional care is needed in these cases, not parental pressure.

CRITICAL THINKING

1. Discuss changes in growth rates between 6 months and 2 years of age and between about 10 and 18 years of age. How would you expect these changes to affect food intake? Consult a child development textbook to find support for your conclusion.

2. Discuss the concept of temperament. Consider how characteristics of temperament can affect eating and food preferences at different times during childhood. Look for information in a child development textbook to include in your discussion.

3. Using the article by Deidrick et al. (2005), explain the connection between genetic problems and serious difficulties of eating and growth.

4. Read the article by Mehler and Crews (2001), and information about eating disorders in a child development textbook. Discuss reasons why an anorexic girl may resist treatment.

5. What role does the desire for autonomy play in reluctance to eat? Would the toddler and adolescent periods of development be times of particular concern with autonomy? Use information from a child development textbook to explain and support your answer.

References

Blinkhorn, A. S., Roberts, B. P., & Duxbury, J.T. (2003). The ability of young children to influence adults in the choice of sugary foods and drinks. *Health Education Journal*, 62, 210–219.

Deidrick, K. M., Percey, A. K., Schanen, N. C., Mamounas, L., & Maria, B. L. (2005). Rett syndrome: Pathogenesis, diagnosis, strategies, therapies, and future research directions. *Journal of Child Neurology*, 20, 708–717.

Ledford, J. R., & Gast, D. L. (2006). Feeding problems in children with autism spectrum disorders: A review. *Focus on Autism and Other Developmental Disabilities*, 21, 153–166.

Mehler, P. S., & Crews, C. K. (2001). Refeeding the patient with anorexia nervosa. *Eating Disorders*, 9, 167–171.

PART III

Preschoolers

Claim 21

Having kids listen to Mozart makes them smart.

Pam and Larry really wanted to do their best by their 2-month-old daughter, Molly. They monitored Pam's diet throughout her pregnancy and read and talked to their unborn child every day. Both parents were highly educated and had jobs that stressed mental abilities, so they wanted to be sure that Molly would grow up to be bright and academically successful. Posters and flash cards of French words surrounded Molly's crib. Only one thing seemed to be missing—the so-called Mozart effect. Pam and Larry had read in a parenting magazine that hearing the music of Mozart helps to "program" a baby's brain to work effectively. They bought some special recordings of Mozart's music that had been put together for just that purpose.

Were Pam and Larry right in what they were doing, or were they just victims of false advertising?

The idea that specific experiences with music can shape brain functioning and improve school performance has been around for some years now. This belief is an appealing one, suggesting as it does that a simple, inexpensive intervention can cut through the worrisome difficulties of intellectual and academic development. The reasoning behind the belief also has some real connection with known effects of experience on brain functioning. For example, flashing lights at different speeds can "drive" parts of brain wave patterns to alter their speeds. People who are good at mathematics are often interested in music, too, so it seems to make sense that experience with music might affect other abilities (Rauscher, Shaw, & Ky, 1993). The plausibility of this belief persuaded the governor of the state of Georgia to distribute

123

classical music recordings to families of newborn babies in the hope that listening to the music would provide a good foundation for the children's mental development.

There is a connection between the belief in the effect of listening to Mozart and research about mental performance, but the association is rather distant and questionable. The original research, suggesting that hearing classical music such as Mozart's work could improve performance on spatial tasks, was conducted with adult participants rather than with children (Bangerter & Heath, 2004). In any case, researchers working with children have not replicated the effect found with adults. For example, in another study, preschoolers who listened to classical music showed no change in their tested spatial intelligence (McKelvie & Low, 2002). It would appear that the Mozart effect is a scientific legend, at least in the version that looks for an improvement in mathematical and spatial ability as a result of listening to classical music's repeated, predictable patterns of rhythms and tones.

But might there be other effects of music on mental functions? Spatial and mathematical skills are important, but they are not the only measurable intellectual abilities. More recent work examined the connection between music and language, an association that may not seem quite as obvious as the Mozart effect on quantitative abilities.

Why would musical experience have anything to do with understanding or using spoken language? All spoken languages depend on changes of pitch (i.e., perception of sound frequency) to convey meaning. The sound represented by one written letter is not just a single pitch but a pattern of extremely rapid pitch changes. Of course, music also involves a pattern of pitch changes, so a child's development of language ability might go hand in hand with the ability to recognize or carry a tune (Nagourney, 2007).

For certain languages, the ability to detect or create pitch changes is especially critical. These languages use *intonation*—a dramatic pitch change in part of a word, with the tone of the voice rising or falling—to indicate different meanings for the same basic sounds. The use of intonation to change meanings of words is common in Asian languages, but in English examples involve only certain actions, for example, using a higher pitch at the end of a sentence to indicate that a question is being asked. English-speaking people often have a lot of trouble learning to process the sounds of languages that use intonation.

Wong and colleagues (Wong, Skoe, Russo, Dees, & Kraus, 2007) compared 10 adult volunteers who had studied a musical instrument with 10 others who had no musical background. None of the adults spoke a Chinese language. All listened to a tape in which the Mandarin word *mi* was intoned in three different ways, which could make it mean "squint," "bewilder," or "rice." The researchers recorded the amount of brain activity devoted to processing the sounds and found that people with musical training showed more such activity than those without the training. In a later interview, one of the researchers speculated that schools should include music training as part of the curriculum because of the possible positive effect on language development.

A somewhat different research approach asked whether music changes mood and motivation, resulting in alterations in performance (Schellenberg, Nakata, Hunter, & Tamoto, 2007). This was reported to be the case for 5-year-olds, but this question would be much more difficult to answer for infants. And, of course, change of mood is temporary, so this evidence is not directly relevant to making kids smart.

Conclusion

Infants and young children do not seem to derive any special mental benefit from hearing classical music, particularly with respect to mathematical or spatial skills. It is possible that music training (rather than passive listening) can alter ways in which people pay attention to sounds, and this might affect language development. Pam and Larry may feel pleased and gratified if they play classical music for Molly, but it is doubtful that this listening experience alone will have much effect on her.

CRITICAL THINKING

1. Consider the study by Wong et al. (2007). What would be two or three other possible differences between the music-trained and untrained groups and how might these confounding variables affect language development? Consult a child development textbook for further information about language development.

2. Read at least the abstract of the article by McKelvie and Low (2002). Did this study involve any of the confounding variables referred to in the last question? Explain your answer.

(Continued)

(Continued)

3. One research team (see Wong et al., 2007) speculated that musical training causes people to process speech sounds more effectively. What would be an alternative explanation of the results of the study? Remember that the participants in the study were volunteers who had made their own choices about whether to study music or possibly had those choices made for them by their parents.

4. Both the original Mozart effect study (see Rauscher et al., 1993) and the Wong et al. (2007) study tested adult participants, but the results were generalized to children. Is this an acceptable approach or not? Are conclusions from studies of children necessarily applicable to adults or vice versa? Explain your answer. Consult a child development textbook to locate information about the period of development in which basic language skills are most easily learned.

5. Using an Internet search engine, find Web sites about the Mozart Effect. Of the first 10 Web sites listed in your search, how many assume that the Mozart effect exists and how many find it questionable? What are two reasons given by Bangerter and Heath (2004) for this situation? (The Bangerter and Heath paper is also available online at www.si.umich.edu/ICOS/Mozart%20Effect-final.pdf.)

References

Bangerter, A., & Heath, C. (2004). The Mozart effect: Tracking the evolution of a scientific legend. *British Journal of Social Psychology, 43,* 605–623.

McKelvie, P., & Low, J. (2002). Listening to Mozart does not improve children's spatial ability: Final curtains for the Mozart effect. *British Journal of Developmental Psychology, 20*(2), 241–258.

Nagourney, E. (2007, March 20). Skilled ear for music may help language. *New York Times,* p. F2.

Rauscher, F. H., Shaw, G. L., & Ky, K. N. (1993). Music and spatial task performance. *Nature, 365,* 611.

Schellenberg, E. G., Nakata, T., Hunter, P. G., & Tamoto, S. (2007) Exposure to music and cognitive performance: Tests of children and adults. *Psychology of Music, 35,* 5–19.

Wong, P. C. M., Skoe, E., Russo, N. M., Dees, T., & Kraus, N. (2007). Musical experience shapes human brainstem encoding of linguistic pitch patterns. *Nature Neuroscience, 10*(4), 420–422.

Claim 22

The time between birth and age 3 years is the most important period of development and learning in a person's life.

Two-and-a-half-year-old Emily lives a highly scheduled life. She goes with her mother to the gym, where they "work out" together in a class with other mothers and preschoolers. She attends nursery school for 2 hours, four mornings a week. She is about to start music lessons with a tiny violin. She has been taking dance lessons for 6 months. Her mother, Patricia, feels that she must help Emily pack as much as possible into the window of learning opportunity during Emily's first 3 years. Their 3-year-old neighbor, Rosie, goes to day care while her mother works 20 hours a week. She has no dance or music lessons, and although the family often goes to run around in the park, Rosie does not have any formal gym attendance. Rosie's mother, Ellen, says, "Oh, let her be a kid! There's plenty of time for that stuff when she goes to school. Anyway, she needs time to relax after hours at the child care center—and so do I."

Which mother has a better understanding of early development?

If it were shown to be true that the most important parts of development occur in the first 3 years of life, a critical step toward a solid theory of human development would be accomplished. Evidence about this issue would also have practical importance for education and for treatment of developmental problems. If the most important steps in development were to occur in the infant and toddler periods, then people would likely agree that most educational resources should be committed to infant education and to early intervention methods. On the other hand, if this early period is no more crucial than any other 3-year period in development, people may want to pour resources into the public schools, which are more cost-effective and easier to run than organizations that work with families and very young children.

When considering a variety of aspects of development, you will find that the claim about the importance of the first 3 years has different levels of support with respect to different types of developmental change. There is no question that brain development is rapid during this period, and it is also true that some problems that interfere with the brain's growth can be corrected if caught early and addressed with intervention. For instance, early brain growth depends in part on diet, with the consumption of high-quality proteins having a significant effect. Brain growth slows and complexity advances less if an infant or toddler is deprived of protein. The poorly nourished child's head circumference is abnormally small, compared to other, better-fed children of the same chronological age. During the first 3 years or so, the problematic development of the malnourished child can be corrected to some extent if the child is given a better diet, with milk, meat, eggs, or other good protein sources included. Catch-up growth can then help bring the brain closer to normal size, although the child's stature may always be short. However, delaying the improved diet until the child is 6 years old will not have the same effect. Although the formerly malnourished child will have better general health with more protein in the diet, brain size will remain small, and poor intellectual functions will be apparent. More specific studies of brain development were difficult to conduct until fairly recent times, when techniques for nonintrusive brain measurements were developed (Chugani, 1999; Papanicolaou et al., 2001).

Functions such as the development of spoken language also depend on both genetic factors and early experience. Newborns normally have good hearing at the time of birth, but they must learn from experience the important sounds of the language that will be their native tongue. Languages are different from each other in some of their basic sound patterns, but babies are not born with innate knowledge about the language their parents speak. Gradually, as a result of hearing older people speak, infants learn to pay attention to the sounds that are most important in their "cradle" language, and they also learn to ignore unimportant, accidental sounds that people make. (We aren't confused when a friend hiccups while talking because we learned long ago that a hiccup sound has no meaning.) By age 6 months— many months before a child can speak—a baby has made a great deal of progress in the task of learning which sounds contribute to meaning and which do not. Hearing impairment delays children's language progress, unless early help is made available. Help that does not arrive until children reach school age is much less effective than early help (Barinaga, 2000).

Development of visual functions has some similar time limitations. Some events need to happen in the first year, or development will not follow the normal pattern. Newborns are limited in their ability to coordinate the use of the left eye and the right eye, so they have poor skill at judging distances—a comparison of the picture seen by the left eye and the picture seen by the right. In the first months, better coordination develops, but good distance judgment requires good coordination and finely tuned brain processes. As a baby looks around and experiences many right-plus-left combined images, frequently used brain cells and connections strengthen; those that are rarely used gradually disappear. For most babies, this process works very well and results in a lifelong ability to judge distances accurately when performing tasks such as driving a car. However, a baby who has poor vision in one eye may lose that eye's function altogether. A baby who is cross-eyed may also have unusual problems if corrective surgery is performed after the brain's fine-tuning has already occurred. In this case, the new, normal-appearing positions of the eyes are not right for the brain functions that were already developed, and the individual sees double images—overlapping but separated pictures from the right and left side. The brain can no longer readjust after the early period of development is past (Chugani, 1999).

In this section, I presented several examples of development that depended on events in the early years. But what happens if young children are deprived of a good diet or experiences and there is no attempt to help them until they are older? This is obviously not a question that should be answered by experimentally subjecting children to deprivation or delayed help. It is difficult to reach a clear conclusion by comparing children who receive early help with those who do not because there are often confounding variables at work, such as family income or level of parental education. One approach to studying the effects of early or late intervention is to examine the effects of the Head Start program, a federally funded intervention program for preschool children that was established more than 40 years ago. According to some research, children who entered Head Start at age 3 years have experienced somewhat more positive effects than those who entered at age 4, but the 4-year-olds have shown some short-term benefits, such as improved vocabularies. Studies of Head Start have not made clear whether the first 3 years are of overwhelmingly powerful effect (Herrod, 2007) or whether later interventions can be useful. Unfortunately, children who do not receive early help do not just remain in a neutral state but are likely to be affected by negative aspects of their environments, such as neglect, abuse, and community violence, so it is quite difficult to read any effect of timing of an intervention.

Very occasionally, students of early development learn about a "wild" or *feral* child, who seems to have survived alone, outside a family or community. Some people speculate that such children were reared by animals and that they therefore offer a wonderful opportunity to see whether later treatment can compensate for poor experiences in the first few years. Even with intense treatment and years of teaching, these children do not develop into normal-functioning adults or even manage to master basic speech. But closer consideration of this situation shows that "wild" children do not necessarily offer a way to measure whether the first 3 years are, or are not, critical to development. First, it is not at all likely that a young infant could survive being reared by animals, so these children probably had some degree of human care for some years of their lives. Second, chances are that the children were abandoned or chased away from their homes because they already showed some problems of development that were too challenging for their caregivers. Therefore, studies of feral children are not useful in understanding the role of the first few years in typical development.

Conclusion

Some aspects of children's development must take place in the first 3 years, or in an even shorter period of time, if they are to happen at all. But some other developmental changes may "catch up" if a later opportunity is offered. Generally speaking, however, the first few years need not be considered the only period of time to learn special skills, such as music and dance. Emily's and Rosie's mothers are making their decisions on the basis of their values and their convenience, which is a perfectly acceptable way for families to operate. Neither can appeal to clear research evidence to support her approach.

CRITICAL THINKING

1. Use a child development textbook to define the term *critical period* (or sensitive period). Do any of the developmental processes discussed in this section indicate that one or more critical periods exist in the first 3 years of a child's development? Explain your answer.

2. Studies of "wild" children have been used to support the view of a critical period for language development. Explain why people might argue that such a critical period exists. What confounding variables make it more difficult to argue that children's social deprivation interfered with their language development?

3. What long-term effects might you predict to occur as a result of experience with Head Start? Explain your answer. Keep in mind that a child's entire family, not just the child, may be affected.

4. Using a child development textbook, define the term *plasticity*. Then briefly summarize the examples used in this section, using the terms *plastic* and *plasticity*.

5. Using the article by Barinaga (2000), create a list of aspects of language development that may have different critical periods. In your opinion, how many of the periods occur in the first 3 years?

References

Barinaga, M. (2000). A critical issue for the brain. *Science, 288,* 216–219.

Chugani, H. T. (1999). Metabolic imaging: A window on brain development and plasticity. *The Neuroscientist, 5,* 29–40.

Herrod, H. G. (2007). Do first years really last a lifetime? *Clinical Pediatrics, 46,* 199–205.

Papanicolaou, A. C., Simos, P. G., Breier, J. I., Wheless, J. W., Mancias, P., et al. (2001). Brain plasticity for sensory and linguistic functions: A functional imaging study using magnetoencephalography with children and young adults. *Journal of Child Neurology, 16,* 241–252.

Claim 23

Day care is like school, so it provides an excellent foundation for children's development.

Lily's mother, Moira, was eager to enroll 2½-year-old Lily in a local child care center, even though Moira's mother was willing to look after the toddler while Moira worked. Moira told her co-worker, "See, day cares are like school. They have regular teachers and little tables sort of like desks. They'll do workbooks, and Lily will learn how to color inside the lines. Then when she goes to school she'll know how to sit still and behave and do what her teacher says. But if she stays with my Mom, she'll just run around all the time—besides, my Mom lets Lily think she's the most important person in the world and doesn't even make her ask for things the way she should."

Was Moira right? Is a group child care setting, called day care or child care, the best environment for a young child's development?

The term *day care* does not describe a monolithic, uniform system. On the contrary, group child care outside the home can have many different characteristics. Child care facilities can be in purpose-built structures (day care centers) or in the residences of child care providers who may be caring for their own children as well as those of other families (often called family day care). A child care arrangement may or may not meet the standards of accreditation set by the National Association for the Education of Young Children (NAEYC) (2005), which attempt to regulate certain facility policies and procedures, such as the ratio of caregivers to children. Child care facilities may or may not be licensed, depending on local and state regulations, and they may not have to meet certain requirements if they are under the auspices of a religious institution. Child care settings can also be very different, depending on the ages of the children attending; standards and practices need to be different for infants and toddlers than they are for preschoolers. Day care arrangements also vary widely in the quality of care offered, with high-quality care more likely for centers associated with universities or hospitals. For-profit centers may take advantage of lax local standards (Morris & Helburn, 2000). In parts of the country where there is little regulation, the quality of day care may be distressingly low. Any simple statement about the effects of day care cannot be true about all group child care arrangements.

This first problem about understanding the connection between development and care experiences is followed by a second. Which aspect of development is being considered and at what point in the course of development is it being examined? Researchers do not necessarily agree on this important issue (Layzer & Goodson, 2006). Experiences in child care can have different effects on emotional, physical, and intellectual development, and those effects can show up differently at different ages (Belsky et al., 2007). For example, the effects of child care on cognitive development might eventually be different than its effects on social and emotional life, even though the two aspects are probably closely related in early life. Similarly, situations might change over time. Undesirable behaviors might occur at 4 years of age but diminish within a few years or might not be seen at 4 years but appear at age 8 (or, of course, be either present or absent in a particular child at all ages). To answer questions about the impact of child care experiences on development, it is essential to consider these and related issues, particularly if the case being considered is about school success, because a child's school achievement is a matter of social and emotional development in addition to knowledge and problem-solving skills.

An ongoing attempt to assess the effects of day care is being made through the Study of Early Child Care and Youth Development (www.nichd.nih.gov/research/supported/seccyd.cfm). This study does not involve children who were randomly assigned to child care experiences in an experimental fashion but instead follows the development of children whose parents make their care and schooling decisions. A discussion of the study suggested a slight increase in classroom disruptiveness, teasing, and bullying, but within the normal range, continuing through sixth grade, for children who had spent a year or more in day care. Surprisingly, this slight change toward worse behavior was seen whether or not the child care center was of high quality (Carey, 2007).

However, children who had spent more time in high-quality child care also had higher vocabulary scores in elementary school.

These mixed results are especially difficult to interpret because of an important confounding variable: The children's parents chose the type of care, and their choices may have included care by a parent, a nanny, a relative, or center-based day care. The family's circumstances and the parents' child-rearing philosophy and practices may have had a major effect on both the care choice and the child's development and behavior. For example, parents who were in a position to choose a high-quality, university-connected child care center are likely to be highly educated adults; therefore, they model for their children a high level of language use (Hart & Risley, 1995). The parents' education and other circumstances are variables that can help to determine both their care choices and their children's vocabulary development, so it is not necessarily correct to conclude that the high-quality child care experience is the cause of the improved vocabulary.

Children's existing characteristics may also help to determine the parents' care choice. An active, aggressive, noncompliant child may not be an acceptable charge for a relative or a nanny. Even a parent who has been staying at home with such a child may feel like a failure and decide that a professional child care provider's training is needed to provide appropriate discipline. The family may feel that a day care center, with its open play space and the companionship of other children, is the right place for a child who is too lively for a small home and too rough-and-tumble for adults to enjoy. It is possible that some children who spend a lot of time in day care are sent there because of their preexisting disruptiveness and difficult temperaments and not, as might be the alternative possibility, that day care experiences cause these children to become disruptive. Quiet, compliant children, on the other hand, may be kept at home or with a relative who finds them very little trouble to care for.

Conclusion

It is a complex task to determine the effect of day care on development, and not enough good information is available on this subject. Information that is available is difficult to interpret because of the many confounding variables. Moira would probably do well to think more carefully about the match between Lily's present developmental needs and specific care arrangements and not to assume that day care experiences shape children in ways that help them in school.

CRITICAL THINKING

1. Read the Carey (2007) article listed in the reference section. According to Carey, what confounding variables did the Study of Early Child Care and Youth Development take into consideration? Hart and Risley (1995) also provide useful information on this topic.

2. In the article by Layzer and Goodson (2006), the authors suggest that researchers tend to measure "the wrong things" about day care. Read the article and comment on the criticized measures and suggested replacements.

3. Examine the NAEYC standards for child care (www.naeyc.org/accreditation/). What five characteristics would apply to a high-quality child care facility? Using a child development textbook for information, comment on the possible connections between these characteristics and good vocabulary development.

4. Do you think the elementary school teachers who were rating children's disruptiveness as described in the Carey (2007) article knew whether the children had been in day care? What might be the impact of such knowledge on the results of the study?

5. In their article about the Study of Early Child Care and Youth Development, Belsky and his colleagues (2007) commented on the problems of concluding that an early experience causes a later outcome. Read the Belsky article and summarize their reasoning about drawing causal conclusions from the data in this study.

References

Belsky, J., Vandell, D. L., Burchinal, M., Clarke-Stewart, K. A., McCartney, K., & Owen, M. T. (2007). Are there long-term effects of early child care? *Child Development*, 78, 681–701.

Carey, B. (2007, March 26). Study finds rise in behavior problems after significant time in day care. *New York Times*, p. A14.

Hart, B., & Risley, T. (1995). *Meaningful differences in the everyday experience of young American children*. Baltimore: P.H. Brookes.

Layzer, J. I., & Goodson, B. D. (2006). The "quality" of early care and education settings: Definitional and measurement issues. *Evaluation Review*, 30, 556–576.

Morris, J. R., & Helburn, S. W. (2000). Child care center quality differences: The role of profit status, client preferences, and trust. *Nonprofit and Voluntary Sector Quarterly*, 29, 377–399.

National Association for the Education of Young Children. (2005). *NAEYC early childhood program standards and accreditation criteria: The mark of quality in early childhood education*. Washington, DC: Author.

Claim 24

If a child is able to complete a task with an adult present, he or she is also able to do it alone.

Jack and his wife, Marian, were arguing about their 4-year-old, Tommy. Jack felt strongly that Tommy should be more independent, but Marian was inclined to help Tommy or even do things for him. She felt that Tommy liked being helped, and what's more, it was so much quicker to do things like button buttons than to wait for Tommy to get through the job. But Jack was very insistent that Tommy could and should put his shoes on alone before he came downstairs in the morning, even though Tommy called downstairs and said he couldn't do it. "I sat there with him every morning last week, and he did it by himself. He can put his shoes on, and you're just trying to baby him. If he can do it when I'm there, he can do it when we're down here."

Was Jack right about the evidence for Tommy's ability? (Never mind who was "right" in the parents' argument!)

When adults master a task, they can do it about as well alone as they do in company. If anything, they prefer to do a difficult job without having anyone watch or bother them. Plumbers are even said to charge more if a homeowner watches while they work!

Observation of children shows a very different kind of behavior pattern from infancy to adolescence. The child may do a task very well when with a familiar adult, even if the adult does not help directly or give advice but is simply present on the scene. But let the adult go away, or sometimes even *look* away from the child, and the skill may seem to evaporate. The child may seem discouraged or distressed by failure and seem unable to do the job that he or she did so well under other circumstances.

This kind of behavior is often seen in infants who have just learned to walk: The baby staggers around and around the living room, smiling and gazing toward the proud and attentive mother. Suppose someone comes into the room or the phone rings, and the mother gets up to respond to the new demand, perhaps even turning her back to the baby so as not to be distracted. Very soon, the baby, who was walking steadily, falls down—and begins to cry.

A similar situation, usually with fewer tears, can be seen among 4-year-olds: With much effort and guidance, the child has learned to put on and button a shirt or put on and fasten shoes with hook-and-loop fasteners (tying shoelaces usually comes later). A parent, who has been supervising this task every day, is finally convinced that the child can do it and one busy morning sends the child off to "do it all by yourself." An hour later, the parent checks to see what is happening and finds that the child is playing and has not made the slightest effort to get dressed. The child and parent may have had quite different ideas of their intentions—the parent assumed that they both shared the goal of getting the child dressed, but apparently this was not so. (Tollefson, 2005, discusses how young children manage to take part in shared actions even though they do not think clearly about what other people intend.)

Teachers may see the same type of behavior in older children: A particular sixth grader seems to need some extra help in arithmetic, for example, and the teacher sits with the student, patiently guiding each step. Then the teacher says she will just watch: "You do the next one by yourself." The student completes the problem successfully, and the teacher is pleased that the student has learned the technique, thinking all the student needs now is reinforcement through practice and repetition. The teacher provides a problem set to practice alone and goes about other business. When the teacher checks back with the student, not a single problem is finished. "It's hard!" explains the student, on the verge of tears. In a case like this, the adult may have as much trouble as the child in understanding another's state of mind (Mason & Macrae, 2008).

Very little research has investigated this childhood behavior, which is so unusual in adults, so typical of children, and so frustrating to parents and teachers who see it as a deliberate refusal to cooperate. However, some ideas about early development can help people understand what these apparently reluctant children are doing. Not surprisingly, different factors may be at work for children of different ages.

Two factors are needed to try to explain the toddling baby's fall when the mother looks away. The first part has to do with the role of the mother's smile and approval of the baby's exploration of the world. As the baby approaches unfamiliar things (and of course everything is a bit unfamiliar when seen from the standing rather than the crawling position) or tries new actions, the baby uses *social referencing* to check whether the mother thinks the situation is frightening. If the mother's voice tone or facial expression shows concern, the baby is likely to back off from the activity. An expression of pleasure and happiness encourages the baby to go on, but in our example, as the mother turns away, her expression is abruptly removed and no longer supports the baby's actions.

A second factor in the baby's sudden failure to walk may involve a very specific way of maintaining balance. Adult dancers and figure skaters keep their balance when turning rapidly by fixing their gaze on an object. New walkers may do the same thing by keeping their gaze on the most interesting and attractive sight in the room, a smiling, familiar face. When this sight is no longer available, balance becomes much more difficult.

What about the older children? They are past the need for help with balance or with social referencing. Nevertheless, the adult's attention and orientation (physical and mental) toward the task may provide a form of *scaffolding* that helps maintain the child's concentration on steps leading to his or her goal. When getting dressed or solving an arithmetic problem, the child must remember the necessary actions and the order in which they have to be done. Distractions such as toys, classroom events, hunger, or anxiety may make this part of the task difficult, whereas the presence of an involved adult may help focus attention. Cultures that stress skills other than literacy make use of these ideas more so than adults in the United States do, and these other cultures provide opportunities for children to be apprentices or to simply spend ample time watching what adults do (Rogoff, 1990).

When children do not seem to be doing a very good job of carrying out a task independently, it is probably best to withdraw adult help gradually (Skibbe, Behnke, & Justice, 2004). Responding with annoyance to the child's poor performance is likely to cause increased emotion and result in even less success in the task.

Parental concerns about children's independent performance usually focus on practical tasks. However, both teachers and parents may have to deal with problems about school performance. Should a child who has once shown mastery of a cognitive ability be expected to continue to do so? When thinking about stages of cognitive development, as suggested by Piaget and others, people usually conclude that they can have this expectation. However, individual children's performance depends very much on the specific task, as well as on other events of the day, and under some circumstances children will not necessarily be able to solve a problem that they did well on another occasion (Willingham, 2008).

Conclusion

When children have not completely mastered a task, they may be able to do the job in the presence of a familiar adult but not when they are on their own. If children fail to complete a task independently, it's likely that they need more guidance and practice for complete mastery, not that the child wants to "boss" the adults or be a baby. Jack and Marian needed to think of Tommy's dressing competence as the learning of a useful skill rather than an interpersonal issue, but chances are that this disagreement was really about other family issues that would not be settled no matter how well Tommy put his shoes on.

CRITICAL THINKING

1. Refer to a child development textbook to find information about the *zone of proximal development* (ZPD) as it was suggested decades ago by the Russian psychologist Lev Vygotsky. How is the ZPD related to the claim discussed in this section? What research approach would be needed to demonstrate the existence of the ZPD?

2. Find the definition of the term *scaffolding* in a child development textbook. Discuss why the teacher's actions with the sixth grader described in this section can be considered scaffolding. Rogoff (1990) provides a number of examples of scaffolding from different cultures.

3. Use a child development textbook to find information about *parental style*. Which parental style would be most likely among parents who encourage a 4-year-old to stay near them when mastering dressing tasks? Explain your answer.

4. Consider a situation in which an adult believes that a child is deliberately refusing to do a task when left alone to do it. Use a child development textbook to read about theory of mind. At what age might a child first be capable of foreseeing the effect of his or her apparent refusal to perform a task that the adult thinks the child can do? Is the adult in this situation using a mature level of theory of mind? Explain your answer.

5. Use a child development textbook to find information about *social referencing*. If toddling babies need their mother's attentive look to maintain balance while walking, what would you expect to be the result of maternal depression or drug and alcohol use? Briefly state how researchers might look for evidence of the outcome you expect. Explain your answers.

References

Mason, M. F., & Macrae, C. N. (2008). Perspective-taking from a social neuroscience standpoint. *Group Process and Intergroup Relations, 11,* 215–232.

Rogoff, B. (1990). *Apprenticeship in learning: Cognitive development in a social context.* New York: Oxford University Press.

Skibbe, L., Behnke, M., & Justice, L. M. (2004). Parental scaffolding of children's phonological awareness skills: Interactions between mothers and their preschoolers with language difficulties. *Communication Disorders Quarterly, 25,* 189–203.

Tollefson, D. (2005). Let's pretend! Children and joint action. *Philosophy of the Social Sciences, 35,* 75–97.

Willingham, D. T. (2008). What is developmentally appropriate practice? *American Educator, 32,* 34–39.

Claim 25

Preschoolers who hold their breath when angry are trying to upset their parents and get their own way.

Four-year-old Marcus did it again. He was startled when his grandmother suddenly grabbed away a sharp knife he had picked up. (She was afraid he would cut himself.) Marcus took one breath and then stood there, not breathing. His lips turned blue, and after a moment he fell to the ground, apparently unconscious. Very quickly he began to breathe again and came to, sniffling a bit and surrounded by some frightened adults. Marcus's mother, Ayesha, rushed to call the doctor and report that Marcus had had another spell of breath-holding. She was terrified that he would die during one of these incidents and wanted some preventive treatment. Marcus's grandmother was concerned too, but she commented, "That boy just does that when he's mad and wants to get back at people. I took the knife he wanted and he thought he'd punish me. But I wasn't born yesterday! Ayesha, don't bother the doctor anymore. We'll just ignore Marcus when he tries to get his way like this."

Were either Ayesha or her mother right about Marcus's breath-holding spells?

Breath-holding spells—more formally known as *cyanotic and pallid infantile syncope*—are frightening, frustrating, and even annoying to parents. These situations usually involve a preschooler who is surprised or suddenly angered by some event. Maybe another child grabbed a toy, or the preschooler's mother snatched the child away from a dangerous road. The child begins to cry loudly or just takes in a breath and holds it; in short order, the child turns pale or ashy or bluish, takes no other breaths, and loses consciousness. As one mother described it, "he went limp . . . his eyes had rolled back into his head. His face was covered with a sheen of sweat and had gone from pink to whitish-grey." A minute or so later, the child "opened his eyes. His pallor faded slowly. . . . His hair was wet from sweat" (Horn, 2007, p. F5).

Naturally, parents are scared by their child's apparent brush with death, especially the first time it happens. They are likely to seek assurance from medical professionals that there is no serious cause for the problem (as indeed they should, because not all loss of consciousness is the same; Stephenson, 2007). Repeat performances may receive a different reaction, especially if the parent forms the impression that the child is trying to manipulate or punish the adults or get his or her own way inappropriately. Parents who frame the situation as manipulative often respond with anger. They may act on advice to walk away and ignore the child or even to throw a bucket of cold water over the unconscious preschooler.

Does the breath-holding spell suggest that the child is trying to influence the adult? Sometimes breath-holding accompanies anger, and sometimes that anger is directed at an adult caregiver. However, breath-holding also can occur when a child is simply surprised, not angry, or when a child is angry at a pet or another child, who probably will not be much concerned at the apparently dangerous physical crisis. Whatever construction a parent may place on breath-holding, the phenomenon is probably not an attempt to manipulate or punish anyone.

Can a preschooler understand adult thinking well enough to plan a show that will frighten a caregiver? This question deals not with a child's capacity to hold his or her breath for a long time but with the child's ability to contemplate the effects of the action. To make such a plan, the child would have to be able to imagine his or her own death or loss of consciousness, envision an adult's response to one of these events, anticipate the adult's deep emotional distress, and anticipate the practical consequences, such as calling an ambulance or doing CPR. Although adolescents and adults can have fantasies about "how they'll feel when I'm gone," preschoolers' limited understanding of others' mental states makes it unlikely that they could manage this complicated cognitive and emotional process. If a preschool child wished to punish or manipulate an adult by causing distress, the child would probably not be able to figure out how to do this. Even when dealing with other preschoolers, children do not usually manage psychological retaliation any more complex than the vague threat, "I won't be your friend."

Given that preschoolers cannot plan to cause others emotional upset, questions remain about the actual events of breath-holding. What is really happening when children suddenly lose consciousness? Can children voluntarily refrain from breathing until unconsciousness occurs? Although it is not always useful to examine adults' abilities to understand children's abilities, it seems significant that few adults can effectively hold their breath long enough to lose consciousness. The urge to breathe becomes irresistible, particularly as the person becomes faint and thinks less clearly about the goal. It seems most unlikely that young children could exert the will not to breathe more effectively than, or even as well as, adults. Even if a preschooler intended to cause emotional distress by losing consciousness, he or she could probably not manage to carry out the plan.

In fact, loss of consciousness following breath-holding seems to be related to a reflex that is characteristic of preschool children and uncommon after 5 years of age. When blood flow to the brain is restricted—perhaps by pressure inside the chest due to loud crying—the child loses consciousness. Movement stops, and with this event the body's demand for oxygen is reduced, allowing the available supply to go to the vulnerable brain. Like other reflexes, this one is not under voluntary control, nor is it obvious what benefit the individual derives from the reflex, except for restoration of breathing. And, also like other reflexes, this one takes place when the right stimulus occurs, not when the individual wants it to happen (Stephenson, 2007).

What about throwing cold water on a child? Such a reaction might be gratifying to the perturbed adult, but it will not prevent another episode of breath-holding. If children do not voluntarily hold their breath, then they cannot decide *not* to do this, even if it means they could avoid punishment. Waking up cold, wet, and confused will not be of any help. Children usually emerge from their loss of consciousness feeling exhausted and frightened, needing comfort rather than punishment. If breath-holding spells occur frequently in a child, the parents need to develop a good response plan. They also need to teach babysitters, relatives, and child care providers what to do when their child loses consciousness and to be sure that everyone understands that the child is not exhibiting "bad behavior." Everyone involved, including the child, can take some comfort in the problem being cured with time. However, some children go on for some years having breath-holding episodes (Goraya & Virdi, 2001).

Conclusion

Breath-holding spells are involuntary and are not a preschooler's way of intentionally distressing adults. Marcus's mother, Ayesha, was overly concerned and did not seem reassured that there was no serious medical problem; his grandmother's approach of ignoring Marcus was based on some incorrect assumptions about preschoolers' thinking and was probably not the best reaction.

CRITICAL THINKING

1. Use a child development textbook to define the term *reflex*. What are some other examples of reflexes that change with age?

2. Horn (2007) described a way to test whether a child has the reflex involved in breath-holding spells. Stephenson (2007) mentions the same method to test the reflex. Under what circumstances would you think this test should be used? Would it be appropriate for most parents or teachers to perform the test?

3. Read about parental styles in a child development textbook. Explain how you would expect parents of each style to respond to a child's breath-holding. What style would you expect to be associated with the assumption that children hold their breath to manipulate adults? Explain your answer.

4. Would you expect a preschooler to have more- or less-frequent breath-holding spells if given much care and comfort after each one? Explain your answer using the concept of positive reinforcement. Remember that breath-holding spells are not voluntary.

5. Would you expect a preschooler to have breath-holding spells less or more frequently if punished after each one? Explain your answer.

References

Goraya, J. S., & Virdi, V. S. (2001). Persistence of breath-holding spells into late childhood. *Journal of Child Neurology, 16,* 697–698.

Horn, J. (2007, July 10). Saving a child, scaring a parent: A fainting reflex. *New York Times,* p. F5.

Stephenson, J. B. P. (2007). Clinical diagnosis of syncopes (including so-called breath-holding spells) without electroencephalography or ocular compression. *Journal of Child Neurology, 22,* 502–508.

Claim 26

Vaccines are a cause of autism.

Laurie and Joe had always thought autism was one of the worst things they could imagine happening to their children. They had seen several movies that featured autistic people, and Laurie and Joe found the images distressing. Even before their twins were born, Laurie and Joe became more concerned that something might happen to cause them to be autistic. Looking up autism on the Internet, they came across the idea that autism was caused by the administration of vaccines that contained mercury preservatives. Little Paula and Peter received their first immunizations on the normal schedule, but as they grew toward their first birthdays Laurie became terribly worried. She read accounts of babies who were perfectly normal, even beginning to talk, then had bad reactions to vaccines and were later diagnosed as autistic. She dreaded having something happen to her children, especially because she felt she knew enough to protect them. Laurie told her neighbor she was thinking about canceling the twins' pediatrician appointment and never going back. "But, Laurie," said her neighbor, "don't you realize what might happen if they got one of the diseases that are prevented by vaccines? They could be brain damaged or even die."

Was Laurie right to want to avoid exposing the twins to vaccines?

Although research has repeatedly disconfirmed the accuracy of the idea, people persist in believing that infants and toddlers who are immunized against childhood diseases may, as a result, be afflicted with autism or similar disorders. Gossip among parents, Internet chat groups, and published books and articles continue to blame vaccines for the existence of autism. Most often, the responsible factor is said to be not the vaccine itself but a mercury-containing preservative, thimerosol, which has not been used for some years.

Although no evidence supports vaccines as the cause of autism (Caplan, 2006), the idea is not without logic. Many immunizations are scheduled in the first months and years of life, and babies usually respond to them with distress—most notably crying and sometimes a slight fever and restlessness. The early toddler period is also the point at which many parents of autistic children notice for the first time that something is unusual about their child's behavior and development, particularly the beginnings of speech (Young, Brewer, & Pattison, 2003). Parents typically seek help for their children when the children reach about 3 years of age and still do not talk or communicate in other ways. The shared timing of immunizations and noticeably unusual behavior makes it easy to assume that one causes the other, even though no evidence supports that conclusion. Some researchers have suggested that variant forms of autism exist: a form that shows symptoms in very early infancy and another that results in developmental regression in the toddler period (Ozonoff, Williams, & Landa, 2005; Woo et al., 2007). The regressive type of disorder obviously raises the question of causation by a recent, preceding event.

There is also a certain logic in placing blame on mercury. This toxic substance has been associated with brain damage in both children and adults. The old expression "mad as a hatter" refers to brain damage sustained by people who were exposed to manufacturing chemicals, including mercury, while making felt hats. It is not unreasonable to speculate that such a dangerous substance can change the pattern of development in a young child's vulnerable brain. However, the use of mercury-containing thimerosol as a preservative was discontinued some years ago, so the idea that recent cases of autistic disorders are caused by mercury in vaccines defies logic.

It is not surprising that families with autistic children seek desperately for an environmental factor causing this pervasive mental and social disturbance. If experts could identify an environmental cause for autism, they could prevent and perhaps cure this very serious disabling condition. So far, though, no evidence exists to support environmental factors as the cause of autism—although some once thought that they did. If environmental causes exist, the responsible events must be quite complex or it would be unlikely that four times as many boys as girls would be diagnosed as autistic; boys and girls have different experiences, but perhaps not that different during the first 3 years of life.

Recent work on a problem similar to autism suggested strongly that genetic factors may play a role in the development of these disorders. The disorder in question, Rett syndrome, is unusual in that it is diagnosed in girls rather than in boys. Rett syndrome appears to be caused by a genetic mutation rather than by a predictable inheritance from previous generations, such as that responsible for eye color or hair texture. Some symptoms of Rett syndrome resemble those of autism, and the genetic changes involved in the disorder are known, so researchers often choose to study Rett syndrome for the clues it may give to autism, whose genetic characteristics are not so well understood (Miller, 2006).

Boys can have the Rett mutation, but those who do die from respiratory problems at a very young age. Girls with the mutation survive, appearing healthy at first. As toddlers, however, they begin to regress in language and social development. They become irritable and show stereotyped hand-wringing movements. Like all children with developmental handicaps, Rett syndrome girls continue to grow and develop, but their developmental pathway involves abnormal breathing and movement as well as serious cognitive problems. Although the language and social problems of Rett girls are comparable to those of autistic children, their other problems are different. The two disorders resemble each other in that parents may not see any developmental problems in the first months of their children's lives and that the onset of symptoms is fairly sudden, as if triggered by an event in the environment.

Researchers have found a strain of mice whose unusual genetic makeup creates an outcome much like Rett syndrome, including similar odd movement patterns. These mice seem to have high levels of stress hormones, and this may also be true of girls with Rett syndrome. Geneticists are able to inactivate and then reactivate the relevant gene in mice but do not have the techniques to do this in humans.

Although a disorder may be partly due to an environmental cause and partly to genetic factors, the information available at this time seems to suggest a strong genetic component as a cause of autism. It does not seem to be the case that vaccines cause autism, although for ethical reasons experimental testing of this idea has not been possible. The persistent belief in vaccines as the cause of autism is regrettable because it can discourage parents from seeking vaccination against potentially dangerous childhood diseases. Such diseases many years ago regularly killed some children and caused others to experience brain damage that led to mental retardation, deafness, or blindness. Parents' concern with the effect of vaccines caused a reduction in immunization of Scandinavian children some years ago, and that change in turn caused some epidemics of the childhood disease pertussis (whooping cough). Bioethicist Arthur Caplan (2006) and others have made education on these issues a major concern and stress the need to counter mistaken beliefs about the causes of autism.

A side issue is the danger inherent in the belief that mercury is the specific component of vaccines that causes autism. When children ingest too much mercury, which has toxic effects, some of the element can be removed from their bodies by a process called chelation. Unfortunately, when chelation therapy is performed on autistic children (or others who do not have excessive amounts of mercury in their bodies), the result may be the child's death ("Pennsylvania," 2007).

An interesting but very new speculation about the vaccine-autism issue has to do with mitochondrial disorders. Mitochondria are components of cells that are inherited from mothers only. Mitochondria contain DNA that is not organized into chromosome structures, and this DNA affects development in poorly understood ways. Disorders resulting from mitochondrial DNA problems are unpredictable and difficult to diagnose. One possibility—at this point totally unconfirmed—is that children with mitochondrial problems may react to vaccines differently than those without such disorders (Harris, 2008).

Conclusion

Vaccines have not been shown to be causes of autism, which is probably largely genetic in origin, and the diseases the immunizations prevent are very serious. Laurie would do well to follow her neighbor's advice and follow a regular immunization schedule for her twins.

CRITICAL THINKING

1. Boys are much more likely than girls to be diagnosed with autism. What does this fact suggest about the causes of autism? Argue for and against the idea that genetic factors are the primary cause.

2. Find a description of the early symptoms of autism in a child development textbook. Compare these symptoms with the description of Rett syndrome given in this section. Are the two sets of symptoms similar?

3. Use a child development textbook to find a definition of *experience-dependent plasticity*. Is the period of time when Rett syndrome begins to affect behavior also a time when high experience-dependent plasticity is expected? Why or why not?

4. Can a child with an unusual genetic makeup have a different period of experience-dependent plasticity than other children do? Explain your answer.

5. Read the article by Miller (2006) to find ideas about combined factors of experience and heredity as causes of Rett syndrome. Do reasons other than genetic makeup explain why girls with Rett syndrome have high levels of stress hormones? Would you expect these reasons to apply to mice, too? Explain your answer.

References

Caplan, A. (2006, Feb. 6). Fact: No link of vaccine, autism. *Philadelphia Inquirer*, p. A11.

Harris, G. (2008, June 28). Experts to discuss one puzzling autism case, as a second case has arisen. *New York Times*, A15.

Miller, G. (2006). Getting a read on Rett syndrome. *Science, 314*, 1536–1537.

Ozonoff, S., Williams, B. J., & Landa, R. (2005). Parental report of the early development of children with regressive autism. *Autism, 9*, 461–486.

Pennsylvania: Charge in death after chelation treatment. (2007, August 23). *New York Times*, p. A17.

Woo, E. J., Ball, R., Landa, R., Zimmerman, A. W., Braun, M. M., & VAERS Working Group. (2007). Developmental regression and autism reported to the Vaccine Adverse Event Reporting System. *Autism, 11*, 301–310.

Young, R. L., Brewer, N., & Pattison, C. (2003). Parental identification of early behavioral abnormalities in children with autistic disorder. *Autism, 7*, 125–143.

Claim 27

Autism rates are rising rapidly, especially in certain parts of the country, so something must be happening to cause more cases of this serious developmental problem.

The Becker family had one child, a 5-year-old boy, and a second baby was on the way. Sherry Becker and her husband, Alan, had discussed many times how much they'd like to have a summer house by the shore, and it seemed that it would be so nice to be able to spend part of each hot East Coast summer at the beach. Sherry mentioned this to her sister, naming the coastal community where they were considering buying. To Sherry's great surprise, her sister was horrified. "You're not going to go there while you're pregnant or when the baby's little, are you? Haven't you read the papers about all the cases of autism they've found in that place? The rates are getting higher and higher. There has to be something dangerous there that gets into the babies' brains. Please promise me you won't do this." Sherry didn't know what to think.

Was it wise for the family to move to such an area at this point in their lives?

Of all mental disorders of early life, autism is the one most likely to receive frightening treatment in the headlines. References to autistic disorders in the movies and on TV have made the diagnosis familiar to most people, but have not provided them much real information about its symptoms or treatment. It is certainly true that autistic children suffer from a number of problems of development and that the lives of their families can be much disrupted by the demands of the children's mental and emotional states. It is also true that although children with autism continue to develop toward adulthood the chances are small that they will manage to attain a fully mature and independent way of life. A small number of high-functioning autistic individuals, such as the noted author Temple Grandin, achieve a great deal of competence, but most autistic people need a good deal of support and protection.

Autism is no picnic for anyone, and it is not surprising that parents are easily alarmed about it. However, some frightening ideas about the disorder may be less disturbing with explanation. Two of these ideas are that rates of autism are increasing rapidly and that an environmental event is causing the problem.

To analyze these ideas, one must first consider the changing rates of autism. It is easy to forget that *rates* are not measures of absolute numbers. In other words, if the number of new cases of autism in a state are cited, the numbers do not refer to a rate. The term *rate* refers to a proportion and is related to the word *ratio*. Information about a rate must state the number of cases of a disorder for a total number of people, both those with and those without the disorder. The more people in an area, the more cases of autism; likewise, the fewer people, the fewer cases. But the actual *rate* (proportion of autistic individuals out of the entire population) could be the same in both situations.

A second important point involves reported rates of diagnosed disorders (Steuernagel, 2005). The reported rates are not based on a magical method of instantly counting how many people have a disorder. Instead, the determination of diagnosed cases involves the process of examining each individual, making the decision about the diagnosis, and collating that information for a given area. If a diagnosis is difficult to make, and few people have received the diagnosis, the rate of a disorder in an area will appear low, even if there are many undetected cases. If the authorities become more aware of a disorder and if practitioners develop more accurate diagnostic techniques, the rate will appear to rise, even though there are no real changes in the underlying facts. The number of diagnosed cases of autism in an area is related to the actual number of cases, but the number of diagnosed cases can rise or fall without any changes in the actual number. The rate of diagnosed cases of autism can vary a great deal from one area of the country to another, without any real difference in children's conditions in different states or towns.

A recent study by the Centers for Disease Control and Prevention (CDC) compared the number of children diagnosed with autism in 14 states, in each state's case comparing the proportion of autistic 8-year-olds to the entire

8-year-old population of the state (Kelley, 2007). Researchers noted large differences among the states. For example, New Jersey had the highest proportion of children diagnosed with autism, with 16.8 boys identified out of every 1,000 boys of this age. Alabama had the lowest rate, with only 5 boys diagnosed as autistic out of every 1,000 boys. The same state difference held for girls, with 4 out of every 1,000 New Jersey girls assessed as autistic, and only 1.4 of every 1,000 Alabama girls receiving this diagnosis.

After reading these data, you may be thinking, what is going on here? Is there a problem in New Jersey? Does the industrial background of parts of this state expose children to lead and mercury, toxic substances whose contribution to autistic disorders has been hypothesized? This might make some sense in comparison with Alabama, a much more rural and agricultural area, where one might expect children to be exposed less to toxic manufacturing materials. But looking back at the data provided by the CDC, readers would see that Utah has a high rate of autism reported for boys and a rather low rate for girls. Now what do readers do with the idea that toxic materials are causing autism? Can it be that in Utah boys are exposed to toxic substances and girls are not?

The CDC data do not explain the causes of autism; however, inspecting differences between states may help readers to detect certain important factors related to reported autism rates as well as the actual number of autistic children, both diagnosed and undiagnosed. It's true that there will probably not be many cases of autism reported if there are not many autistic children present, but it is also true that there can be few cases reported when there actually are many children with the disorder. Before a case is reported to CDC and entered into the records, one or more adults must have been aware of symptoms of autism, ready to take a child to be evaluated, and able to make and communicate the diagnosis and file the record in a state data system. The presence or absence of adults able to do these tasks may be one of the essential factors that determine the reported rate of autism in a state. Autistic symptoms are both subtle (Jones, Carr, & Feeley, 2006) and pervasive (Herbert, 2005). Paradoxical as it may seem, larger numbers of educated and competent adults in a state may cause the reported rate of autism in the state to rise. (But few people would argue that autism is caused by exposure to educated adults.)

Whether New Jersey really has more than its fair share of autistic children is difficult to determine, but it is clear that the state's population has characteristics that encourage correct diagnosis of autistic children, including an elaborate state record-keeping system, good public education with special education services, and a high proportion of parents who are college graduates and may thus have some knowledge of developmental disorders.

A distressing issue about autism involves clusters of cases in specific geographical areas. Reports of clusters lead people to think that an unidentified characteristic of an area is making children autistic. Parents who are aware of clusters may also think that if they stay away from the implicated areas their children will not become autistic. However, the real cause of a cluster may be a statistical one. Random distribution of cases, which is expected for natural disorders, does not mean absolute uniformity of occurrence in all places. It would be surprising if there were no natural variation—the phenomenon that causes some areas to have higher and some to have lower numbers of cases of autism (or any other disorder). In addition, mistakes in identifying a cluster may be made if the expected number is not accurately determined or even if the definition of autistic symptoms has changed (Baron-Cohen, Saunders, & Chakrabarti, 1999).

Experts seem to have a much better understanding of how autistic children receive a diagnosis, and what statistical factors are at work, rather than of how children become autistic. However, one thing is clear: When people see an increase in rates of autism and want to make related decisions for their families, they need to consider whether the increase results from better reporting or from real changes in children's conditions.

Conclusion

Changes in reported rates of autism are influenced by many factors other than the actual proportion of autistic children in the population, so people cannot use information about only those changed rates to determine causes of autism. Sherry's sister has misinterpreted the significance of high reported rates of autism in a geographical area.

CRITICAL THINKING

1. Use a child development textbook to find a description of autism. Basing your answer on this description, explain why 8-year-old children were chosen for the CDC study. Isn't it possible to diagnose the disorder in much younger children?

2. If no autistic children were in a group, would none be diagnosed? If several autistic children were in a group, would any or all be diagnosed? Read a textbook description of autism and use it to explain your answer to this question. Be sure to consider whether all autistic individuals behave in the same way or whether there are individual differences.

(Continued)

(Continued)

3. Why is it important to compare proportions of children diagnosed with autism (e.g., 16.8 boys per 1,000 in New Jersey and 5 per 1,000 in Alabama) rather than absolute numbers (e.g., 722 in one state and 135 in another)?

4. Read the article by Kelley (2007). Why does the author think it is significant that a state diagnoses many autistic children while they are still very young? Provide more than one reason that supports this attitude.

5. Each state in the CDC study reported that the number of boys diagnosed with autism was at least 3 or 4 times more than the number of girls diagnosed with autism. Comment on two possible causes of autism that might explain this fact.

References

Baron-Cohen, S., Saunders, K., & Chakrabarti, S. (1999). Does autism cluster geographically? A research note. *Autism, 3,* 39–43.

Herbert, M. R. (2005). Large brains in autism: The challenge of pervasive abnormality. *The Neuroscientist, 11,* 417–440.

Jones, E. A., Carr, E. G., & Feeley, K. M. (2006). Multiple effects of joint attention intervention for children with autism. *Behavior Modification, 30,* 782–834.

Kelley, T. (2007, February 18). An autism anomaly, partly explained. *New York Times,* p. WK2.

Steuernagel, T. (2005). Increases in identified cases of autism spectrum disorders. *Journal of Disability Policy Studies, 16,* 138–146.

Claim 28

Children with brain injuries can be rehabilitated by using practices like patterning, and other problems can be treated with similar approaches.

People in Tyra's neighborhood were standing on the sidewalk talking about an accident that had recently occurred. Six-year-old Mikey, who was entirely too brave with his new bicycle, had been hit by a car, and was transported, unconscious, to the hospital. He had been in the hospital for several days. Mikey's mother told Tyra, "I'm sure he'll get well, but they want to keep him in the hospital to see if he has any brain damage. He would never mind me when I said to wear his bike helmet." "Don't worry too much about that," Tyra told her. "There was a boy where I used to live who had brain damage, and his mother and the neighbors used to work on him every day, moving his arms and legs around. There are things you can do that help."

Was Tyra right? Can a child's damaged brain be restored by exercises at home?

Professional treatments for brain damage may involve exercises that help strengthen muscles and restore muscular control and can include practice sessions in which the patient works toward recovering lost functions of other kinds. But patterning is a method usually considered outside the range of conventional medical treatments. It is a controversial method that involves techniques different from those ordinarily employed by physicians, physical therapists, and occupational therapists. Controversial treatments are those practices that are claimed to cure a problem when they do not actually do so (McWilliam, 1999). Like many conventional interventions (Barry, 1996),

155

controversial treatments may be difficult to evaluate, but their logic can be examined.

Patterning is a treatment in which adults, usually volunteers and relatives, move the limbs and head of a child through a series of motions that are thought to resemble the reflex movements of a very young infant. This treatment is usually done for a child who has severe brain damage as a result of accidental injury or a disease, such as cancer.

Patterning is usually, but not always, implemented with children whose severe brain damage leaves them without apparent consciousness or the ability to move their bodies voluntarily. Even simple movements such as swallowing may be difficult or impossible for these children. Their level of disability makes it impossible for them to participate in therapy that includes practicing movements or speech sounds. Adults who practice patterning move the limbs and head of the passive, unresistant child; the child does not try to make the movement, so the situation is not like the spontaneous movements of a very young infant.

Patterning is not usually part of a conventional medical or rehabilitation treatment, but some readers may have heard of relatives or neighbors who used the method or may even have been asked to participate. Because five adults are needed each time patterning is done, and because it is supposed to be carried out every day, several times a day, families often need to organize a large number of friends and acquaintances to help them.

The idea behind patterning is the speculation that damaged brain structures can be recreated by providing stimulation resembling that experienced during the growth period of early infancy. This hypothesized gradual restructuring, which would, if it worked, restore the normal, undamaged brain condition, can be called *recapitulation*, or repetition of a process from the beginning. Sadly, for families whose children have suffered severe brain damage, no evidence supports the effectiveness of patterning for successful recapitulation and recovery of function.

The idea that damaged brain functions can be retrained is not such a very strange or wrong one. Even adults who suffer a brain-damaging stroke are likely to recover some or all functions, especially with appropriate physical, psychological, and speech therapy. Young infants show a surprising ability to recover completely from devastating injuries, such as the loss of half of the cortex. It is clear that a damaged brain can do some healing, and uninjured parts of the brain can take over some of the functions of injured parts. But this process involves the continuing development of the brain from the time the injury occurred. It does not involve a return to "square one" of brain development and a repetition of earlier, normal brain-development processes.

A common error in thinking about brain functions is the assumption that a brain injury (or even the experience of an emotional trauma) simply stops brain development in its tracks or causes it to "rewind" to earlier stages. In reality, the injured brain continues to develop in a pattern determined in part by the injury, in some ways parallel or identical to normal development but in other ways quite different. The situation is similar to the body growth of a severely brain-damaged child, which is slowed and perhaps distorted by a lack of movement but does not stop altogether.

Although some families have persisted for years in using patterning, no evidence supports the effectiveness of the treatment, and the American Academy of Pediatrics has twice issued policy statements advising against its use (American Academy of Pediatrics Committee on Children with Disabilities, 1999). Children treated with patterning are not likely to recover consciousness or move by themselves, and if they do the outcome is not caused by the patterning treatment. However, the frequent handling and movement of the injured children's bodies may prevent some physical problems that might otherwise develop in an unconscious, immobile human being.

Families who implement patterning must be enormously motivated to carry out this difficult work. Organizing help and scheduling daily treatments are demanding tasks. For patterning with school-age children or adolescents, the physical task of moving the "dead weight" of a limb or the head is a challenge to helpers. It is not surprising that highly motivated and engaged parents may notice any little change in their child's face or body and interpret these as evidence of returning consciousness and voluntary movement.

Research on physical or psychological treatments such as patterning ideally involves *blind* studies. This means that the people who evaluate a child's condition do not know what treatment the child has been receiving and thus are not influenced by their own expectations of the value of the treatment. Studies of treatments like patterning, however, are often not blind, and the parents often evaluate their child's condition following treatment. It may seem unsympathetic to say that a parent of a sick child is not a good source of evidence about a treatment's outcome, and certainly parent support groups stress parents' personal knowledge as more important than objective measurement. But many professionals argue that high research standards need to be applied to treatments for children and that the emotional involvement of families prevents them from accurately judging their children's performance.

If conventional treatment can offer little help for severely brain-damaged children, what harm is there in encouraging parents to use patterning and keep up their hopes? In some cases, no harm is done, but in other cases the stress placed on the family is overwhelming, leading to marital rifts and the denial of time and resources for other children in the family. In addition, beliefs associated with patterning have been applied in other cases besides that of brain damage. For example, some people claim that normally developing children might need a form of patterning if they are slow to learn to read. Crawling movements have been stated to be an essential way to cause brain and cognitive development, and many years ago some elementary schools actually implemented remedial programs that required children to crawl or to practice more complex motor skills like skipping, in the belief that their school work would suffer otherwise. These related beliefs can misdirect school and family resources and cause other problems.

Conclusion

Although many brain-injured children recover well, they do so spontaneously or as a result of conventional treatments. Family treatments such as patterning are not known to be effective. Although Tyra's statement may have comforted Mikey's mother and was valuable in that way, it was not a reliable piece of information.

CRITICAL THINKING

1. Use a child development textbook to define *plasticity*. Explain how plasticity of brain development is related to the possible effectiveness of patterning.

2. In normal development, certain movement patterns and certain brain developments occur at about the same time. Does this mean that one causes the other? Explain your answer.

3. Search the Internet for comments by a parent support group devoted to any early childhood problem you choose. Do the parents seem interested in evidence from formal research, or do they feel that their group's personal experiences are more meaningful? Explain the reasons for your answer.

4. Are the current debates about persistent vegetative states relevant to the patterning issue? How might these arguments affect parents' decisions to use patterning?

5. Read the comments by former Surgeon General Everett Koop (2002). How do Koop's remarks apply to parents' decisions about patterning?

References

American Academy of Pediatrics Committee on Children with Disabilities. (1999). The treatment of neurologically impaired children using patterning. *Pediatrics*, *104*, 1149–1151.

Barry, M. J. (1996). Physical therapy interventions for patients with movement disorders due to cerebral palsy. *Journal of Child Neurology*, *11*(Suppl. 1), 51–60.

Koop, E. (2002). The future of medicine. *Science*, *295*, 233.

McWilliam, R. A. (1999). Controversial practices: The need for a reacculturation of early intervention fields. *Topics in Early Childhood Special Education*, *19*, 177–188.

Claim 29

Preschoolers who try to bargain with their parents really want to manipulate and control adults, and they should not be allowed to negotiate.

"Oh, Mom! I want to play some more. Can't I have one more game? Can I wait until the long hand is on the 6?" One more game, one more minute, one more hug, one more drink of water, one less spoonful of green beans—these were the requests 4-year-old Hamid made of his mother, many times every day and on into the night. Hamid's mother found life much simpler if she gave in and agreed to some of these bargains, although she usually drew the line at some point. Hamid generally did what she asked him to after a little negotiation had taken place. But Hamid's grandfather did not approve. "You're just letting him get his own way all the time. You've already spoiled him. Otherwise, he wouldn't be trying to control you so much. You'd better insist he does things your way, whether he cries and begs or not! He'll become a monster if you don't!"

Is Hamid's grandfather right? Are all of Hamid's requests aimed at taking command of the adults, who ought to be in charge?

Like human beings of any age, preschoolers want what they want (it would be pretty silly for them to want what they don't want). In that sense, bargaining with parents is an attempt to be in control of their own lives. But parents of preschool children often feel that some bargaining goes far beyond matters that the child actually wants or needs. It seems to some parents that bargaining is a way of life for their preschooler, and many parents become concerned that their child wants to take control of everything in the household. Could this be true? Is a child's wish to be in control for the sake of control itself? Is the preschooler's goal to exploit adults and to win a secret game that is being played without the adults' knowledge? These questions are probably most accurately answered in the negative. Bargaining and negotiating over bedtime, meals, and departure for child care are most likely normal steps in a preschooler's development of social skills and close relationships.

Late toddlerhood has been labeled "the terrible twos," in part because of children's strenuous efforts to get their own way in matters that sometimes seem ridiculous to their parents. Exactly why preschoolers behave in this sometimes very trying way is difficult to explore through empirical research, unfortunately. Children of this age group are not able—and might not be willing—to explain their motives. Indeed, even if researchers waited until the children were older to investigate this issue, and perhaps tried to link parent reports of toddler argumentativeness with later attitudes toward other people, they would find their research embroiled with multiple confounding variables.

Because research approaches are difficult, attempts to explain early childhood bargaining have usually been in the form of theoretical statements based on clinical observation and have sometimes stemmed from the study of working relationships between parents and children. The famous attachment theorist John Bowlby (1982) and some of his successors consider negotiation and bargaining to be a natural and desirable stage in the growth of an internal working model of social relationships. An internal working model is a set of thoughts and feelings, in this case the ideas and emotions that help to determine how a person behaves toward others and expects them to behave toward him or her. In Bowlby's view, negotiation with parents follows a child's establishment of an emotional attachment to a few preferred, familiar people, and such negotiation is part of a child's efforts to handle separation. The young child cannot avoid all experiences of separation from familiar adults, but the child can have some sense of security, control, and confidence as a result of negotiating about separation. The ability to delay the parent's departure from the day care center by asking for five more kisses or to put off saying "good night" by arguing over the exact amount the door is to be left open is sufficient to help buffer the young child against the fear of separation and possible loss.

Bowlby's (1982) view of bargaining stresses the comfort the preschooler can derive from negotiating with adults. Such comfort and security can provide a good context for exploring and learning about the world, much like the secure base a toddler needs for exploring the world. A child who cannot bargain and negotiate may experience anxiety that interferes with learning and thinking. In addition, the experience of bargaining with adults is an excellent way to practice negotiation and compromise skills that will be beneficial in the future. Children can also work on such skills with peers, but an adult's ability to bargain provides a more advanced model from which a child can learn.

Because negotiation and bargaining involve at least two participants, they can be considered from a transactional point of view, with the assumption that each person affects and is affected by the other. Modern research on this topic studies the contributions of both the parent and the child to their conflict and its resolution.

Although it may seem most important to study what the children do, parents play a powerful role in a child's learning about negotiation. Parents frequently introduce their own strategies of bargaining and reasoning to a preschool child's resistance or expression of distaste (e.g., rejection of a food item) (Crockenberg & Litman, 1991). Experience with these parental strategies is a factor in developing a child's later willingness to cooperate and compromise. Parents who respond to conflict with coercion, and stress their authority, may be setting the stage for their children to be poor and reluctant negotiators.

Why does parental negotiation have a positive effect on a child's cooperativeness and social skills? One reason may be the use of language and reasoning modeled by the parent, learned by the child, and later employed by the child in interactions with other children and adults. Language of some sort is essential to bargaining. Parents who react coercively to children's behavior may model little useful language because they may remain silent or shout in ways that convey little except their anger.

The process of negotiation also requires some knowledge of what another person might know or want and how that knowledge or motivation may be different from one's own. A child who offers a teddy bear as an incentive for a parent to forget about bedtime will probably be unsuccessful, but one who promises to stay quietly on the sofa wrapped in a blanket may succeed, especially if the parent's real wish is for a little peace rather than for the child actually to be asleep. Similarly, a parent who is trying to say good night may find the promise of a distant trip to Disneyland unsuccessful, but a child who really wishes to postpone separation might accept a promise to come back in 10 minutes and look in the door. Parents' and children's negotiations help children learn how other people's needs and wishes are different from their own, knowledge which will contribute greatly to later abilities to compromise and cooperate. For example, both preschoolers and older children frequently find themselves in conflict with their peers (David, Murphy, Naylor, & Stonecipher, 2004), and negotiating skills that were learned earlier can be helpful in these situations.

Adults who lack the ability to understand a child's needs may find negotiation a demanding and frustrating task, as may those who find it hard to articulate a compromise position between their wishes and their child's. The same difficulties can occur when parents feel anxiety about the outcome of negotiation and believe, as it has traditionally been claimed, that "either you rule your child or your child rules you." These parents' beliefs about human relationships can lead them to avoid compromise rather than to encourage their children's negotiating skills. Parents who have better empathic abilities, on the other hand, may both foster secure attachment in their children and negotiate with them more successfully (Gini, Oppenheim, & Sagi-Schwartz, 2007).

Conclusion

Difficult as it may be to deal with a preschooler's bargaining demands at times, negotiations between parents and young children have real advantages for social development. Children who have healthy bargaining experiences, where both sides compromise, can develop useful social skills. Hamid's mother is right in negotiating with him, but of course she is also right in stopping when a reasonable compromise has been achieved.

CRITICAL THINKING

1. Use a child development textbook to find a description of a parental style that avoids negotiation with young children and relies on exertion of the parent's authority. Explain your choice.

2. Read the study by Crockenberg and Litman (1991). Why do you think the authors chose to study this particular group of mothers and children? Do you think the findings would be different if this study were done again today? Explain your answer.

3. Studies of family interactions often have difficulty in separating the effects of variables such as mothers' styles and child gender or age. What confounding variables were present in the Crockenberg and Litman study (1991)? Explain your choice.

(Continued)

(Continued)

4. What relationship do you see between the use of physical punishment, such as spanking, for preschoolers and the encouragement of compromise and cooperation? Can parents use physical punishment regularly and still have opportunities for bargaining? Explain your answer.

5. List and describe several situations in middle childhood in which the ability to bargain and compromise would be useful. Consider events at home, in school, and in play or sports. Use information from a child development textbook to support your view.

References

Bowlby, J. (1982). *Attachment*. New York: Basic.

Crockenberg, S., & Litman, C. (1991). Effects of maternal employment on maternal and two-year-old child behavior. *Child Development, 62*, 930–953.

David, K. M., Murphy, B. C., Naylor, J. M., & Stonecipher, K. M. (2004). The effects of conflict role and intensity on preschoolers' expectations about peer conflict. *International Journal of Behavioral Development, 28*, 508–517.

Gini, M., Oppenheim, D., & Sagi-Schwartz, A. (2007). Negotiation styles in mother-child narrative co-construction in middle childhood: Associations with early attachment. *International Journal of Behavioral Development, 31*, 149–160.

PART IV

School-Age Children

Claim 30

Children who play with matches will grow up to be seriously disturbed and violent and will probably be serial killers, especially if they are also cruel to animals and wet their beds.

Seven-year-old Joshua was in trouble with his mother, Emily. She had told him a dozen times to stay away from her kitchen matches. She had just found him in the backyard trying to set fire to some newspapers. Fortunately, he wasn't very good at striking the matches, so the flames kept going out. Emily mentioned this to her aunt, who was horrified. "I just read about this on the Internet," she said. "This is really bad when kids do these things. And I saw him chasing my cat, and he wet the bed last time he slept over here. It said on the Internet that those three things mean he'll grow up to be a serial killer. You better get him straightened out." These comments worried Emily enough to mention the problem to Josh's father, Will, who had a different response. "I don't care if he kills that cat; it'll save me the trouble. But you didn't tell me he still wet the bed. I'll beat that out of him."

Were any of Josh's family right in their beliefs and concerns about his behavior?

People often believe that there is a very specific connection between childhood fire setting and later homicidal violence in adulthood. The idea that fire setting is a predictor of murder is often discussed with an additional emphasis on an associated group of childhood behaviors. This group, sometimes called MacDonald's triad, involves fire setting, cruelty to animals, and persistent bed-wetting after the age of 5 years. Quite a few years ago, a researcher who interviewed and investigated serial killers reported that those three childhood behaviors were characteristic of the people he interviewed (MacDonald, 1968). The belief that MacDonald's triad of symptoms can predict serious adult violence has received much attention but little research support.

MacDonald (1968) conducted a *retrospective study*. In these studies, adults with certain characteristics are questioned about their life history. (Adolescents and older children can also be participants in a retrospective study, but the MacDonald study focused on adults.) Retrospective studies may also include interviews with other people, such as parents, brothers, sisters, neighbors, or teachers of the participants, who are likely to have memories of the participants' childhoods. It can also be possible to find objective information, such as school or medical records.

Retrospective studies may be conducted when no other research approach is possible. For example, in the case of fire setting, locating children who play with matches and following them for years to see how many committed murder would be extremely difficult. However, retrospective studies are by no means the perfect solution to this type of research problem. One difficulty with any retrospective study is that memory reports are not always reliable. Even well-meaning informants may forget or confuse several memories or fill in a memory gap with an explanation of what "must have" happened. People who have reason to hide facts may simply fail to report what they remember. Similarly, people can exaggerate a memory to communicate that they "always knew" there was something strange about a relative.

A second, very serious problem of retrospective research is that it may consider only those who have certain adult characteristics and ignore the population as a whole. How many children set fires, torment pets, and wet the bed but grow up to be quite respectable, normal, noncriminal citizens? Studies like MacDonald's (1968) cannot answer these questions. To provide such answers, a retrospective study would need to examine information about a large number of people, some proven to be serial killers and some not. Ideally, interviewers would be "blind" to the homicidal status of the people being questioned. After data collection, childhood characteristics of the killing group would be compared statistically to those of the nonkillers, showing whether the two groups are similar or whether the serial killers show significantly more past fire setting, cruelty to animals, and bed-wetting, or perhaps just one of these behaviors.

An even better research approach would involve a *prospective study*. Instead of trying to find out whether serial killers set fires when they were children, researchers would collect information about a large group of children, including some who set fires and tormented animals and some who did not. The researchers would keep in touch with the children as they reached adulthood and at some point would compare the record of serious antisocial behavior among those who had set fires to the same type of behavior among those who had not. The advantage of the prospective approach is that researchers can gather clear evidence about childhood characteristics, without problems related to informants' forgetting, exaggerating, or deliberately tailoring their reports to fit what they know of a person's adult life.

Unfortunately, many serious research problems cannot be handled by either prospective or retrospective studies. Children who set fires or are cruel to animals may not be caught, or if caught they may not be reported to any authority. Some parents consider these behaviors acceptable, or at least tolerable. Bed-wetting may be handled (appropriately or inappropriately) at home, without any outsider ever knowing about it. Older children who continue to wet their beds may try to keep the problem secret to avoid punishment, embarrassment, and social disapproval. People who commit serial murders make serious efforts to conceal their crimes and may not be apprehended for a long time, if ever. Even individuals of markedly low intelligence are aware that others will stop or punish violent behavior. In addition, serial killing is an exceedingly rare behavior, and very large numbers of people would have to be studied before one such individual could be detected. Thus, research on this subject does not easily find connections between childhood behaviors and serious adult violence, even if such connections exist. Small numbers of case studies (Wright & Hensley, 2003) provide weak foundations for understanding this matter.

Research that investigates the evidence for or against mistaken beliefs is usually best focused on large numbers of people, not on an individual case history. With respect to beliefs about childhood behavior and violence, however, one reported case seems highly relevant (Sereny, 1999). This case involves a girl who at 9 years of age killed a little boy but grew up to feel remorse for her action and wanted to make a productive life for herself and her daughter. The girl, Mary Bell, probably never would have been caught had she not gone to her victim's house and asked to see him in his coffin. As an adult, after serving a prison term, she confided in a journalist because she wanted to tell the story herself before her daughter heard it elsewhere. Mary Bell's story suggests that any statistical connection between childhood and adult violent behavior tells only part of the story of individual development.

The existence of treatments for both bed-wetting (Ronen & Rosenbaum, 2001) and fire setting (Sharp, Blaakman, Cole, & Cole, 2006) may also be relevant to the possible connection between MacDonald's triad and adult violence. If these behaviors are so deeply embedded in personality that they cause very unusual and unacceptable adult behaviors, it seems unlikely that childhood interventions would be able to eradicate them. However, this line of reasoning would have to give way to empirical evidence, if such evidence existed.

Conclusion

No reliable evidence supports the belief that certain childhood behaviors such as fire setting are predictors of severe violence in adulthood. However, research related to this question is very difficult to conduct. Emily would probably do best to try to protect Joshua from violent experiences and abusive treatment and to make sure he is well supervised, rather than to label him as a murderer in the making.

CRITICAL THINKING

1. With reference to retrospective studies on this topic, explain why research results are more trustworthy if an interviewer does not know whether an individual is a serial killer.

2. Why might it be difficult to ensure that a researcher not know the criminal history of an interviewee, particularly whether the participant is a serial killer? Explain your answer. Keep in mind the rarity of serial murder.

3. In a prospective study, how can you ensure that a researcher interviewing participants in adulthood does not know which interviewees set fires during childhood?

4. Describe how cases like that of Mary Bell (Sereny, 1999) are useful for understanding child development and how, on the contrary, the use of such anecdotal material might confuse rather than help researchers' comprehension.

5. Conduct an Internet search of fire setting. Locate 10 references to fire setting as a predictor of violence. Do most of the sites base their comments on published research other than that of MacDonald (1968)?

References

MacDonald, J. M. (1968). *Homicidal threats.* Springfield, IL: Charles C Thomas.

Ronen, T., & Rosenbaum, M. (2001) Helping children to help themselves: A case study of enuresis and nail biting. *Research on Social Work Practice, 11,* 338–356.

Sereny, G. (1999). *Cries unheard.* New York: Metropolitan/Holt.

Sharp, D. L., Blaakman, S. W., Cole, E. C., & Cole, R. E. (2006). Evidence-based multidisciplinary strategies for working with children who set fires. *Journal of the American Psychiatric Nurses Association, 11,* 329–337.

Wright, J., & Hensley, C. (2003). From animal cruelty to serial murder: Applying the graduation hypothesis. *International Journal of Offender Therapy and Comparative Criminology, 47,* 71–88.

Claim 31

Children have different learning styles, depending on whether they are left brained or right brained.

Melody's teacher was concerned about 10-year-old Melody's poor math skills, and she said so at a parent-teacher conference with Melody's mother, Tasha. But Tasha was not concerned or even very impressed by the teacher's statements. "Melody has always liked to draw and sing and dance. She's one of those right-brained people who isn't good at schoolwork like reading and arithmetic. She's more intuitive, like her daddy. I'm not going to worry about this, because I know she has talent and will be a great performer someday."

Was Tasha right to think that people who are good at the arts are not good at schoolwork? Can Melody's teacher use other special methods to teach her in a "right-brained" way?

The idea that human beings have learning styles that depend on their tendency to use one side of the brain more than the other became popular about 40 years ago and has remained a common assumption. Generally, this belief includes the idea that left-brained activities are analytical, whereas right-brained activities are creative, holistic, and intuitive. Some educators find this point of view very appealing; others take a more general view of individual learning styles that contribute to academic achievement (Hadfield, 2006).

Most children and adults are right-handed, and only about 10% use their left hands for fine movements, such as writing. Right-handed people fairly consistently use their two hands in predictable ways, using the right hand for skilled small muscle tasks and the left for less delicate movements, such as holding the top of a sheet of paper or steadying an object by gripping it. Left-handed people do things the other way around, although they are usually a bit more skillful with their right hands than "righties" are with their left.

The brain's control over motor skills follows a predictable pattern, too. The left side of the brain sends the signals that control the right hand's movements, and the right side of the brain controls the left hand. So, in that sense, people are left brained if they are right-handed and right brained if they are left-handed.

So far, so reasonable. But what about learning styles? Why have some people associated the dominant activity of one side of the brain with particular ways to learn, or even particular skills other than movements such as hand use? In fact, the idea of being right brained or left brained in learning style is a big jump in reasoning from studies of brain surgery. Surgical treatment of brain-damaged patients, beginning in the 1940s, was the source of the idea that one or the other cortical hemisphere could do much of people's brainwork. Patients who had epileptic seizures because of an injury to one side of the brain (e.g., a man who was clubbed in the head while a prisoner during World War II) were treated by surgery that cut many of the neural connections between the right and left brain halves. This procedure allowed the healthy side of the brain to take more control over the body and to prevent the seizures caused by the injured side.

After surgical treatment, the health of these patients improved, but they had some other interesting changes, too. Because communication between the two sides of the brain was interrupted, each side was much more isolated from the other. Normally, much of the information about something seen with one eye is communicated to both sides of the brain, but following split-brain surgery, only one side of the brain received information from one eye. The same held for hearing. In a person with normal auditory functioning, sounds that come into one ear are signaled to both sides of the brain, but after the split, sounds entering the left ear were communicated only to the left half of the brain.

This unusual isolation of left and right cortical hemispheres allowed researchers to observe whether each side of the brain had specialties or tasks that it could perform especially well. Researchers had long known that the left hemisphere of a right-handed individual had a special connection to spoken language and that injury to the left side of the brain was more likely than right-side injury to damage language ability. The split-brain research confirmed this fact and suggested other differences between the two sides—information that quickly spun into the claim that brain preferences somehow determine preferred tasks and ways of learning.

However, there were some problems with the left-brain, right-brain idea. First, an intact brain—with the hemispheres normally connected—does not work like a split brain. The two sides of the brain ordinarily function together, in coordination, although one may do a bit more of some tasks (especially language) than the other. To look at one hemisphere alone gives an inaccurate view of normal functioning—as inaccurate as studying how a person's right leg would be used after the left had been amputated, as a way of understanding normal walking. Brain imaging studies, which were not available in the early split-brain research, showed that both sides of the brain act together under normal circumstances.

Many important tasks require something from each hemisphere, so, for example, in an emotional conversation between two right-handed people, the right hemispheres work to comprehend emotion in speech, and the left sides work to understand and remember stories that have emotional meaning. A person who had one of these abilities, "right" or "left," and not the other would not be an effective sender or receiver of emotional information. Similarly, in carrying out tasks in school, children use both sides of their brain to deal with cognitive tasks and the emotional—and motivating—aspects of their assignments (Willingham, 2006).

Many educators are especially interested in sex differences in the brain. Could these differences explain some of the apparent differences between boys' and girls' learning? Although some small but consistent differences exist between groups of boys and groups of girls, there is also a great deal of overlap between the two, and this outcome may have as much or more to do with interests and values as it does with actual brain functions (Kimura, 2002).

Are there individual differences in children's styles, or preferred ways, of learning? Yes, of course. Such individual differences originate in temperamental differences, past experiences of success or failure, and beliefs about the world—for example, that only boys can do math or only girls are good at art. Individual differences are also based on interests, motivation, and opportunities to practice tasks. Such individual differences are connected to brain functioning, but not in the simple way implied by the terms *right-brained* or *left-brained teaching/learning*. Certainly, different types of instruction are not magical cures for teaching and learning problems (Willingham, 2006).

Abilities in the arts and in academic subjects are not necessarily connected to specific sides of the brain, nor are they mutually exclusive. Research in particular topics supports this idea. For example, a small number of musicians have absolute pitch, the ability to identify or sing a note in isolation from other notes (rather than as part of a tune). They are reported to be more likely to have this ability if they had musical instruction before school age and if they also have an analytical, cognitive learning style (Chin, 2003).

In light of this evidence, people should reject the simple claim that artistic ability is a right-brain characteristic because this aspect of musical skill was partly dependent on training and not innate. In addition, it seems that people should reject the idea that ability in the arts is associated with a nonanalytical cognitive style.

Conclusion

Individual children can prefer certain school tasks and have preferred ways of learning, but these are not solely the result of dominance of one side of the brain or of specialized abilities that belong to the left or to the right cortical hemisphere. Being skilled in the arts does not mean a child cannot be good at math or vice versa. It would be good for Tasha not to suggest to Melody that she is not the kind of person who does math; instead, Tasha should encourage Melody to practice her math skills and see them as abilities all adults need, no matter how talented they are in other ways.

CRITICAL THINKING

1. Refer to a child development textbook to find information about the connection between handedness and hemispheric dominance. What proportion of people would you expect to be right brained, considering the proportion of left-handed people? How does this proportion relate to the proportion of U.S. children who perform poorly in math?

2. Search the Internet to locate a popular (nonscholarly) book or article that explains how people can use a particular side of their brain. How does the publication's approach to brain functioning compare to the comments in this section?

3. Explain the role that temperament might play in preferences for particular learning activities or topics. Choose several temperamental factors for examination. Refer to evidence from your child development textbook in your explanation.

4. Using your child development textbook or other sources, such as the article by Kimura (2002), find the proportion of boys who are left-handed as well as information about the cognitive abilities of typical school-age boys. Find the same information for girls. Do these facts combine in a way that matches popular beliefs about right-brain and left-brain functions? Explain your answer.

(Continued)

(Continued)

5. Read the article by Willingham (2006). Describe the parts of the brain surgeons cut during split-brain surgery. Search the Internet or print sources to find information about people who never had one or both of these brain structures (this situation will be described as *agenesis* of the structures). Would you expect the abilities of these people to be similar to those of people in the surgical cases? Explain your answer.

References

Chin, C. S. (2003). The development of absolute pitch: A theory concerning the roles of music training at an early developmental age and individual cognitive style. *Psychology of Music, 31,* 155–171.

Hadfield, J. (2006). Teacher education and trainee learning style. *RELC Journal, 37,* 367–386.

Kimura, D. (2002). Sex differences in the brain. *Scientific American, 12*(1), 32–37.

Willingham, D. T. (2006). "Brain-based" learning: More fiction than fact. *American Educator, 30*(3), 27–33, 40–41.

Claim 32

Karate lessons help schoolchildren achieve self-discipline and improve their schoolwork.

Eleven-year-old Lee was having a lot of trouble with arithmetic. His parents yelled at him, grounded him, and offered him rewards, such as a trip to Disneyland, if he improved his math grade, but all to no avail. Lee couldn't explain the problem—he just said "It's hard!" When he was supposed to be doing his homework, he sat and daydreamed most of the time or gave most of his attention to what he could hear of the TV program the rest of the family was watching. One afternoon, Lee's mother noticed an advertisement on the bulletin board at the supermarket. A new karate school was opening in their neighborhood, and the advertisement said that karate instruction was good for children: It raised their self-esteem and improved their grades. This seemed like the answer to their problems, and it wasn't very expensive either. Lee's parents discussed the matter that evening and decided to sign Lee up for karate lessons.

Did they make the right choice for the right reasons?

The claim that karate classes do anything for children other than develop their karate skills is, of course, usually made by commercial organizations or other groups with a financial interest in encouraging study of the martial arts. Examination of the claims about karate instruction usually shows that they are founded on personal anecdotes or testimonials rather than on systematic research evidence. Cases where children experience no benefit from their karate training—or even cases where they seem to have been harmed in some way—are not likely to be included in such evidence as, of course, they would be in a scientific investigation.

What would researchers have to do to collect information before making a valid claim about the positive effects of karate training on children's schoolwork or general behavior? Ideally, the children would need to be randomly assigned either to karate classes or to some other type of training. The two types of training would need to be equal in difficulty and other factors, such as the amount of time spent away from home. It would be difficult to keep parents from knowing which type of training their child receives, but the children's teachers could and should be prevented from knowing this information. Improvement in school grades and behavior would be monitored and the achievements of the two groups of children compared with each other. The results of statistical analysis of this comparison would make it possible to conclude that karate training had a superior effect on the children's school performance—or, alternatively, that the other training method had a better effect or that the two seemed to be about the same.

Why not just compare children who take karate lessons with those who do not? Anecdotal evidence about one or two children might not be useful, but what if many children were involved in such a study? As usual in studies of self-selected groups such as karate students, confounding variables confuse the issue and make it difficult to isolate the causes of any differences that may appear between groups. Families who can afford to pay for karate (or other) lessons are different from less affluent families in many ways, including health care and educational background. Families who can afford lessons but are too overscheduled or disorganized to bring their child to class may be quite different from better organized or less harried families, especially in terms of the self-discipline sometimes claimed to result from karate training. Families with many children, or with some children with special needs, often have scheduling and financial difficulties. Those difficulties affect enrollment in karate lessons and supervision of homework and sometimes even school attendance. As for characteristics of the children, impulsive, poorly behaved children are likely to perform badly in school and to be kicked out of extracurricular activities in which they are enrolled. Children who are self-regulated and self-controlled are likely to do well in school and be well-thought-of members of karate and other classes.

Confounded variables make it far from a simple matter to demonstrate the possible benefits of karate training. But the idea that such an experience could have many benefits is not a silly one. Research on children's play suggests that some important rules about social interactions are learned through play activities, especially rough-and-tumble play that involves pretend aggression (Smith, Smees, & Pellegrini, 2004). Children participating in such play activities learn to tell the difference between intentional aggression—that intended to hurt or intimidate another person—and pretend chasing and yelling, which are designed to prolong social interactions for fun. This kind of learning is linked to self-discipline because it helps children learn to react with anger only when appropriate—that is, when another child is launching a real attack. Children who learn this response from play experiences will less frequently lose their temper and respond aggressively to someone who does not mean harm. More formal sports activities can have similar learning effects, helping children to establish different behaviors to use in different situations—for example, aggression used in a physical fight versus aggression in a hockey game. Martial arts activities that focus on pairs who "fight" for limited time periods also have the potential for teaching suitable times for aggression.

What about the idea of *catharsis*, or venting, of angry feelings? Can play aggression in the form of karate neutralize negative emotions that have accumulated during daily life? This popular belief is often put forward as an advantage of any kind of aggressive sport or game; however, it does not seem to be true. The ancient idea of catharsis of anger or other distressing feelings has been rejected by empirical research. Behaving angrily or aggressively is more likely to increase the frustrated person's feelings of anger rather than to relieve the emotional tension. Experiencing anger about past events, in the absence of any other treatment, does not eliminate the resentment and frustration a person has been feeling (Littrell, 1998). Although most research on this topic has studied adults, it seems likely that the same conclusion would apply to children and teenagers.

What about the role of self-esteem in helping improve academic achievement? Assuming that karate lessons improve self-esteem, it is still unlikely that self-esteem alone will help increase school success (Marsh & O'Mara, 2008). Research on this topic has generally concluded that general self-esteem is not a factor in academic achievement, although a more specific academic self-concept may be.

It is possible that some advantages result from martial arts training for children, just as positive outcomes result from participation in other types of sports. However, those advantages may be based on the involvement of parents and their resulting increased interaction with their children (Kremer-Sadlik & Kim, 2007). A similar conclusion may be made about the effect of parent involvement on school achievement.

Conclusion

Although karate or other sports training may help children develop some aspects of self-control—and greater self-control can improve school performance—it is also possible that children with self-control do well in sports. There is no evidence that improved self-control and academic success are results of karate training. Lee's parents would be better advised to work with him on his arithmetic homework, or arrange for someone else to give him more instruction, rather than expect classes on another topic to help him with schoolwork.

CRITICAL THINKING

1. Suppose a study simply compared children who study karate with those who do not. What three or four confounded variables would interfere with a clear conclusion? Explain your answer.

2. Identify a suitable type of training to compare to karate instruction when evaluating the effect of karate training on schoolwork. Explain your choice, identifying any confounding variables that would be present.

3. Refer to a child development textbook for information about age differences. Explain whether the confounding variables in a study of kindergarteners in karate classes would be the same as those in a study of teenagers. Would fewer confounding variables be present for one age group than for the other? Explain your answer.

4. Search the Internet for claims from commercial and professional groups about the benefits of karate training. What evidence do these groups offer for these claims?

5. Read the article by Smith et al. (2004). Compare the learning from rough-and-tumble play with learning from structured sports or lessons.

References

Kremer-Sadlik, T., & Kim, J. L. (2007). Lessons from sports: Children's socialization to values through family interaction during sports activities. *Discourse and Society, 18,* 35–52.

Littrell, J. (1998). Is the experience of painful emotion therapeutic? *Clinical Psychology Review, 18*(1), 71–102.

Marsh, H. W., & O'Mara, A. (2008). Reciprocal effects between academic self-concept, self-esteem, achievement, and attainment over seven adolescent years: Unidimensional and multidimensional perspectives of self-concept. *Personality and Social Psychology Bulletin, 34,* 542–552.

Smith, K., Smees, R., & Pellegrini, A. D. (2004). Play fighting and real fighting: Using video playback methodology with young children. *Aggressive Behavior, 30,* 164–173.

Claim 33

Learning to read is mainly a matter of recognizing letters and reciting the alphabet, so watching TV programs like *Sesame Street* is the most important preparation for school success.

Six-year-old Isabel stayed at her neighbor's house every day after school because her parents, Robin and Ivan, had to work until 5 p.m. The neighbor, Mrs. Atkins, let the children watch TV most of the time, but she was careful for them to see some educational programs. Her home was safe and convenient and an inexpensive arrangement for Isabel. Isabel was not reading much yet, and her grandmother suggested that she might need a different kind of after-school program. "That Mrs. Atkins just has the TV on all the time, and you two don't ever have time to read to Isabel. Don't you think that might have something to do with her being slow in school?" Ivan replied, "I was slow too and I'm okay now, right? Anyway, Mrs. Atkins always makes sure they see *Sesame Street*, and Isabel knows her alphabet and can name all the letters. She'll read when she feels like it, same as me."

Who was right? Is reading simply a matter of knowing the alphabet and recognizing letters?

If a child care provider or a parent shows a child several episodes of educational television each day, are they helping a child build a good foundation for literacy? Certainly, educational television offers children a better start than working in a coal mine would. However, examining the process of reading suggests that *Sesame Street*—no matter how cute and engaging the program may be—is only the beginning of the learning process for reading. Reciting the alphabet is exciting for children and necessary for efficient use of a dictionary but otherwise not needed for reading. (In fact, how many younger children think there is one letter with a long name between *K* and *P*, a letter they call "elemento"?)

Modern research on reading stresses the process by which children learn *grapheme-phoneme correspondence*, the relationship between the shape of a letter and the sound it represents. In many languages, this relationship is reasonably consistent. However, English is unusual in that it contains many words derived from other languages. In English, the shape-sound connection can be very complicated. A single letter within a word can indicate several sounds, requiring readers to choose the appropriate sound by looking at other letters in the word or even other words on the page. In other words, several letters can be combined to represent a single sound, and in some words letters are "silent."

In English, as in other languages, the names of letters are not the same as the sounds they indicate. The name for the letter *m* ("em"), for example, is not the same as the sound "mmm." Some English letter names include the sound the letter represents, but others, such as *W* ("double-yew") and *Q* ("kyew") do not. Some research in early reading studied children's understanding of letter names and found that the related sounds were most easily learned when the letter name contained the sound at the beginning of the letter name rather than the end. Letter names that did not contain the indicated sound were hardest to learn. In other words, the sound for *T* ("tee") was easier for participants to learn than the sound for *F* ("eff"), and *W* and *Q* were more difficult than either *T* or *F*. Although the children in the study had an easier time pronouncing certain sounds, the actual nature of the sounds did not seem to affect their learning of the sound-shape connection. The authors of this study suggested that new readers would benefit from extra practice with letters whose names did not stress the speech sounds they represented (Treiman, Tincoff, Rodriguez, Mouzaki, & Francis, 1998).

It is possible that some aspects of learning to read are primarily matters of maturation, not of experience or instruction. For example, the alphabet used to write English and many other European languages has some letters with similar shapes but different spatial orientations. For example, the letter *W* is like an upside-down *M*; until children are mature enough to pay attention to the different positions, they may think of the two as the same letter. The problem is even greater for the lowercase letters; for example, the letters *p* and *q* and *b* and *d* are the same shape, with different right-left or up-down orientations. Lowercase *f* and *t* have similar problems, especially when printed by hand. Research conducted many years ago showed that large numbers of children pay little attention to right-left or up-down differences until they are 5 or 6 years old; they reverse letters in their printed writing as well as in their early reading attempts (Howard & Templeton, 1966).

As children become more experienced with reading or being read to, they learn that written language is different from the familiar spoken version. This is evident in the traditional first-reader pattern of language, which uses expressions that are rarely heard in speech (e.g., "Run, Spot, run!") and avoids more common, less repetitive constructions with the goal of using fewer different words. Written language sometimes inverts word order (e.g., "Away he went" rather than "He ran away"), which is rare in ordinary speech. Certain written texts, such as fairy tales and other stories for young children, present an unpredictable world of events that are completely disconnected from children's life experience: Kings favor their handsomest sons, girls are shut up in towers by jealous stepmothers, cows know the answers to riddles, and billy goats get the better of trolls. These traditional written language and story patterns are unfamiliar and puzzling to young schoolchildren who have experienced only everyday spoken language, but the patterns are familiar to those who have been read to regularly from an early age. Although modern children's authors have written realistic stories, individual children's backgrounds may or may not coincide with the language and subject matter of a particular book. Even for modern stories, much time spent listening to stories is the best aid to understanding written language.

In the years since the first airing of *Sesame Street*, research on early literacy has provided new insights into learning to read. The process of understanding how children learn to read is by no means finished. New curricula and views on reading are still emerging (Cooper, 2005; Dickinson, 2002). It is clear, however, that learning the alphabet is only a first step in learning to read; other experiences with the written language are also very important.

Conclusion

The tasks of learning letter names and shapes and reciting the alphabet are only a small part of a child's work toward learning to read. Children need other experiences in preparation for reading, and being read to by adults is of great importance. Some aspects of reading are maturational, however, and cannot be hurried by experiences. Isabel's grandmother is right in thinking that Isabel would benefit from a child care provider who stresses reading experiences, especially because her own parents do not read to her often; however, Ivan's statement that Isabel will read "when she's ready" holds a grain of truth.

CRITICAL THINKING

1. Read the article by Treiman and colleagues (1998). What do the authors mean when they refer to the properties of a sound? How are sound properties different from letter names? What characteristics of a letter other than the name might affect how easily it is learned?

2. Different languages use different names for some letters, even though they employ the same alphabet. For example, the French pronunciation for the letter G is "zhay" and the letter J is "zhee." Would it be possible to further test the conclusions of Treiman and colleagues (1998) by comparing children who are learning different languages? Would confounding variables make it difficult to draw conclusions from such a study?

3. In research on learning to read, is it reasonable to study the effects of being read to by comparing a group of children whose caregivers liked to read aloud with a group whose caregivers did not enjoy it? What problems and confounding variables would be associated with such an approach?

4. Howard and Templeton (1966) indicated that older children performed better than younger children at paying attention to letters' right-left or up-down orientation. What factors might be responsible for this difference? Explain your answer.

5. What might be the advantages and disadvantages of exposing preschoolers and kindergarteners only to realistic stories in everyday language and not to fantasy stories and literary language? How could data be collected to test the claim that realistic stories are more beneficial than fantasies?

References

Cooper, P. M. (2005). Literacy learning and pedagogical purpose in Vivian Paley's "storytelling curriculum." *Journal of Early Childhood Literacy*, 5, 229–251.

Dickinson, D. K. (2002). Shifting images of developmentally appropriate practice as seen through different lenses. *Educational Researcher*, 31, 26–32.

Howard, I. P., & Templeton, W. B. (1966). *Human spatial orientation*. New York: Wiley.

Treiman, R., Tincoff, R., Rodriguez, K., Mouzaki, A., & Francis, D. (1998). The foundations of literacy: Learning the sounds of letters. *Child Development*, 69, 1524–1540.

Claim 34

Birth order is an important factor that determines children's intelligence and personality.

Justin was doing moderately well in fifth grade, but he was certainly not the academic leader of his class. He was much more interested in art and music than in math and science, and the subjects that interested him did not contribute to his grade average. Justin's parents were convinced that he could do much better, especially because his second-grade sister was reading far above her grade level. Justin's mother told her friend, "I know he could do much better if he just decided to. I don't know what makes him so stubborn. But I read that firstborn kids have higher intelligence than the later ones, so there's no question in my mind that Justin ought to do better in school than his sister does."

Is Justin's mother right? Should his position as firstborn make him more intelligent and therefore more academically successful? Or are there other reasons that help determine both tested intelligence and academic achievement?

"She's a typical middle child; she doesn't care a bit about school"; "he's an oldest child, always worried and trying to manage things, studying all the time"; "she's so selfish—what an only child!" Popular beliefs about the effects of birth order involve some clear statements about personality and school achievement, and those beliefs stand to reason—that is, most people think they make some kind of intuitive sense and some research evidence confirms them (Sulloway, 2007). However, other factors, such as temperament and experiences outside the family, may be able to override any effects of birth order. That multiple factors determine a child's development provides a strong hint that the situation cannot be a simple one.

In examining the effects of any factor that influences development, one task researchers must do is consider the possible *mechanisms* at work—the series of measurable events that links the cause to the outcome. Any effects of birth order, for instance, might be based on biological events. An illustration of this mechanism would be changes in a mother's reproductive system caused by events during each pregnancy, changes that result in a different prenatal environment for a later-born than for an earlier-born child. A different mechanism might involve social and emotional change: Parents may be more skillful in the care of but less excited about the birth of later-born babies, resulting in caregiving differences between firstborn and later-born children. Another factor that might cause birth order effects involves experiences with younger or older siblings—a firstborn child has no older siblings by definition, whereas a later child has at least one older sibling and sometimes several older and several younger. All of these possible mechanisms may be involved in the effect of birth order on any aspect of development. These mechanisms can work separately, together, or in different ways at different periods in an individual's life, so simply naming mechanisms is only the beginning of understanding birth order effects. However, to figure out which questions to ask about birth order, researchers first need to identify various important factors and mechanisms.

Whether birth order affects personality is one of the most intriguing questions for most readers, who even in old age may still be trying to understand how they differ from their brothers and sisters. But studying personality factors can be difficult because personality is not easy to measure. Many different personality characteristics can be considered. A somewhat simpler approach is to try to determine how birth order affects tested intelligence. This is the approach taken by many researchers of birth order effects.

A good deal of the empirical research conducted on birth order and IQ focuses on the very slightly higher intelligence test scores of adults who were firstborn children. But not all research reports the same relationships of IQ and birth order. Some studies found no difference between firstborn and later-born adults, and some studies of children showed that later-born children actually have higher IQ scores than their older brothers and sisters (Kristensen & Bjerkedal, 2007). (This does not mean that the younger children answered more questions correctly than the older ones but that the *intelligence quotients* calculated on the basis of age were higher for the later-born children.)

It is confusing that the research findings for children seem to be the opposite of those for adults, but this is actually not unusual. This situation is an example of an important concept in the study of development: that differences between groups or measurements commonly seen among children may not hold up as the individuals grow into adulthood, and they may even be reversed in later life. Characteristics of groups of adults may not explain what they were like as children, and, discouragingly, characteristics of children may or may not predict who they will be in the future. Of course, it is possible that some early events will positively correlate with later ones, but researchers know this only by careful evaluation and comparison of people at different times in their lives. It would be very unwise to assume that people do not change.

Why might birth order influence IQ? What mechanisms would make firstborns slightly superior in adulthood or later-borns superior in childhood? A biological explanation might make sense for the adult comparison but cannot simultaneously explain what happens in childhood. No simple biological cause seems capable of creating superior performance in adulthood but lower performance in childhood.

Can a social cause account for the higher intelligence test scores of adults who were firstborn? The usual explanation is that firstborn children are provided with undiluted parental interest, attention, and stimulation and model themselves on competent and affectionate adult behavior. This situation applies particularly to the learning of speech. Firstborns are primarily around adults, who demonstrate large vocabularies and complicated grammar, whereas later-born children are primarily around other children, which can limit the scope of speech that they hear. Firstborn children thus receive a head start on development and are able to stay ahead of others as they grow into adulthood—experiencing many successes, being expected to do well, and possibly also striving to be like competent adults.

This explanation stands to reason. But how can researchers explain the evidence that, during childhood, later-born children score higher on intelligence tests? This phenomenon seems to indicate that older siblings promote the development of later-born children, that older children are hindered by having toddlers in the house, or possibly that both of these situations are true. It may be true that older brothers and sisters help to educate their younger siblings, offering them models that are not too difficult for them to follow (as adults' models might be). It is also a possibility that having younger children to care for removes parents' attention from their older children and temporarily slows the older ones' development. Again, however, empirical research, not simply speculation, is needed to help understand these possibilities.

A recent study in Norway compared IQ scores for men of different birth order positions, including some whose older siblings had died (Kristensen & Bjerkedal, 2007). This study examined both the real birth order, based on the number of children previously born to a mother, and the *social order*, or number of older children living in a household with a given child. The social order was reported to be the more significant factor, and second-born sons whose older sibling had died were equal in adult IQ to firstborn sons. This study seems to indicate that experience is the mechanism by which birth order affects adult IQ. But differences as they seem to exist in childhood are still difficult to explain—and it is possible that different mechanisms are at work at different times of life. For example, birth order seems to influence the behavior of parents toward young children (Keller & Zach, 2002), but this effect may not persist for long and of course will no longer be present after the parents die and the children are middle-aged or older.

An important issue in the study of birth order effects involves method. Most birth order studies have used a cross-sectional approach, in which individuals from various families are grouped according to their birth order within their families (e.g., all firstborns together). However, a preferable method may be to study individuals within their own families, comparing firstborns to their own later-born siblings. When this method is used, the birth order effect on intelligence is no longer apparent (Wichman, Rodgers, & McCallum, 2006). Are the differences previously reported for birth order just a matter of differences between families, not differences in birth order? This is possible, but the best way to study this question has not yet been determined.

Conclusion

Information about the effects of birth order on development indicates that adults born early in the family sequence may have slightly higher tested intelligence than those born later, and the children's different experiences may be responsible for this. However, comparisons during childhood give different results. Justin's mother is mistaken in thinking that he should do better academically than his little sister—and she is forgetting that school achievement depends on interest, motivation, and effort as well as intelligence.

CRITICAL THINKING

1. Read the Sulloway article (2007) to find the average IQ difference between firstborn and later-born adults. Using information from a child development textbook as evidence, compare this difference with the measurement error associated with standardized intelligence tests. Would you expect the intelligence difference to have any practical effect? Explain your answer.

2. Kristensen and Bjerkedal (2007) concluded that individuals whose siblings died are disadvantaged on some factors associated with intelligence. Locate several such factors in a child development textbook and summarize the article, using more specific terms.

3. Read about intelligence tests in a child development textbook. Find out how the tests for younger children are different from those for older children. How would you connect those differences with the reports of higher IQ in later-born children during childhood? Are early developing aspects of intelligence encouraged by the presence of older children?

4. Identify some personality factors that have a strong genetic basis, referring to a child development textbook for information. Do genetic factors override the effect of birth order on personality? Explain your answer.

5. What do Kristensen and Bjerkedal (2007) mean when they say that birth order effects might be an artifact? In your explanation, focus on their reference to the lower IQs of children from larger families.

References

Keller, H., & Zach, U. (2002). Gender and birth order as determinants of parental behaviour. *International Journal of Behavioral Development, 26*, 177–184.

Kristensen, P., & Bjerkedal, T. (2007). Explaining the relation between birth order and intelligence. *Science, 316*, 1717.

Sulloway, F. J. (2007). Birth order and intelligence. *Science, 316*, 1711–1712.

Wichman, A. L., Rodgers, J. L., & McCallum, R. C. (2006). A multilevel approach to the relationship between birth order and intelligence. *Personality and Social Psychology Bulletin, 32*, 117–127.

Bullying is a natural behavior for children, and there's nothing you can do to stop it.

Will was a stocky, strong 12-year-old, but his size and muscles did not keep him from getting pushed around by older kids at school. On the playground or at the bus stop, someone was always threatening him, shoving him, or tearing up a few pages of his homework. Taking his lunch money was a regular thing, of course. Will became depressed and anxious and dreaded Monday mornings when he would have to go to school after a peaceful weekend. His grades were suffering, and he was waking up everyone in the house with nightmares. Finally, he told his father everything and begged for help. Will's father said he would talk to the teacher and the principal, and even though Will was reluctant about this, he accepted the idea that it might be the only way to get help. Both members of the school staff were sympathetic and friendly, but the principal said, "Look, there's not a thing we can do about this. That's just the way kids are. It's human nature. If I tell them not to bully Will, they'll bully him more. Why don't you get him boxing lessons? Then maybe they'll respect him."

Was the principal right? Is there nothing schools can do to help children who are bullied?

Oddly, behaviors that people attribute to human nature always seem to be unpleasant. No one seems to include compassion, empathy, or charity as part of human nature. Calling a behavior natural usually implies that the behavior is undesirable and cannot be modified or altered. Even teachers often take this point of view about bullying or feel that a teacher who is good at dealing with bullying has a "natural" ability to deal with the "natural" behavior (Crothers & Kolbert, 2008).

There is no doubt that bullying in schools is highly undesirable. At its worst, bullying causes physical injury or even death. Long-term bullying and rejection are associated with suicide. In the short term, bullying affects school attendance because bullied children often avoid attending school as often as they can, resulting in missed academic work and fewer positive social interactions with other children. Unfortunately, there is also no doubt that bullying and intimidation of children is widespread.

Is it possible to reduce bullying in schools? Personnel who implement antibullying programs have a difficult job to do because the act of bullying is presumably gratifying to the bully, who experiences a sense of power and may also gain material items, such as money extorted from victims. Children who bully or are bullied may have personality characteristics that are related to their actions or at least a long history of related behaviors (Pellegrini & Bartini, 2000; Tani, Greenman, Schneider, & Fregoso, 2003). Programs need to have sufficiently powerful components to deal with actions that have been punished many times but are consistently rewarding to the bully.

Since the 1990s, a variety of antibullying programs have been developed. Application and testing of these programs help determine whether bullying behavior can be modified, at least by the approaches that are now available. Studies of the outcomes of antibullying programs are especially helpful if they show whether programs have both initial effects and long-term influence in reducing bullying in school.

Some antibullying programs assume that bullies turn to inappropriate behavior because of a lack of skills for positive social interaction. For example, one program, studied some years ago, focused on school aggression in general, rather than specific bullying behavior, and attempted to guide elementary school boys to think about the causes of other people's behavior. Considering that aggressive boys were likely to interpret others' actions as hostile when they were actually accidental, this program, Brain-Power, provided lessons in interpreting others' intentions and responding to the motive rather than the behavior. Four schools were studied, and some children in each school were randomly assigned either to the BrainPower program or to one of two control conditions, either a problem-solving program or a no-attention condition. The researchers reported that the BrainPower program reduced aggression by a small amount, but the effect disappeared within 12 months (Hudley et al., 1998).

More recent antibullying programs tend to be much more complicated than the BrainPower approach. For example, in the Steps to Respect program, teachers present classroom lessons about empathy to elementary school children and provide instruction in how children should act when someone tries to bully them (the suggestion is to make eye contact and use a strong voice). In addition, when teachers observe bullying among children, the teachers provide on-the-spot coaching in more appropriate behavior for both the bully and the victim. To test the effects of the Steps to Respect program, one study (Hirschstein, Van Schoiack Edstrom, Frey, Snell, & MacKenzie, 2007) randomly assigned schools, not children, to either the antibullying program or a comparison condition. Both children and teachers were asked to rate children's social skills and playground behavior. A reduction in bullying was reported for the Steps to Respect schools.

The study raised an interesting question: In the Steps to Respect program, the best results occurred when the teachers provided the lessons as they had been instructed. Why might teachers not follow instructions? Sometimes teachers preferred teacher-led activities to the program's required role-plays. Another problem may have involved the difficulties teachers experience in carrying out one-to-one coaching while involved in other important activities. Success or failure of a program may depend on teachers' ability and willingness to follow through with the program, inside and outside of the classroom. The teachers' involvement may in turn depend on the quality of the instruction they received in the program, the commitment of the school administration, and the number of bullying problems the teachers address each day. Teachers who must contend with a high turnover of students or with poor and unpredictable attendance may become discouraged because they have to repeat lessons children have missed or provide repeated instruction to children who enter the school later in the year.

Recent related research (Menon, Tobin, Corby, Menon, & Hodges, 2007) suggests that it would be unwise for antibullying programs to try to raise bullies' self-esteem in an effort to improve their social behavior. Longitudinal studies showed that aggressive children with high self-esteem become more, not less, aggressive over time; they increasingly enjoy aggression and its rewards; they become less concerned about the harm they do to their victims.

Conclusion

It seems to be possible for some programs to reduce the amount of bullying in schools, but not all programs are successful, and some programs work only in good situations. Effective programs may need to focus on changing victims', as well as bullies', behavior. Will's principal could take some action to help reduce bullying, but he would have to have financial resources and quality teacher training to accomplish this goal.

CRITICAL THINKING

1. Review a child development textbook and federal Web sites, such as the National Institutes of Mental Health site, to find information about consent to research. Explain the rationale for parental consent and the consent of older school-age children for playground observations. What rules govern this kind of research?

2. One of the studies discussed in this section (Hudley et al., 1998) randomly assigned children to programs; the other study (Hirschstein et al., 2007) assigned schools to programs. What unwanted factors might affect the outcome of the first study but not the second? Explain your answer.

3. Imagine a study in which the participating teachers who present antibullying information are also the observers who report changes in bullying behavior. What factors might affect the outcome of this study? Explain your answer.

4. The BrainPower study excluded girls. In the Steps to Respect study, about half of the child participants were girls. Explain how this difference might affect reports of bullying behavior in school-age children. Consider both cognitive and physical gender differences and the changes that occur between third grade and the end of sixth grade. Refer to a child development textbook for information to support your explanation.

5. Why wouldn't researchers simply measure children's social skills at the beginning of a school year, then compare them to measures of the same children after a year's exposure to an antibullying program? What problem might result from this method? Would the problem be more serious in a study of sixth-graders or a study of third-graders? Explain your answers.

References

Crothers, L. M., & Kolbert, J. B. (2008). Tackling a problematic behavior management issue: Teachers' intervention in childhood bullying problems. *Intervention in School and Clinic, 43*, 132–139.

Hirschstein, M. W., Van Schoiack Edstrom, L., Frey, K. S., Snell, J. L., & MacKenzie, E. P. (2007). Walking the talk in bullying prevention: Teacher implementation variables related to initial impact of the Steps to Respect program. *School Psychology Review, 36*, 3–21.

Hudley, C., Britsch, B., Wakefield, W. D., Smith, T., Demorat, M., & Cho, S.-J. (1998). An attribution retraining program to reduce aggression in elementary school students. *Psychology in the Schools, 35*, 271–282.

Menon, M., Tobin, D. D., Corby, B. C., Menon, M., & Hodges, E. V. E. (2007). The developmental costs of high self-esteem for antisocial children. *Child Development*, *78*, 1627–1639.

Pellegrini, A. D., & Bartini, M. (2000). A longitudinal study of bullying, victimization, and peer affiliation during the transition from primary school to middle school. *American Educational Research Journal*, *37*, 699–725.

Tani, F., Greenman, P. S., Schneider, B. H., & Fregoso, M. (2003). Bullying and the Big 5: A study of childhood personality and participant roles in bullying incidents. *School Psychology International*, *24*, 131–146.

Claim 36

Sugar is a major cause of hyperactive behavior.

It was Sally's first year as a second-grade teacher, so of course she kept her ears open to hear the opinions of more experienced teaching staff. In the teachers' lounge, several people expressed their dread of the first of November. "Oh, boy, is that going to be the day from hell!" exclaimed one experienced teacher. "It's like this every year—fighting, crying, nobody can stay in their seats. The whole day is ruined. They go out for Halloween and then it's just sugar, sugar, sugar until they finally go to bed. The parents always say they'll limit the candy, but they don't—and I don't blame them because my kids are exactly the same way!" Sally listened carefully and was not surprised when her classroom was chaotic on the first day of November.

Were Sally and her colleagues right in thinking that Halloween candy was the cause of the disruption?

Since at least the 1950s, parents and teachers have been assuring each other that sugar causes children to become overactive and inattentive, with symptoms characteristic of ADHD (attention-deficit/hyperactivity disorder). As evidence, believers in this connection often point to the day after Halloween, an occasion when adults anticipate seeing, and often do see, children behaving disruptively, especially in the classroom. Many of these children went out trick-or-treating on Halloween night, received large amounts of candy, and undoubtedly ate a good deal of it, even though their parents tried to set limits. Reports of candy consumption and observation of hyperactive and inattentive behavior are interpreted to mean that sugar consumption causes a behavior change.

Parents who limit sugar and food additives in their children's diet often report improvement in child behavior and conclude that past undesirable behavior was caused by an unsuitable diet (Smucker & Hedayat, 2001). Although the food additive factor complicates this conclusion, these parent reports are also taken as evidence that ADHD and related problems are caused by ingestion of sugar, especially refined sugar.

Some people who accept the sugar-ADHD link argue for a commonsense connection: Sugar is easily digested and converted to energy, hyperactive children seem to have too much energy; therefore, limiting children's sugar intake will make them less energetic.

Considering the difficulties created by impulsiveness and hyperactive behavior, it is too bad that these claimed connections do not seem to be correct (Lilienfeld, 2005). Contrary to the reasoning stated in the last paragraph, all food must be converted to the sugar glucose before it is used to fuel cell functions, so dietary sugar has no more direct connection to energy than any other food. Of course, children who are actually starving become lethargic, but this is because of a lack of nutrients and calories, not because they are calmed by their candy-free diet. In addition, scientifically controlled studies show no association between sugar in the diet and undesirable behavior.

Although parents seem to have more accurate information about the facts of ADHD than teachers do (West, Taylor, Houghton, & Hudyma, 2005), some groups of parents hold mistaken beliefs about certain issues, such as the links between diet and hyperactivity (Bussing, Gary, Mills, & Garvan, 2007). In the absence of much systematic research, it is all too easy for teachers and parents to forget that most human behaviors have multiple causes rather than a single simple factor at work. It is also easy to forget that multiple causes are often confused with each other in ways that make it difficult to know the effects of a specific cause. More confusion comes from letting personal experiences influence one's understanding of complex matters.

If sugar does not cause hyperactivity, why, then, do teachers and parents commonly report disruptive behavior on November 1? For an explanation, the confounding variables contributed by the noncandy aspects of Halloween need to be examined, and there are many to consider. Features of Halloween experience and behavior include children's reluctance to eat dinner when more exciting things are happening; scary stories and costumes; activities outside after dark, which parents usually discourage in the colder fall weather; the perceived dangers and delights of visiting strangers' homes, which is usually forbidden, even for fundraising sales (e.g., Girl Scout cookies); and a lack of sleep caused by the extension of bedtime and difficulty falling asleep after an exciting night. Alterations of normal diet and sleep patterns, added to exciting or even frightening experiences, are enough to change mood and behavior in adults as well as children. (In fact, both parents and teachers may be affected by Halloween events and eat sweets and lose sleep.) Although this logical analysis cannot rule out the contributions of sugar ingestion, it does show that alternative explanations can be made, suggesting confounding variables that may influence teacher and parent reports of post-Halloween disruption. Systematic research is needed before claims can be made about the causes of children's behavior changes.

How can systematic research be carried out to test the assumptions often made about sugar and behavior? A reliable study of this issue requires that neither adults nor children know whether the children's diets contain components that might affect their mood and behavior. Adult expectations about the effect of diet can cause parents or teachers to notice and report children's behavior in ways that match the adult expectations—or even to act toward children in ways that contribute to behavior alterations. Children who expect sugar to make them excited and impulsive may feel justified after Halloween if they abandon their usual efforts to behave calmly. Just as adults may excuse inappropriate drunken behavior as "the alcohol talking," children may believe that candy bars make them jump up and down or push in line.

Of course, in everyday situations, both adults and children know when children have consumed extra candy. The same holds when parents use special diets for children. The parents obviously know what they are doing, especially because some diets are rather demanding and effortful for the cook, and the children are likely to recognize from the appearance and taste of the food that their meal is not ordinary. Children may also hear their parents discuss their expectations about the diet, or the parents may tell the children directly that they will be able to behave better after they eat different foods.

Can the effects of beliefs about diet and ADHD be limited by research designs? To do this, researchers need to make sure that neither the children nor the adults who assess children's behavior know the diet a child is receiving (i.e., both groups must be blind to the children's diets). Obviously, an adult must decide which child receives which diet, but that adult should not be in contact with the children. How can this be accomplished? Certainly, this research must be done in a restricted environment, such as a residential camp or boarding school, where the children are limited to the food provided by adults (e.g., children should not be allowed birthday cupcakes sent from home). In addition, the children's basic diet needs to be made from scratch, without the flavor or appearance of a food cooked with refined sugar. All of the children in the study must receive the same diet (even though they may not like it), but a randomly selected half should receive daily capsules containing sugar or any other dietary additives to be tested. The other half of the group should receive capsules of identical appearance but without potentially active ingredients. A comparison of behavior changes in the two groups will reveal any connections between diet and behavior, without any effect of beliefs and expectations. Past research that met these requirements did not show a connection between sugar in the diet and inappropriate behavior.

It is possible for some children to have sensitivities to sugar or to other dietary components, and parents' reports can provide hints about this. Nevertheless, for real understanding of diet as a cause of impulsive behavior, researchers always need to control parents' and children's expectations and prevent these confounded variables from confusing the outcomes.

Evidence and logical argument about the effect of sugar say nothing about the possible effect of food additives on children's attention, mood, and behavior. Each type of food additive needs to be tested individually, following the same rules discussed earlier, and some researchers have conducted well-designed studies suggesting that some food additives have the effects once ascribed to sugar (Rosenthal, 2007).

Conclusion

Well-controlled research does not show that sugar consumption is a cause of ADHD or other impulsive or inappropriate behaviors. Confounded variables usually accompany children's eating of extra candy, especially at parties or on holidays, including the expectations of teachers, parents, and children that bad behavior will follow. It may be that Sally's own attitude and behavior contribute to the disruption she expects and finds in her second-grade classroom.

CRITICAL THINKING

1. Using a child development textbook, find information about the effects of parental styles. Describe the ways parents' behavior can influence children's behavior, making the children more, or less, inattentive and hyperactive.

2. Find information in a child development textbook about the role of genetics in impulsive behavior. What nongenetic influence might impulsive parents have on their child's behavior? What genetic influence might they have?

3. How would you expect impulsive children to influence a parent's or teacher's behavior toward them? Would it make any difference if the adult were impulsive as well?

4. Review information about temperament in a child development textbook. Explain how temperamental differences between a child and a parent might cause the parent to describe their child as impulsive and inattentive.

5. What confounded variables are removed by having children randomly assigned to Sugar or No sugar groups? How might the research outcomes in this design differ from those where parents select their children's diet? Read the article by Rosenthal (2007) for other ideas about design of this kind of research. Explain how the designs discussed in the article can be applied to the study of dietary sugar effects.

References

Bussing, R., Gary, F. A., Mills, T. L., & Garvan, C. W. (2007). Cultural variations in parental health beliefs, knowledge, and information sources related to attention-deficit/hyperactivity disorder. *Journal of Family Issues, 28,* 291–318.

Lilienfeld, S. O. (2005). Scientifically unsupported and supported interventions for childhood psychopathology: A summary. *Pediatrics, 115,* 761–764.

Rosenthal, E. (2007, September 6). Some food additives raise hyperactivity, study finds. *New York Times,* p. A3.

Smucker, W. D., & Hedayat, M. (2001). Evaluation and treatment of ADHD. *American Family Physician, 64,* 817–829, 831–832.

West, J., Taylor, M., Houghton, S., & Hudyma, S. (2005). A comparison of teachers' and parents' knowledge and beliefs about attention-deficit/hyperactivity disorder (ADHD). *School Psychology International, 26,* 192–208.

Claim 37

Adopted children have many more problems of social and emotional development than nonadopted children do.

Sixteen-year-old Jazzmin was delighted when a new neighbor asked her to baby-sit 8-year-old Terence one weekend. Terence seemed like a nice enough kid, and Jazzmin definitely needed some money for prom expenses. Jazzmin was very surprised when her mother hesitated about the job. "But Mom—they live right down the street! What could happen? And I really really need some money to get my nails done!" Jazzmin's mother said, "You're young yet. Maybe you don't understand this. I heard that that boy is adopted . . . adopted kids can really have problems. Some people even say they can be killers. I don't want you to have to deal with any craziness. We'd better see if you can find another way to earn your nail money."

Was Jazzmin's mother right about the problems of adopted children, if not necessarily about Terence?

Like many other myths and misunderstandings about child development, the claim that adopted children are emotionally disturbed involves a tiny portion of reality and logic, mixed with a large dose of fantasy (Demick, 2007). Knowing some facts about early social development, and knowing the impact of early separation and loss, people might guess that adoption is a disturbing experience. But guesses are not necessarily accurate because individual experiences involve differences in timing, conditions, personality, and family characteristics as well as the experience of separation.

Adopted children, by definition, have experienced separation from their birth parents and may have been separated from later caregivers as well. Studies of toddlers who experience abrupt, long-term separations from familiar adults show that these children respond with intense and long-lasting grief. Separated toddlers go through a lengthy mourning period, withdraw from social contact, become uninterested in play, and eat and sleep poorly. With sensitive, responsive care from new adults, the children gradually recover and form new emotional connections, returning to their normal developmental pathways. Lack of sensitive care, or repeated separations, may make it difficult for toddlers to recover completely from their losses, and, possibly, their social behavior and capacity for relationships may be negatively affected.

So far, it seems that evidence supports the claim about adopted children. Some children are greatly distressed as they proceed through the adoption process. However, it would be a mistake to assume that all children and all adoptions are alike. The effects of adoption depend on three highly significant factors that may be quite different for different adopted children: the child's age at separation, the circumstances surrounding the adoption, and the caregiving abilities of the adoptive parents. (These factors may be related to each other, as, for example, the age of a child at adoption is often related to the circumstances under which the adoption occurred.)

The child's *age at adoption* helps to predict the developmental outcome of the experience. Toddlers, as explained earlier, respond with severe distress to abrupt separations and need help to recover. But what about children of other ages? Are there developmental differences in children's reactions to adoption? In fact, infants who are adopted in the first months of life show very few differences in development compared with nonadopted children. Children who are older than 5 or 6 years of age when moved from their familiar family to another home are likely to be sad and confused, but they do not grieve inconsolably. In fact, the period between about 6 months and 3 years of age seems to be the time when children are most intensely affected by adoption events. Children in this age group are not able to understand what is happening, but they are old enough to have formed an attachment to familiar people; as a result, they are more likely than children in other age groups to have behavioral or mood disorders that require professional help. However, resilient children even of this vulnerable group may recover well with the support of responsive caregivers.

What about the *circumstances* of adoption? Children adopted immediately following birth have no more problems than nonadopted children. There are more difficulties among those who remained with birth parents, were abused or neglected, then finally placed for foster care or adoption. Children adopted from foreign orphanages may have experienced severe neglect and often show physical and cognitive delays when placed in the care of their adoptive families (Pomerleau et al., 2005). However, most foreign-adopted children do very well and catch up developmentally within several years of adoption (Rutter, 2002).

Discussion of circumstances of adoption should also include individual characteristics of children. Some infants are placed in foster care (and later adopted) because they tested positive for drugs at the time of birth. Others are separated from their birth parents because the children have actual or potential disabling conditions that are challenging to the birth parents. Birth parents who have disabilities, such as mental retardation, may be persuaded or even forced to give up their child, who may or may not share or be affected by the parents' conditions. Toddlers with emotional disorders may be mistreated or abandoned by immature or incompetent parents, placed in long-term foster care, and possibly later adopted. In all of these cases, developmental risks are present before the child is adopted—problems that may not be cured by adoption but were certainly not caused by adoption, either.

The third factor, adoptive parents' *caregiving abilities*, involves the adoptive parents' understanding of developmental changes in emotional needs and their capacity and willingness to respond to those changes. Some adoptive parents do well with young infants because the parents expect and want to cuddle and comfort a baby; however, they do less well with older children, who need a sense of autonomy and may be concerned with school and friends. In this situation, the adopted infants progress well, but the older children may be more likely to display emotional or behavioral problems. The reverse can also occur if the adoptive parents have different preferences and skills. It seems, too, that adoptive parents are anxious and concerned about the children's needs and are more likely to seek services for adopted rather than for non-adopted children (Le Mare, Audet, & Kurytnik, 2007).

One issue that confuses people's understanding of adoption is the periodic change in adoption rules and standards. Experiences of children adopted today may be very different from those of children adopted 20 or 30 years ago, and future adoptees may have different experiences from adoptees of previous periods. For example, today's adoptions involve "falsified" birth certificates that conceal children's actual parentage, so children grow up without knowing about their biological background and may not be able to find this information when they are adults. A number of states are considering altering this arrangement (Raymond, 2007). Some families, of course, participate in *open adoptions*, which encourage a connection between the biological parents and the adoptive family. How these changed circumstances influence adopted children is still unknown.

It appears that most adopted children do very well and that differences between adopted and nonadopted groups are small. Social and emotional problems in adopted children are caused by a combination of risk factors, not by adoption alone (Rutter, 2002). And, of course, children who are not adopted may have serious problems, too. People should not expect all adopted children to be completely without mental health difficulties, but neither should they assume that serious emotional problems are characteristic of all adoptees. Some adopted children may experience difficulties resulting from a combination of factors, such as the adoptive parents' lack of readiness for their parenting tasks and past sexual abuse or neglect of the children (Simmel, 2007). Most will do well in a family environment that provides what they need.

Conclusion

Adoption alone does not cause social and emotional problems, although some problems may exist before adoption. The differences between adopted and nonadopted children are small, especially if adoption took place in the first months of a child's life. Serious mental illness and violent behavior are not particularly associated with adoption. Jazzmin's mother was naturally concerned about her daughter's safety at the neighbor's house, but she need not worry that adoption alone makes Terence dangerous.

CRITICAL THINKING

1. Read about social reactions in a child development textbook. Present a description of reactions common in children between birth and 6 months of age and those common in children about 18 months old. In which period of time would adoption cause less stress? Explain your answer.

2. Describe three confounded variables that make it difficult to interpret comparisons of adopted and nonadopted children. You can find some further information about this in Rutter (2002). (This is a lengthy and complex article, and you will probably find the discussion section most helpful.)

3. In a child development textbook, find information about genetic factors in behavior. Discuss the accuracy or inaccuracy of the old belief that adopted children might be "bad seeds." Review the article by Demick (2007) for other mistaken beliefs about adoption. What evidence does Demick offer to refute such beliefs?

(Continued)

(Continued)

4. Describe three confounded variables that might make it difficult to compare the results of international and domestic adoptions (variables that are characteristics of either international or domestic adoptions, not variables shared by both groups). Be sure to include characteristics of the adopting family. Search the Internet to find what foreign adoption Web sites tell prospective parents about adoption and include this information in your description.

5. Read about adolescents' emotional needs in a child development textbook. Explain why parents might be challenged by these needs after adopting a school-age child. Keep in mind the amount of time that may pass between the adoption and the child's entry into adolescence.

References

Demick, K. (2007). Challenging the common myths about adoption. *Brown University Child and Adolescent Behavior Letter*, 23(4), 8.

Le Mare, L., Audet, K., & Kurytnik, K. (2007). A longitudinal study of service use in families of children adopted from Romanian orphanages. *International Journal of Behavioral Development*, 31, 242–251.

Pomerleau, A., Malcuit, G., Chicoine, J.-F., Seguin, R., Belhumeur, C., et al. (2005). Health status, cognitive and motor development of young children adopted from China, East Asia, and Russia across the first 6 months after adoption. *International Journal of Behavioral Development*, 29, 445–457.

Raymond, B. B. (2007, July 29). Mystery-free adoption. *New York Times*, p. NJ15.

Rutter, M. (2002). Nature, nurture, and development: From evangelism through science toward policy and practice. *Child Development*, 73, 1–21.

Simmel, C. (2007). Risk and protective factors contributing to the longitudinal psychosocial well-being of adopted foster children. *Journal of Emotional and Behavioral Disorders*, 15, 237–249.

Claim 38

It is important for parents to be fair and treat all their children in the same way.

Their parents had different ways of dealing with 12-year-old Dave and 10-year-old Martin. Martin had always been very hard to wake up in the mornings, so he was supposed to go to bed an hour before his brother, especially on school nights. Dave was becoming a bit overweight as he approached his teen years, so the boys' parents were limiting the number of ice cream cones he could have, which they did not do for underweight Martin. Dave and Martin frequently told their parents how unfair these rules were. "We're almost the same age!" Martin declared. "Maybe I should go to bed 15 minutes earlier than he does, but not a whole hour. He keeps me awake banging around, too. But anyway, you're supposed to be fair, and it isn't fair to have different rules like this. You should treat us exactly the same." The boys' parents listened seriously to this complaint.

It's not pleasant to be accused of unfairness. Should Dave and Martin's parents change their approach and apply the same rules to their sons?

The word *fair* pushes many adults' emotional buttons. A child who accuses a parent or teacher of unfairness is likely to get attention, if not immediate sympathy. Adults are easily engaged on this issue because they agree that fairness is an important quality, and they do not want to find that they actually have been unfair. Parents and teachers generally agree with children that fairness is something adults should value and practice.

Given a chance to think it over, many adults would probably say that being fair is complicated. It can involve giving the *same* attention to different people's *different* needs. Children, on the other hand, have a simpler concept of justice and may believe that being fair means treating everybody exactly the same. Their complaints about unfairness usually mean that they think people have not been treated identically (or, of course, children may simply mean that they do not like the outcome and are arguing on the basis of what seems to be a legitimate complaint).

Should adults follow children's wishes and treat all their children with scrupulous equality? Is it even possible to do such a thing? Most parents with more than one child, if they are honest, have to admit that they have not behaved the same toward all their children, even though they wanted to be fair. How did this come about?

One reason that parents behave differently toward different children is that the parents change over time. The idea that children are growing and maturing is common; however, people often think that development ends at some point (perhaps at about the age where readers are now). But people continue to develop through adulthood. In addition, although aware that adults rear and teach children, people tend to forget that children also raise parents and teach teachers. From infancy, children communicate to adults what they need and like, both by subtle cues and by loud or violent actions.

Having learned by experience with one child (or one class), parents and teachers can never return to their original expectations and beliefs about children. With increasing experience, adults' anxiety, conscientiousness, and (perhaps) too-high expectations give way to confidence, relaxation, and more realistic views of children's abilities. Adults' ways of behaving toward children go through related alterations. The oldest children are quite right—Mom *did* make them go to bed earlier than the youngest children; which children received the best care is more difficult to determine, of course.

Parental changes over time cause older and younger children to be treated differently. But there are other reasons for "unfair" differences in parental behavior. One reason is the inborn individual differences in children's personality patterns. These differences, thought to be present from birth, are called *temperamental* factors. Temperamental differences are among the reasons why one newborn cries easily and becomes upset unless fed often and in small amounts, whereas a sibling is calm and cheerful, sleeps for long periods, and eats a good deal at a meal. Temperamental differences seem to have biological causes, although it is not yet clear whether genetics plays a role, and to what extent, or whether the differences are caused by prenatal events.

Temperamental differences can make it difficult for parents to treat their children in the same way, even if the parents believe they should do this. In a sense, babies won't let them treat their children equally. Babies who need frequent feeding and comforting are likely to get what they need. If they do not, the consequences involve, in the short term, the discomfort of family members who listen to babies' cries and, in the long term, problems of physical growth and health. Later-born babies, if they happen to need less frequent feeding, will respond unhappily to parents' efforts to wake them for feedings. Each baby and parent pair or trio develops patterns of communication and habits that are unique to that pair, patterns that will continue—with some variations—into later childhood.

Temperamental differences also make it appropriate for parents to use different disciplinary approaches with different children. Children who are temperamentally inclined to fearfulness may respond poorly to punishment, which is so distressing that they cannot pay attention to the lesson being presented. Less fearful children may be little impressed by gentle discipline and may need methods that are based on their affectionate relationships with parents (Kochanska, 1997).

Family circumstances can also make it impossible or undesirable for parents to treat all children the same. The death or serious illness of one parent might mean that the other parent has to change his or her ways of dealing with a child. Divorce may cause even more drastic changes in parenting. Loss or gain in income, or even simply moving to a new neighborhood, might make a difference because socioeconomic status is an important factor that buffers children's risk of antisocial behavior (Veenstra, Lindenberg, Oldehinkel, De Winter, & Ormel, 2006). But one of the most influential factors is the illness or disabling condition of one child, which might require other children to take more responsibility or lose some parental attention. In all of these situations, parents have little choice but to model a more adult view of fairness and to treat each family member as appropriately as they can. School-age children may complain that this treatment is unfair, but with help they can learn some important life skills from their experiences.

Although adults should recognize the impossibility, and even the undesirability, of making children's lives exactly fair, children's complaints about unfairness should not be dismissed entirely. In fact, both parents and teachers sometimes behave unfairly without realizing it. A child's sense of unfair treatment may be associated with unexplained irritability, hostility, and aggressive behaviors (Evans, Heriot, & Friedman, 2002), and alleviating the feeling of unfairness may be an important step toward improved family relationships.

Conclusion

Although parents should not display obvious favoritism, differences in the way they treat their children are inevitable. In addition, it is in some ways desirable to fine-tune child-rearing methods to the needs of individuals. This does not mean that children will necessarily agree with or approve of this complex way of thinking about family life. Dave and Martin's parents are making the right decisions, but they might do well to discuss their reasoning with the boys.

CRITICAL THINKING

1. Read about the development of theory of mind in a child development textbook. What level of theory of mind development would be needed before a child could take an adult view of fairness? Explain your answer.

2. In a child development textbook, read about concepts of temperament. Imagine parents who had an "easy" baby first, then a "difficult" baby. What problems about fairness of treatment might arise when these children reach school age? The article by Kochanska (1997) will help you think about this.

3. What problems of fairness might arise in a family with one son and one daughter? Would it matter if the boy were older? How might the situation compare to an all-boy or all-girl family? Use a child development textbook to review gender differences and their effects and explain your answers.

4. As parents change with age and experience, would you expect their ways of parenting to have better or worse effects on their children? Be sure to explain what you would consider better or worse effects. It would be helpful to read about children of large families before you answer this question.

5. In a child development textbook, read about families' adjustment to divorce and remarriage. Would you expect the most demanding parenting behavior to come from a stepparent who already had children or from one who did not? How would adjustments to family change be related to the fairness of parents' behavior as seen by the children?

References

Evans, I. M., Heriot, S. A., & Friedman, A. G. (2002). A behavioural pattern of irritability, hostility and inhibited empathy in children. *Clinical Child Psychology and Psychiatry, 7,* 211–224.

Kochanska, G. (1997). Multiple pathways to conscience for children with different temperaments: from toddlerhood to age 5. *Developmental Psychology, 33,* 228–240.

Veenstra, R., Lindenberg, S., Oldehinkel, A. J., De Winter, A. F., & Ormel, J. (2006). Temperament, environment, and antisocial behavior in a population sample of preadolescent boys and girls. *International Journal of Behavioral Development, 30,* 422–432.

Claim 39

A child's personality is formed by his or her experiences, especially those within the family.

Mia had always been the "shy one" in her large and lively family. Now, at age 11, she seemed more reluctant to be sociable. She would not sleep over at friends' houses and did not participate much in summer church camp. She even hesitated to go to school at times, especially if she had to speak in class. Mia's dad blamed her grandmother for this situation. "Mia's the only grandchild you took care of, and look how you made her turn out. You always kept her so quiet and didn't even take her to the park to play with other kids. I know you thought you were teaching her good manners, but I don't know what we're going to do with her now. I just wish she'd come up like the other kids—they're friendly people. And her mother and I treated them all the same."

Was Mia's father right? Was it the caregiving of Mia's grandmother that produced this unsociable personality?

Everyone "knows" that families make children what they are. The belief that experiences shape personality is an extremely strong one, with a foundation in "common sense" as well as in theoretical emphases left from decades ago. For many years, popular ideas derived from psychoanalytic theory have stressed the effects that parents have on their children's emotional development. Studies of parenting "styles" (Baumrind, 1971) have emphasized behavioral differences among children who were brought up in different ways.

However, recent research showed that variation among personalities within families is greater than variation between families. This means that personality differences among children of the same family can be very high—actually greater than differences among children of different families. Although these facts do not indicate that family experiences have no effect on personality, they certainly suggest that cause and effect are quite complicated.

An important point to keep in mind is that children in a family have many *nonshared* experiences as well as some shared ones (Dunn & Plomin, 1991). Shared experiences are usually factors such as the house the family lives in or the educational level of the parents (although these may be different for children with a large age difference between them). Nonshared experiences involve gender differences, differences in school or athletic success, and the consequences of being a younger or an older child, to name a few. Nonshared experiences may have stronger influences on personality development than do shared experiences within the family, and they may occur outside the family as well as at home. Some nonshared experiences, such as those related to gender, can determine other important experiences, especially within traditional societies. For instance, in some cultures, boys may have more personal freedom than girls do and less anxiety about the implications of others' behavior toward them. Nonshared experiences can begin within the family but can also connect with or cause individual experiences in school and in the community.

Personality development is also influenced by a factor that is present so soon after birth that it is thought to be innate, not learned. This factor, temperament, involves an individual's constitutional or biological tendencies to respond to the world in certain ways. Temperamental characteristics remain fairly consistent from birth through childhood and adolescence and appear to play a major role in the determination of behavior patterns.

Of course, 12-year-old children will not behave in exactly the same way they did when they were 12 months old, and the concept of temperament does not suggest that they do. However, temperamental aspects of personality involve similar patterns in the context of different ages and stages of development. For example, 12-month-old infants who show a temperamental pattern of withdrawal from new situations may scream with fear when approached by a friendly stranger. As 12-year-olds, these same children may not scream but perhaps may appear sulky and unfriendly when they are introduced to a new neighbor (Kagan, Snidman, Kahn, & Townsley, 2007).

Various ways of assessing temperament offer some understanding of innate personality differences that seem to exist independent of experiences. The fact of early and persistent individual differences suggests strongly that experience is only one of many factors that determine later personality.

An interesting possibility for personality development involves the interaction between temperament and experience. Although it is common to assume that parents rear children and shape their personalities, it can also be true that children "make" parents treat them in certain ways. Parents may respond positively to an outgoing child and have little concern for the child's social skills (but perhaps encourage the child to calm down and be quieter). With a child who tends to withdraw—who may belong to the same family—the parents may coach the child on social responses, scolding the child for appearing unfriendly or even punishing the child for seeming disrespectful or even ungrateful to adults. These two children, who began with different temperaments, can also have different experiences, which in turn might act to shape their behavior patterns. A child who begins life with an inhibited or sensitive temperament and encounters adverse experiences, such as domestic violence or abusive treatment, may develop a long-term pattern of shyness (Aron, Aron, & Davies, 2005).

The different family experiences of children with different temperaments may depend in part on the parents' own temperaments and related factors. Parents who withdraw from new situations may respond with sympathy to their timid children—or may push their children to participate because the parents are aware of the disadvantages of social withdrawal. Other family members may also contribute to the pressure placed on the child (or have an indirect effect through pressure on the parents). Such pressures result from the relatives' perception of a temperamental pattern as desirable or undesirable. To complicate matters further, the parents and other family members may regard certain temperamental characteristics, such as shyness, as acceptable for girls but not for boys, creating another interaction between the child's temperamental makeup and nonshared experiences created by the family.

A difficult issue in the study of personality development involves the timing of experiences. Researchers have suggested that changes in resilience (the ability to overcome adverse experiences) occur as children age and that the timing of these changes is different for boys than for girls (Chuang, Lamb, & Hwang, 2006). Family situations and other experiences may have different outcomes if they occur at different points in development—if they have any effects at all.

Conclusion

Although family experiences contribute to the shaping of personality, they do so through complicated interactions with temperament and social expectations. Mia's grandmother may have encouraged Mia to be quiet and unsociable, but she is not entirely responsible for Mia's later personality characteristics.

CRITICAL THINKING

1. In a child development textbook or in the article by Baumrind (1971), read about the connections between parenting style and personality as reported by Diana Baumrind. Explain how it might be possible for child personality to affect parenting style, rather than the other way around.

2. Use a child development textbook to find information about children's responses to divorce. Describe how children might respond to their parents' divorce as if it were a nonshared experience. What factors might cause the children to experience divorce in different ways?

3. Read about temperament in a child development textbook. Describe how a specific temperamental characteristic might be displayed by an individual in two stages of development: infancy and adolescence. Additional helpful information may be found in the publication by Kagan et al. (2007).

4. What are some confounding variables that may be present in studies of parenting style? These factors might include education, socioeconomic status, and gender (they are typically associated with one parenting style rather than another). Explain your answer.

5. Read about shared versus nonshared experiences in a child development textbook or in the article by Dunn and Plomin (1991). List the possible shared and nonshared experiences of two children born to the same parents 10 years apart. Be sure to consider how parental characteristics may change during this period of time.

References

Aron, E. N., Aron, A., & Davies, K. M. (2005). Adult shyness: The interaction of temperamental sensitivity and an adverse childhood environment. *Personality and Social Psychology Bulletin, 31,* 181–197.

Baumrind, D. (1971). Current patterns of parental authority. *Developmental Psychology Monographs, 4*(1, Pt. 2).

Chuang, S. S., Lamb, M. E., & Hwang, C. P. (2006). Personality development from childhood to adolescence: A longitudinal study of ego-control and ego-resiliency in Sweden. *International Journal of Behavioral Development, 30,* 338–343.

Dunn, J., & Plomin, R. (1991). Why are siblings so different? The significance of differences in sibling experiences within the family. *Family Process, 30,* 271–283.

Kagan, J., Snidman, N., Kahn, V., & Townsley, S. (2007). The preservation of two infant temperaments into adolescence. *Monographs of the Society for Research in Child Development, 287*(72, Serial No. 2).

PART V

Adolescents

Claim 40

Children are more likely to become delinquent if their fathers are absent or uninvolved.

Marta and Jack had struggled with each other throughout their marriage. Now, with their children, Sean and Kylie, 12 and 9 years old, Marta feels that divorce is inevitable. Jack is drinking heavily, and Marta sometimes joins him. Domestic violence between the parents is occurring more frequently, and the children were once so frightened that they called the police even though they knew they would be punished. One day, Marta told her mother that she was going to see a lawyer and start divorce proceedings. "Oh, honey, I wouldn't do that," her mother commented. "How are you going to control Sean by yourself when he's a teenager? Boys need a father in the house to keep them from getting in trouble."

Is Marta's mother right? Are the chances better for Sean's adolescent life if his father continues to live with the children?

Curiously, in past history, people expected widows' sons to do very well in life. For example, the unusual leadership and other abilities of George Washington are sometimes attributed to his mother's childrearing. Washington's mother was a widow who did not remarry but devoted herself to her son's interests. The belief that father involvement is essential to good development is a more modern attitude, but today, of course, the absence of a father is much more likely to be a result of divorce (or no marriage) rather than death.

A large number of U.S. children and adolescents rarely see their fathers, as a result of high divorce rates and the high rate of births to unmarried couples. In many cases, fathers never live with the children; after a legal custody decision, it is common for primary custody to go to the mother. The fathers in these cases may end up living some distance from their children, may marry and have other children, or for many other reasons may reduce their contact with their children.

Marriage of a father to a child's mother has been suggested as a way to ensure the child's good development and to prevent delinquent behavior. One reason given for this suggestion concerns the economic viability of the family unit: Two adults should be able to earn a living and care for children more effectively than one adult can. But the suggestion of marriage as a cure is also associated with the assumption that fathers can control children's behavior—especially that of boys—more successfully than mothers can. However, this may not be the case when mothers are authoritative (firm but reasonable) in their parenting style (Simons & Conger, 2007).

Research on large numbers of children concluded that the effect of fathers depends not just on their presence but also on who they are and how they behave. One study of fathers' parenting styles found that in intact families a father with an authoritarian parenting style is more likely than fathers with other parenting styles to have a son involved in delinquent activity and drug and alcohol use. If the father-son relationship is positive, however, the ill effects of authoritarian parenting are less than in families where the relationship is hostile and negative. These effects are stronger for boys than for girls (Jaffee, Moffit, Caspi, & Taylor, 2003).

The study just described emphasized the role of attitudes toward children and the quality of parent-child relationships. However, intensely negative attitudes may culminate in actual maltreatment, and when this occurs in adolescence teenagers are more likely to be involved with antisocial behaviors, such as drug use, drinking, and violence. The presence of a maltreating father may thus be more harmful than his absence.

Many studies of father involvement and delinquency are correlational studies, in which a statistical connection between the two factors is calculated. In these cases, it can be difficult to interpret correlations and to conclude which factor caused the other—or, indeed, whether additional factors caused both of them. Most readers will assume that father involvement causes the level of child delinquency rather than the other way around, but is this necessarily the case?

One correlational study examined connections between adolescents' perceptions of their parents' antisocial behavior and reports of adolescents' own behavior. The authors discussed the possibility that the parents' behavior and parenting skills could be disrupted by the extremely challenging behaviors of their children. Anger and frustration with child behaviors might be "medicated" by drug and alcohol use or expressed through aggressive behavior toward the children. Resident or nonresident fathers might feel especially challenged or disrespected by child delinquency because the fathers accept popular beliefs about their powerful position and expectations that they can exert control over their children. The result might be maltreatment of a challenging child, either by the annoyed father or by a mother who does not want the father to be agitated (Smith, Ireland, & Thornberry, 2005).

To understand the effect of fathers on children's development, genetic factors as well as the children's experiences in the family need to be considered. Detailed analysis of the effects of antisocial fathers suggests that their children receive a "double whammy" of genetics and environmental pressures toward behavior problems—that is, the children may inherit their father's genetic makeup and experience his behavior. Researchers reported that these children do better with less contact with their antisocial fathers, whereas children of socially appropriate fathers benefit from father involvement. Children of socially appropriate fathers have a double advantage rather than a whammy because they carry genetic material associated with positive social behavior, and they experience good social interactions with their fathers. The separate roles of heredity and environment suggest that children of antisocial fathers may be positively influenced by socially appropriate stepfathers, but a child who is genetically directed toward appropriate social behavior can be negatively influenced by an antisocial stepfather.

Attempts to understand father influences are complicated by the possibility that families may function differently within different demographic groups. Groups with large numbers of single-mother households may respond in their own characteristic ways to father absence (Salem, Zimmerman, & Notaro, 1998). Thus, it may be unreasonable to compare effects of father involvement in intact families with events in divorced or never-married families, unless the family patterns of others in the neighborhood or demographic group are considered. Family experiences that are strikingly different from those of relatives, friends, or neighbors may have their own effect on children's behavior. Of course, the effects of father presence or absence can be different for different groups—for example, for boys versus girls, in large versus small sibling groups, or in extended families versus nuclear families. One study of the rare but growing phenomenon of the father-only family suggested that children in these families are more likely to become delinquent (Demuth & Brown, 2004).

Conclusion

Although an intact and well-functioning family provides many benefits for children, the simple presence of a father is not necessarily beneficial to children's social development, and the presence of an antisocial father actually may be harmful. Marta's mother is mistaken in advising her daughter to stay in a violent marriage as an alternative to having a delinquent son. If Sean's father is hostile to him, the continuation of the marriage is likely to encourage delinquency in adolescence. In addition, other factors, such as Marta's own drinking, will continue to have negative effects on Sean whether the parents stay together or not.

CRITICAL THINKING

1. In a recent study, the authors analyzed data from the National Longitudinal Study of Youth 1997 (Bronte-Tinkew, Moore, & Carrano, 2006). Read the study and describe how the researchers chose the participants.

2. Read the article by Jaffee et al. (2003). According to the authors, what confounded variables confuse comparisons between intact and single-parent families? Do Salem et al. (1998) suggest different confounding variables?

3. Read a child development textbook to find out about girls' delinquent behavior. Explain why father involvement might influence girls differently than boys. (Hint: Is adjudication based on different reasons for girls than for boys?)

4. What genetic factors might make both fathers and children more antisocial than the average person? What evidence suggests the presence of these factors? Use information from a child development textbook to support your answer.

5. Demuth and Brown (2004) reported a greater tendency toward delinquent behavior in father-only families. (Under what circumstances do you think such a family would come into existence?) What variables may confound and confuse this conclusion? How would those confounded variables be associated with delinquent behavior?

References

Bronte-Tinkew, J., Moore, K. A., & Carrano, J. (2006). The father-child relationship, parenting styles, and adolescent risk factors in intact families. *Journal of Family Issues, 27,* 850–881.

Demuth, S., & Brown, S. L. (2004). Family structure, family processes, and adolescent delinquency: The significance of parental absence versus parental gender. *Journal of Research in Crime and Delinquency, 41*, 58–81.

Jaffee, S. R., Moffitt, T. E., Caspi, A., & Taylor, A. (2003). Life with (or without) father: The benefits of living with two biological parents depend on the father's antisocial behavior. *Child Development, 74*(1), 109–125.

Salem, D. A., Zimmerman, M. A., & Notaro, P. C. (1998). Effects of family structure, family process, and father involvement on psychosocial outcomes among African-American adolescents. *Family Relations, 47*(4), 331–341.

Simons, L. G., & Conger, R. D. (2007). Linking mother-father differences in parenting to a typology of family parenting styles and adolescent outcomes. *Journal of Family Issues, 28*, 212–241.

Smith, C. A., Ireland, T. O., & Thornberry, T. P. (2005). Adolescent maltreatment and its impact on young adult antisocial behavior. *Child Abuse and Neglect, 29*, 1099–1119.

Claim 41

Violent television programs and video games cause increased aggressive behavior.

Fourteen-year-old Jared and his younger brother Jimmy were "addicted" to violent TV programs. They had a television set in their bedroom, and it emitted a constant roar of bangs, booms, shrieks, shouts, and emergency sirens. Their parents often told them to switch programs or at least turn the volume down, but Jared and Jimmy begged, whined, and sulked until they were allowed to watch what they wanted, as loud as they wanted. But their mother was worried because the boys seemed so explosive in some ways, especially if their favorite teams lost a game. This problem became apparent when Jared reached his teen years. Their neighbor—who had to listen to the loud TV in the summertime—commented that a cause and effect phenomenon was at work. "Those violent shows make kids so angry and aggressive. If you didn't let them watch that stuff, there wouldn't be any problem." The boys' mother wasn't so sure. She remembered that her father had been in a lot of trouble for fighting as a kid, and that was before violent TV programming.

Who is right? Is aggressiveness caused by violent TV programs and videos?

Aggressive behavior, aimed at hurting or distressing another person, is very much a part of human life, beginning in the toddler period. (It might begin earlier, but infants are not physically or cognitively able to organize aggressive acts.) People do not have to seek a cause of general aggressive tendencies because they are a part of normal human behavior. However, the amount of aggression displayed, its circumstances, and its targets are not necessarily the same for different individuals or for a single person at various times in his or her life. Although young children share characteristic modes and situations of aggression, older children and adults may have extensive individual differences. It is thought that previous experiences and present circumstances help to determine how often an individual behaves aggressively and the type of aggressive action the person displays (Loeber & Stouthamer-Loeber, 1998).

Most if not all human groups want to *regulate* aggressive behavior. They want to foster aggression used instrumentally and for the perceived benefit of the group, as in war or contact sports, but they want to limit harmful aggression that has no perceived benefit, such as attacks on other group members—although certain individuals may be permitted aggression against their own group as they carry out police or disciplinary functions. Parents are often permitted or even expected to use limited aggression toward their children for disciplinary purposes, and in traditional societies husbands are permitted this type of aggression against their wives.

Regulating aggression in teenagers and young men is a concern common to many societies and one that is evident in the United States today. Excessive aggression among these large, strong, quick members of the community can be frightening and even harmful to their targets. These facts have led to an examination of adolescents' preferred activities as potential causes of aggression, with the hope that controlling such possible causes might help to regulate aggression within the community.

Past studies of children and adolescents who watch many hours of violent television programs demonstrated that these individuals show unusually high levels of aggressive behavior, a fact that can be interpreted as evidence that viewing of violent programming causes aggressiveness. However, because these studies did not involve experimental designs that controlled confounding variables, it is important to consider alternative interpretations.

One alternative conclusion is that adolescents who behave aggressively also prefer violent television programs and choose to watch them frequently, just as teenagers who play baseball might choose to watch sports programs. The choice of television program in this case is caused by the existing general tendency toward aggressive behavior, not the other way around. A second alternative is that a third or fourth factor, such as family income or neighborhood characteristics, influences both aggression and television choices. Another possibility is that parental preferences for or against violent programs play a role in determining which television shows are seen in a home—the parents may provide role models for violence or an opposing system to be rejected by adolescents. These alternative explanations are less obvious than the original idea (that violent television causes violent actions), and their existence weakens the argument for the first interpretation.

An important and relevant question is whether inquiries should focus on violent television programs or on television viewing in general. Violent events are common even in programs that are not classed as violent. For example, an average prime-time hour of programming shows three to five violent events, and an average hour of children's programming includes 20 to 25 acts of violence, according to one study.

However, even completely nonviolent TV programs might be associated with aggressive behavior. What is known about the association between all television watching and aggressiveness? One study investigated this connection, collecting data about the amount of television watching by adolescents and young adults. The researchers found more aggressive behavior among those who spent more time watching television. Boys who watched more than 3 hours of television a day at 14 years of age were involved in five times as many assaults or fights as those who watched less than 1 hour a day. In addition, the behavior exhibited by the children in this study was specifically one of aggression against other people, not general antisocial behavior, such as theft or other property crimes (Johnson, Cohen, Smailes, Kasen, & Brook, 2002).

Of course, a statistical association does not allow people to conclude that an excessive amount of television viewing causes aggressive behavior. Once again, aggressive adolescents may choose to watch television rather than entertain themselves in other ways. Or factors such as childhood neglect may cause both aggressive behavior and high levels of television watching.

Other factors may be involved in even more complicated ways. For example, adolescents who watch less television may use their time in sports or other social activities in which they develop improved social skills that permit them to compete without resorting to physical violence. Alternatively, aggression-prone adolescents may be so lacking in social skills that they are excluded from social groups or sports teams and have few entertainment options except television and association with other antisocial adolescents. Poor educational achievement may prevent aggressive adolescents from doing homework, reading, or pursuing hobbies that require instruction, thus limiting their activities and making television the easiest choice of entertainment for them.

Certainly, the research on television and violent behavior is contradictory. The question is a complex one that needs to be considered with respect to factors such as brain development and resilience; even so, research may never yield a simple answer (Twemlow & Bennett, 2008). Some studies showed significant, but quite small, effects of television on behavior (Savage & Yancey, 2008). Other work emphasized the role of protective factors, such as satisfactory mental health and good social relationships (Comstock, 2008).

Conclusion

Although research has shown associations between television viewing and aggressive behavior, it is not clear whether violent television programs cause aggressiveness. Jared's and Jimmy's mother is right to be concerned if they are watching violent television to the exclusion of other social and physical activities, especially if their behavior is unacceptable, but simply removing the TV is not likely to solve the problem of explosive aggressiveness.

CRITICAL THINKING

1. Read the article by Johnson et al. (2002). List the factors (other than television viewing) that the authors mention as possible causes of adolescent aggressiveness. Explain briefly the logical connections between these potential causal factors and the outcome of increased aggression.

2. What differences between boys and girls are described in Johnson et al. (2002)? Read Section E of the paper by Loeber and Stouthamer-Loeber (1998). What gender differences do they discuss?

3. If someone were to conduct a quasi-experimental study of aggression in teenagers who watch violent television programs, comparing them to those who do not, what possible confounding variables would need to be considered? Explain your answer. (Don't forget the hint about gender differences given in Question 2.)

4. Refer to a child development textbook to find out about how children learn to regulate aggressiveness through rough-and-tumble play. What opportunities are missed by children who are socially rejected? How might these missed opportunities alter social interactions for these individuals when they reach adolescence or early adulthood?

5. Discuss the possible effect of parents' and older siblings' choice of television programming on the children in the Johnson et al. study (2002).

References

Comstock, G. (2008). A sociological perspective on television violence and aggression. *American Behavioral Scientist, 51,* 1184–1213.

Johnson, J. G., Cohen, P., Smailes, E. M., Kasen, S., & Brook, J. S. (2002). Television viewing and aggressive behavior during adolescence and adulthood. *Science, 295,* 2468–2471.

Loeber, R., & Stouthamer-Loeber, M. (1998). Development of juvenile aggression and violence. *American Psychologist, 53*(2), 242–259.

Savage, J., & Yancey, C. (2008). The effects of media violence on criminal aggression. *Criminal Justice and Behavior, 35,* 772–791.

Twemlow, S. W., & Bennett, T. (2008). Psychic plasticity, resilience, and reactions to media violence: What is the right question? *American Behavioral Scientist, 51,* 1155–1183.

Claim 42

If parents are not strict enough, children will behave badly and may become criminals.

Fifteen-year-old Daniel's parents were recently divorced and still argued frequently about Daniel's upbringing. Daniel's mother, Christin, insisted that Daniel needed strict rules and heavy punishments if he broke them. If Daniel were even 5 minutes late in coming home from school, she grounded him for a week. Christin did not tolerate any excuses or even discussion of the rules and their consequences, and she secretly feared that she would lose control of Daniel if she did not insist that he toe the line. Daniel's father, Mike, was more relaxed about rules and somewhat pleased to think Daniel had more fun at his house than at Christin's. But Christin argued this point. "Daniel's the one who's going to suffer if he gets his own way all the time. He has to learn to tell right from wrong and to respect authority. You're too lazy to keep after him, but how are you going to feel if he ends up in jail because you're not strict enough? It'll be too late then!"

Was Christin right about this? Is parental strictness necessary to ensure children grow up to be respectable citizens?

The first step in understanding this common belief is to examine the meaning of *strictness*. A small number of people who deplore laxity in childrearing support treatment that most people consider abusive, such as locking children in dark closets or beating them with electrical cords. A larger number reject such extreme severity but advocate some level of physical punishment and consider parents "not strict enough" if they do not spank their children occasionally. Much existing research on strictness focused on the use of physical or other punishment, though researchers also studied parents' expectations and rules for their children. For example, one study asked parents whether they agreed or disagreed with statements such as "I expect my child to obey without questioning me" and "I don't let my child complain." Understanding strictness requires knowing what a child might be punished for, what the family rules are, and what kind of punishment is used. When examining strictness of parenting, the kind of control parents are aiming for must also be considered—for example, behavioral control achieved through attentive monitoring and discipline or psychological control achieved through guilt and other emotional influences on children.

Research on parenting strictness is difficult to conduct and interpret because family life involves many confounding variables. Parental strictness is associated with characteristics of children, such as their activity levels, and characteristics of their living situations. For instance, a family living in an upstairs apartment may be under more pressure than a family in a house to keep children quiet. If children from strict families behave better—or, possibly, worse—than children with laxer parents, it is hard to know whether the children's development was determined by the parenting behavior or by one or many related factors. Nevertheless, this issue is so important that ongoing research is exploring a variety of issues connected to strictness.

Past research on psychological control looked at a factor called *intrusiveness* as an important aspect of strict parenting. Intrusive parenting involves high levels of personal control by parents who can be described as both possessive and unusually protective of their children. This personal control is manifested in negative, critical remarks that use the parent-child relationship for leverage. One researcher (Barber, 1996) concluded that intrusive parenting "potentially inhibits or intrudes upon psychological development" (p. 3297) and is "a consistently negative and inhibiting experience for children" (p. 3314).

Other related research investigated the effect of parents' control on school-age children's *internalizing* problems (e.g., excessive worry, stomachaches with no physical cause) and *externalizing* problems (e.g., getting into fights). In addition to examining behavioral and psychological control by parents, these researchers also studied how much affection the parents showed their children. Surprisingly, the children with high levels of both internalizing and externalizing problems were those whose mothers showed much affection and exercised high psychological control. The smallest numbers of externalizing problems, such as fighting, were shown by children whose mothers used high levels of behavioral control and low levels of psychological control (Aunola & Nurmi, 2005).

An intriguing but confusing factor related to the effects of parental strictness is ethnicity, which seems to be important in determining outcomes. African American children whose parents are restrictive, and might even be classed as harsh disciplinarians, are reported to have good developmental outcomes, as measured by school success and low anxiety. This is not the case for European American children. What might cause this ethnic difference? Do genetic factors cause children of different ethnicities to respond differently to strict parenting practices? This may be a possibility, but it may also be that ethnic differences in living conditions play a powerful role.

Recent research tried to explore the effects of ethnicity by examining environmental confounding variables—experiences that may be different for most African Americans than they are for most European Americans. Ethnicity in the United States is strongly associated with living conditions, employment, education, and family income, although there is a good deal of overlap in the experiences of different ethnic groups. In the study discussed here, the researchers compared a group of African American families who were living in poverty with a group of European American families with similar life circumstances. The families were evaluated for the number of stressful events (e.g., a family member's death, homelessness) that they had experienced in the previous year. The restrictiveness of the parents' behavior toward their children was measured with a questionnaire and observations of parents playing a game with their children. The children of the *less* restrictive parents had more behavior problems as family stress levels increased. In families with more restrictive parents, the children had little stress-related change in problem behaviors. For these very poor families, parental restrictiveness seemed to protect the child from the impact of family stress, for both African American and European American families. It may be the case that apparent ethnic differences in the effects of restrictiveness are related to the effects of different living conditions rather than specific genetic or cultural differences (Bhandari & Barnett, 2007; Hill & Bush, 2001). Cultural differences in values may also make a good deal of difference in the ways children respond to various parenting styles (Dwairy et al., 2006).

Much of the past research on strictness focused on obvious, important influences, such as the frequency of delinquent behavior. However, the effect of strict or more relaxed parenting may be a more subtle factor that results in less obvious outcomes. For example, children familiar with different parenting styles may expect adults to use different reasoning about rules, some expecting that rules will be based on equality of social relations, others expecting rules to be associated with consequences of their actions for other people (Leman, 2005).

Conclusion

Strict parenting practices, in general, do not seem to support good development or behavior in children, but such practices may be positive when used by families living in poverty or experiencing other types of stress. Christin probably does not need to be so strict to keep Daniel on the right path, although she may feel the need to control her child as the family goes through the changes inherent in divorce.

CRITICAL THINKING

1. Some of the work described in this section assessed parental strictness by means of a questionnaire, but one study (Bhandari & Barnett, 2007) used an observational approach. Read about the methods used in the observational approach and describe the advantages and disadvantages of each method.

2. Describe variables that may be confounded with parenting practices. Locate information that supports your answer in a child development textbook or in Hill and Bush (2001).

3. Identify characteristics of children that may help to determine the parenting practices used in their family. Refer to a child development textbook or to Aunola and Nurmi (2005) for information to help you form your answer.

4. Consider the effect of homelessness on a family. What are some direct effects of homelessness on school-age and adolescent children? How might the effects of homelessness on parents indirectly affect the children?

5. It is not uncommon to hear people claim that the level of parental strictness they experienced as children is correct and suitable for all children. Explain whether changes in the social environment during a few decades determine the level of parental strictness of a generation. Refer to the conclusions of Bhandari and Barnett (2007) in your response.

References

Aunola, K., & Nurmi, J.-E. (2005). The role of parenting styles in children's problem behavior. *Child Development, 76,* 1144–1159.

Barber, B. K. (1996). Parental psychological control: Revisiting a neglected construct. *Child Development, 67,* 3296–3319.

Bhandari, K. P., & Barnett, D. (2007). Restrictive parenting buffers Head Start students from stress. *Infants and Young Children, 20*(1), 55–63.

Dwairy, M., Achoui, M., Abouserie, R., Farah, A., Sakhleh, A. A., Fayad, M., & Khan, H. K. (2006). Parenting styles in Arab societies: A first cross-regional research study. *Journal of Cross-Cultural Psychology, 37*, 230–247.

Hill, N. E., & Bush, K. R. (2001). Relationships between parenting environment and children's mental health among African American and European American mothers and children. *Journal of Marriage and the Family, 63*, 954–966.

Leman, P. J. (2005). Authority and moral reasons: Parenting style and children's perceptions of adult rule justifications. *International Journal of Behavioral Development, 29*, 265–270.

Claim 43

Adolescents' brains go through some rapid changes; as a result, teenagers develop new ways of thinking about the world and about themselves.

Fifteen-year-old Sarah was annoying a lot of adults with her constant criticism and sarcasm. No mistake made by her teachers went unnoticed or escaped remark. Her parents also received daily doses of withering scorn. A crisis was reached when Sarah commented unpleasantly on the makeup and hairstyle of one of her grandmother's closest friends, a recent widow who was just beginning to socialize a bit. Sarah's grandmother was deeply offended and even hurt by the idea that Sarah might think the same things about her. Sarah's mother, Meg, was concerned and discussed with her sister how they might persuade Sarah to keep her criticisms to herself more often. But Sarah's aunt felt this would not be possible. "I was reading an article about this," she said. "The thing is, their brains are changing, and their brains make them think and talk that way. You can't change Sarah's brain—you'll just have to put up with it. She just sees how things could be better and has to talk about it."

Is Sarah's aunt correct about this, or is it possible for Meg to help Sarah learn not to make other people feel as if they are under attack?

Several different thoughts are packed into this claim. One idea is that quick changes in brain structure and function occur during adolescence. The second idea is that adolescents show rapid changes in thinking ability and patterns. Third is the possibility that the first event, brain changes, is responsible for the second, thinking changes.

Evidence from modern imaging techniques shows changes in the brain throughout childhood and even more changes from age 12 to age 20 (Beckman, 2004). The size of the brain increases along with the size of the body, but puberty is also a time when certain types of brain cells multiply rapidly. These cells are then gradually "pruned" away, year by year, throughout adolescence. Brain structures that connect different brain areas become more organized, and the cells are more likely to be coated with myelin, a substance that helps neural messages travel quickly to specific areas of the brain without spreading to other areas. Developmental changes are extensive in the parts of the frontal lobe that work to inhibit impulses—such as emotional surges—from other parts of the brain (Scharfman & Hen, 2007).

Experts gather that all normal adolescents experience these brain changes. But what about changes in thinking? Are similar predictable, nearly universal changes evident in the way adolescents think and solve problems? Decades ago, the Swiss researcher and developmental theorist Jean Piaget described what he considered to be an almost universal cognitive change from more concrete to more abstract thought. He spoke of a formal operational period of thought, when adolescents, like adults, were able to consider factors separately from each other, to be systematic in problem solving, and to check their thinking for errors. Piaget considered formal operational thought to emerge as a rather abrupt change in developing children's thought patterns, involving a reorganization of thinking similar in some ways to earlier developmental events.

More recent research, however, suggested that Piaget was mistaken in his belief that greater ability for abstraction comes with adolescence. The idea that cognitive changes happen abruptly has also received criticism. Instead, researchers suggested that teenagers may have one or all of a variety of cognitive advantages over younger children, including improved information-processing speed, improved capacity (amount of memory available), and improved inhibition (the ability to ignore distractions, including the person's own impulses). One or all of these improvements increase adolescents' executive control—the ability to manage processes of learning and problem solving, such as deciding the order of tasks to be completed. Improved executive control, rather than abstraction, may be the reason teenagers succeed in mental tasks that younger children fail.

Can changes in the adolescent brain explain changes in memory, thinking, and problem solving, as Claim 43 states? Making this assumption invites problems. Although imaging of normal brain development does not show large anatomical differences between individuals, there are large individual differences in cognitive development. If brain development alone were responsible for cognitive change, then anatomical and cognitive changes would demonstrate similar amounts of variability; otherwise, one pattern of brain development would have to cause many different outcomes. (Of course, I refer only to aspects of brain development that can be shown by current imaging techniques; other developmental changes cannot presently be measured.)

Individual differences in cognition are well-known. During childhood and puberty, there are individual differences in both brain growth and cognition. After puberty, many individuals show little further cognitive development, whereas many others show distinct cognitive advances during this period. Most people realize that individuals have advanced cognitive abilities in some areas ("I was always good at that!") but not in others ("I just can't do math, carry a tune, learn foreign languages").

Some differences in cognitive ability might be explained by genetic factors or by earlier experiences. Cognitive differences between boys and girls exist from an early age, although the two genders overlap a great deal in their abilities. A person who became hearing impaired at an early age may not have developed brain circuitry that is responsible for certain cognitive tasks. Some individual differences may also stem from experiences during the early adolescent "pruning" period, which can shape the brain so that more of its resources go into certain cognitive areas.

When people think of teenagers' cognition and behavior, they need to consider aspects beyond individual differences in specific brain functions, such as the idea of teenagers as instigators or producers of their own cognitive development. Some information teenage learners encounter is received with indifference—or even against the learner's will; conversely, topics an adolescent finds interesting and chooses to practice are practiced and mastered. Success in these favored areas is highly motivating and leads the adolescent learner to choose even more engagement in the subject. The sense of expertise is thrilling and acts as a far more effective reward than a good grade or parental approval. The particular cognitive area favored by an individual probably involves a combination of factors: some possible genetic advantages, early experiences of success, and interests that develop through individual experiences in environments that promote further learning. Another adolescent may have the same brain development (as far as experts can measure) but different cognitive abilities produced by different individual factors.

Despite the changes and variations in adolescents' brain functions and cognition, evidence is clear that most adolescents are able to exercise empathy (Jensen-Campbell & Malcolm, 2007). Further research suggested that even adolescents with attention disorders can learn to use meditation to achieve some control over their own thoughts and feelings (Zylowska et al., 2008). The relevant research findings do not support the belief that adolescent behavior is out of control because of changes in brain functioning.

Conclusion

Although adolescent brains undergo distinct developmental changes, cognitive changes and related behaviors are probably not entirely caused by brain maturation. Sarah's behavior is not simply a matter of increased ability for abstraction due to brain changes; rather, her behavior is also a product of her experiences and motivation. Because adolescent development includes an increased ability for inhibition, Sarah is capable of learning to refrain from using sarcasm in inappropriate situations. Yelling at her or making sarcastic ripostes will not help; calm guidance and modeling of appropriate behavior are more likely to help her behave more appropriately.

CRITICAL THINKING

1. Compare the discussions of early childhood and adolescent cognitive development in a child development textbook. Which topic provides more details about individual differences in development? Which describes more connections between cognitive and emotional life? To what extent are details of brain development emphasized? Give examples to support your answers.

2. In a child development textbook, find information related to instigation of one's own development. In what new ways can adolescents influence their own development? How does this behavior compare with school-age children's abilities? Would your answer differ if the children were from a traditional society? An industrialized society? Explain your answers.

3. Kuhn (2006) uses the term *disposition* to describe one aspect of adolescent cognitive development. Define this term and give an example of how this factor might function.

4. Read about adolescent brain functioning in a child development textbook. Describe the changes in adolescent brain and cognitive function, referring to the concept of plasticity. The article by Scharfman and Hen (2007), which contains information about the effects of increased neuron production, may be helpful to you in forming your answer.

5. Kuhn (2006) stated, "Positively valued activities lead to behavioral investment, which leads to greater expertise and hence greater valuing, in a circular process that has taken hold by early adolescence" (p. 65). How might this process interfere with academic achievement? Is this concept discussed by Beckman (2004)? Explain your answer.

References

Beckman, M. (2004). Crime, culpability, and the adolescent brain. *Science, 305, 596–599.*

Jensen-Campbell, L.A., & Malcolm, K.T. (2007). The importance of conscientiousness in adolescent interpersonal relationships. *Personality and Social Psychology Bulletin, 33,* 368–383.

Kuhn, D. (2006). Do cognitive changes accompany developments in the adolescent brain? *Perspectives on Psychological Science, 1,* 59–67.

Scharfman, H. E., & Hen, R. (2007). Is more neurogenesis always better? *Science, 315,* 336–338.

Zylowska, L., Ackerman, D. E., Yang, M. H., Futrell, J. L., Horton, N. L., Hale,T. S., Pataki, C., & Smalley, S. L. (2008). Mindfulness meditation training in adults and adolescents with ADHD. *Journal of Attention Disorders, 11,* 737–746.

Claim 44

High self-esteem makes children perform better in school.

Fourteen-year-old Eric was not doing very well in his ninth-grade algebra class. Eric's mother met with his teacher to discuss how to encourage him to do better work. "He seems so depressed and withdrawn sometimes," his mother told the teacher. "I don't think he has much self-esteem, and that's probably the problem with his schoolwork." Eric's teacher agreed, and they planned a program to help increase Eric's self-esteem. The teacher had stickers to place on work that Eric failed and "congratulations" stickers on work that showed effort. Eric's mother said that she would take Eric somewhere he would like to go every weekend and tell him what a special person he was. They discussed the possibility of hiring a math tutor for Eric but decided extra work on the subject would just lower his self-esteem even further because it would call attention to his poor school performance.

Were Eric's mother and teacher right to assume that low self-esteem caused his poor schoolwork and that their plans will raise both self-esteem and algebra grades?

Gold stars, Student of the Month awards, and the oft-repeated refrain "good job!" are outgrowths of a national concern with self-esteem and the belief that raising self-esteem raises performance. Research reports have contradicted this view (Baumeister, Campbell, Krueger, & Vohs, 2005), although some authors maintain that raising self-esteem is important in itself.

Despite research evidence to the contrary, the conviction that raising children's self-esteem raises their academic and extracurricular performance has created a self-esteem industry focused on methods and materials for increasing the sense of self-worth (Humphrey, 2004). Why, after all, should teachers and parents drill children on multiplication tables if making the children feel better about themselves will provide the motivation to work? Although this approach to solving children's problems has some logic, the possibility of finding supportive research evidence depends on researchers' ability to measure both performance and self-esteem.

In considering the effects of self-esteem on academic performance or sports or social activity, the first problem is to decide how to measure an individual's assessment of himself or herself. As is the problem for so many aspects of psychology, researchers cannot get inside people's heads and directly examine their experiences nor can researchers necessarily estimate from observed behavior what is felt about the self because people, even school-age children, have learned to behave in socially approved ways.

Measures of self-esteem are indirect and usually involve asking individuals to agree or disagree with statements about the self. For example, in one self-esteem scale for children (Battle, 2003), individuals are asked to say whether they agree with certain statements, such as "Most boys and girls are better at doing things than I am," "My parents make me feel that I am not good enough," and "Boys and girls like to play with me." These statements seem to be related to self-esteem as people usually think of it. Unfortunately, this kind of measurement is problematic: Both children and adults might shape their answers in the direction of social desirability. Rather than respond in a way that reveals their true feelings, participants may provide answers expected of a "good" person. In fact, children with low self-esteem are probably more likely to bolster their reported thoughts about themselves and to try to claim that they are "better" than they think they are. However, measures of self-esteem have consistent associations with some objective measures (e.g., school grades), so the self-esteem measures seem to be assessing something, although it might not be self-esteem.

There appears to be a correlation between high school academic achievement and measures of self-esteem, with higher self-esteem accompanying higher marks. But, as is usual with correlational studies, readers need to ask the following questions: Which factor causes, and which is caused? Do teenagers feel highly motivated to study and achieve because they think well of themselves? Or, alternatively, do they think well of themselves because of a long history of high achievement? Or do other additional factors, such as parents' education, ability to model confidence, and support for school success, influence both self-esteem and academic work?

The belief that high self-esteem causes high academic performance has been associated with practices such as social promotion and grading policies that focus more on effort or social cooperation than on objective achievement. These well-intentioned efforts may help some children through the occasional period of academic difficulty, but they probably do not have positive effects on self-esteem or later school performance. After the first school years, children are aware of their own performance and accurately assess whether it is better, worse, or about the same as that of their classmates. To the extent that self-esteem is influenced by school, children's feelings of self-worth are likely to alter with their actual sense of achievement. Undeserved passing grades may be a relief but will probably not communicate to most children that they have done well and can feed into the belief that a good grade is given "because the teacher likes me." This type of grading may communicate to children that adults are unpredictable and also poor judges of performance or that grading is concerned with personal charm rather than ability combined with effort. Unearned grades, promotion, and excessive rewards or praise also can make children feel that they are worse in school than they previously thought; otherwise, they would not be receiving unusual treatment.

Can a reward system of the type planned by Eric's mother and teacher affect his school achievement? Behavior can be changed by rewards, whether self-esteem is affected or not. However, with this approach, behavior change occurs only through effective planning and management of the plan. The individual must want the reward, and it is doubtful that Eric, a ninth-grader, wants stickers on a paper. Rewards must be reserved for desirable behaviors, such as completing a homework problem, not distributed in ways unrelated to the behavior changes that can help school performance. To give rewards appropriately, adults must be attentive to the child's behavior and observe carefully whether desirable actions are occurring. Paradoxically, minimum rewards are most effective, and over time more performance should be required before a reward is given—perhaps two homework problems rather than one, then three, and so on. This use of reward, or *operant conditioning*, assumes that the adults know which behaviors need to be increased in frequency to improve school performance and that the child can do what is wanted. If it is not clear what the child needs to do to improve, or if the child is not capable of the action, reward is not an effective way to improve academic achievement. It seems unlikely that the reward in Eric's case will make a difference: His mother and teacher do not know what he can do and what he cannot—nor are they planning to reward actual achievement.

A final consideration about Eric involves his mood. His mother said he was sad and depressed often, but rather than considering those problems alone, she moved quickly to what they meant for his self-esteem. Children and teenagers can be depressed, just as adults can, and it is possible Eric's depression is linked to his present lack of academic achievement (Grimm, 2007).

Conclusion

Although self-esteem measures and academic achievement are positively correlated, it is not clear that one causes the other. Neither is it clear that reward programs, including unearned high grades, cause an increase in self-esteem, although appropriate use of reward may cause improved academic work. Eric's mother and teacher mean well, but their plan will probably not improve either Eric's mood or his schoolwork. Tutoring for his academic weakness and consideration of a possible mood disorder might be more effective ways to help him.

CRITICAL THINKING

1. Discuss factors that can influence measures of self-esteem and also affect school performance. Explain your answer, using evidence from a child development textbook for support.

2. Search the Internet to find a program that claims to raise children's self-esteem. What does the program recommend as a way to raise self-esteem? What evidence is given to support this claim? What is the cost of the program and materials, such as books and videotapes?

3. If you were designing a quasi-experimental study to compare school performance of children with high self-esteem scores versus children with low self-esteem scores, what confounded variables would you consider? Keep in mind characteristics of home and school environments as well as characteristics of the children. What does Battle (2003) say about cultural issues in the measurement of self-esteem? (If you cannot find Battle's book, you may be able to find a useful summary or review of the work.)

4. Read the article by Baumeister et al. (2005). What evidence in the article suggests that there might be advantages to lower self-esteem rather than to higher? Explain your answer.

5. In a child development textbook, read about activities during the high school years. Explain whether school performance is an important factor in determining self-esteem in most adolescents.

References

Battle, J. (2003). *Culture-free self-esteem inventories: Manual.* Austin, TX: Pro-Ed.

Baumeister, R. F., Campbell, J. D., Krueger, J. I., & Vohs, K. D. (2005). Exploding the self-esteem myth. *Scientific American Mind, 16*(4), 50–57.

Grimm, K. J. (2007). Multivariate longitudinal methods for studying developmental relationships between depression and academic achievement. *International Journal of Behavioral Development, 31,* 328–339.

Humphrey, N. (2004). The death of the feel-good factor? Self-esteem in the educational context. *School Psychology International, 25,* 347–360.

Claim 45

The DARE program is an effective way to prevent children and adolescents from dealing or using drugs.

The Riverside town council and the town's high school principal were discussing the problem of drug dealing and use among teenagers. Although drug use was not blatant in Riverside, many people worried enough about it to try to prevent any increase. "We need to think of the future," commented the principal. "It makes no sense to try to fix a problem after it's started. Preventive measures are the way to go, and there are good antidrug programs out there. I think it would be worth the money to buy one." The Riverside chief of police, who was on the council, agreed. "Let's get the DARE program," he suggested. "I think it's great the way they have police officers go to the schools. The men enjoy it, and they get to know the kids. What's more, I saw on the DARE Web site that the program really works." The other members of the group agreed. They liked the idea of a positive interaction between police officers and teenagers.

What does the evidence say, though? Was the council right in thinking that DARE is an effective program?

DARE (Drug Abuse Resistance Education) is a program conducted in schools by police officers for the purpose of preventing children's use of recreational drugs and other harmful behaviors associated with drugs. The program is widely advertised through bumper stickers and other public announcements. An extensive Web site (www.dare.com) includes claims that

"DARE works." Yet some research provided no more than weak support for the DARE program, and some studies indicated worse outcomes for children who participated in the DARE program than for children who didn't.

It appears that the claim that DARE effectively reduces drug use is not only a myth but a myth supported and advertised by governmental and private organizations. Analysis of the DARE myth provides a valuable example for understanding the rare but important phenomenon of publicly advocated erroneous beliefs about child development.

An analysis of the program should begin with some of DARE's own claims. An assessment on the DARE Web site as evidence for the effectiveness of DARE shows a serious conceptual difficulty. The DARE site includes two stated goals: to provide children with information that will change their belief that "everyone is doing drugs" and to provide them with social skills that will help them refuse to use or sell drugs. Achievement of these goals can be measured by comparing information gathered from children who have completed the program and children who have not participated in the program. The evaluation DARE offers as "proof," however, involved a survey of parents, teachers, and principals, with their ratings of the DARE program and the extent to which it effectively prevents drug use. Tests of students' attitudes were also performed before and after DARE exposure, but the Web site does not report whether attitude changes occurred. Actual drug use was not measured, although of course there are many reasons why this would be difficult to do.

Pre- and posttesting (testing before and after a treatment or lesson) is usually a poor way to collect information about children and adolescents because an important variable, *maturation,* becomes confounded with the treatment. Children age, and as they become older, they change. The longer the time period involved in the research, the more natural maturational change is expected; consequently, researchers cannot easily determine whether a change was caused by maturation or by an intervention such as DARE. The only way to understand the effect of the intervention is to use a comparison (control) group of students who did not experience the intervention. The amount of change seen in the comparison group is compared to the amount of change in the treatment group (i.e., those who attended DARE presentations). Any difference between the two measured changes may have been caused by the treatment, provided that the two groups are similar in other characteristics.

One difficulty in evaluating a program like DARE, which is taught in many different schools by hundred or thousands of police officers, is the possibility that the program alters over time or that different versions are used by different instructors. Such possible changes or variations in the program are unidentified confounding variables that can interfere with interpretation of evidence about effectiveness.

Even if an intervention program were clearly shown to be effective in one study, repeated assessments would be wise because the program—or the children participating in it—might change in meaningful ways. According to the DARE Web site, a new assessment program is in progress. This program employs random assignment of schools either to the DARE program or to a drug education program already in use at a school. This design is much better than the pre- and posttest design mentioned earlier, but some of schools in the evaluation used existing curricula that were very similar to the DARE program, making it difficult to interpret any differences in outcome.

A difficult design issue involves *blinding* problems. For an objective assessment of the effects of a program, it would be best if children, parents, and teachers did not know which program was used. If they know, their attitudes and expectations can affect the outcome of the treatment. But of course it is impossible to prevent everyone in the school from identifying the program in use. In fact, the whole community may know, if the well-known DARE bumper stickers begin to appear on local cars. (Other drug prevention programs do not seem to use this ploy as often.)

In a progress report on the DARE Web site, the researchers carrying out this new evaluation noted two factors that may be challenges to their interpretation of the data: Police officers were reported to use the appropriate instructional method considerably less than 100% of the time, introducing an additional confounding variable, and several New Orleans schools participating in the study were so badly affected by Hurricane Katrina in 2005 that they had to drop out of the study after having participated for 4 years, making a complete data analysis impossible.

Studies comparing DARE and other drug education programs have used a technique called *meta-analysis*, a statistical procedure that takes many small studies and combines them in a way that allows better identification of causes and effects. One meta-analysis found that the DARE program's lecture format was significantly less effective than other programs' use of interactive, peer-oriented discussion techniques (Tobler & Stratton, 1997). The DARE program currently being evaluated includes discussion groups and role-play methods that add an interactive component; thus, this new version of DARE may be more effective than the earlier one.

Programs like DARE were originally put together in ways that agreed with the assumptions and convenience of police officers and other sponsors. In recent years, however, these programs have been evaluated by the standards of *evidence-based treatment* (EBT). EBT criteria are stringent requirements for detailed analysis of data and for research designs, including factors such as randomization and comparison to standard treatment (Gandhi,

Murphy-Graham, Petrosino, Chrismer, & Weiss, 2007; Petrosino, 2003). It is not surprising that high-powered assessments are sometimes in disagreement with the views of police officers who are involved with the DARE program and feel the experience is positive.

Conclusion

As of 2007, published research on the DARE program did not demonstrate that DARE effectively prevented child and adolescent drug use. However, the new program, still in the process of evaluation, includes new methods that have been shown to have good results. The Riverside town council should consider a variety of programs and review the independent research evidence about them, rather than accepting what program advocates advertise.

CRITICAL THINKING

1. Examine the DARE Web site, particularly the posted research reports. How do the methods and conclusions of those reports compare with the comments in this section?

2. In a child development textbook, find information about cognitive and social development in adolescence. List the reasons why an interactive, peer-oriented program might be more effective than a lecture program. What do Tobler and Stratton (1997) say about this issue?

3. What might be the effect of a drug prevention program on children's responsiveness if they and their families frequently see program advertising, such as the DARE bumper stickers? Is advertising a potential confounding variable? Explain your answer.

4. Read in a child development textbook about adolescent cognitive and emotional development. Explain the advantages and disadvantages of asking adolescents to indicate the frequency and extent of their drug use on a survey form. What factors might make this information less than accurate?

5. Read about cognitive and social development in a child development textbook. Describe the amount of change expected of children between 7th and 12th grade, even in the absence of a program such as DARE. Be specific about the kinds of changes that occur and how they might affect attitudes toward drugs. How can these changes be considered and kept from interfering with the assessment of DARE or similar programs? List any relevant research design issues.

References

Gandhi, A. G., Murphy-Graham, E., Petrosino, A., Chrismer, S. S., & Weiss, C. H. (2007). The devil is in the details: Examining the evidence for "proven" school-based drug abuse prevention programs. *Evaluation Review, 31*, 43–74.

Petrosino, A. (2003). Standards for evidence and evidence for standards: The case of school-based drug prevention. *Annals of the American Academy of Political and Social Science, 587*, 180–207.

Tobler, N., & Stratton, H. (1997). Effectiveness of school-based drug prevention programs: A meta-analysis of the research. *Journal of Primary Prevention, 18*(1), 71–128.

Claim 46

Children and adolescents learn bad behavior from their peers.

Sixteen-year-old Wanda used the "F word" in front of her grandmother and grandfather and didn't apologize or even look embarrassed. When her mother, Lisa, reprimanded her, Wanda just rolled her eyes and muttered, "Get a life!" Later, Lisa tried to smooth over the incident that had offended her parents. "She's really a good girl," Lisa explained. "She never used to talk like that, but when we moved here she started running with some bad kids, almost delinquents, I guess you'd call them. They apply a lot of peer pressure and get Wanda to misbehave. She stays out too late, and I think she's even skipped school some days. I just wish she'd make some nicer friends and get a better attitude."

Was Lisa right? If Wanda decided to befriend classmates who were not anti-social, would the result be more appropriate behavior from Wanda?

Most children and adolescents manage to learn from their friends some behaviors that adults don't like. For preschoolers, these behaviors might include spitting and calling people "poopy face"; for older children and adolescents, the behaviors might be gross jokes, swearing (or saying words close to swear words), and efforts to go to R-rated movies. But what about really bad behavior, such as stealing, drug and alcohol use, and extended school truancy? Are these learned from bad companions?

School-age children and adolescents who commit crimes (or status offenses that bring them into the juvenile justice system) often have friends who show similar behaviors; they are less often associated with well-behaved peers. It seems reasonable to assume that a child who is in trouble "fell in with" undesirable companions by chance, then copied their behavior, becoming delinquent as a result of exposure to delinquent society. Some might also assume that if the same child had made friends with a socially appropriate group, the child would not have become delinquent.

Obviously, a child who associates with delinquent friends can learn from them some new techniques of robbery, fighting, or drug use. Delinquent peers may also encourage antisocial behavior in members of their group by threatening to exclude them if they do not participate. Younger group members may be required to commit antisocial acts that benefit older ones, with the argument that the younger children will not receive serious penalties if caught, but the older ones will. Delinquent groups can also be rewarding to their members, admiring them for daring acts and emphasizing their contempt for conventional behavior, although some research suggested that members are only indirectly rewarded for their actions (Rebellon, 2006). Such groups offer role models and acceptance to adolescents who are struggling to find an identity and who fail to find one in school or other conventional activities.

However, the idea that learning from a delinquent group is the main factor in becoming antisocial assumes that the individual was equally ready to go in either a "good" or a "bad" direction. According to this view, the child was pushed toward delinquent attitudes and behavior by a chance association with delinquent peers. Is this a possibility? Can any child who enters a delinquent group adopt and commit to the views and actions typical of delinquents?

It appears that children who become delinquents had some undesirable characteristics before they began to associate with delinquent peers. Their impulsive, aggressive, antisocial behavior causes them to be rejected by nondelinquent children. Delinquent children and adolescents, on the other hand, may have no objection to antisocial acts and may in fact admire bold, aggressive, unconventional behavior. For this reason, an alternative interpretation of the association of delinquents with other delinquents is that an antisocial person seeks out similar peers, rather than learning bad behavior through an accidental association.

Why is it that antisocial children leave the rejecting group rather than trying to fit in with well-behaved peers? Most school-age children and adolescents receive some criticism and rejection from peers (who may not be very subtle) as well as from teachers (who may use sarcasm and public ridicule in their efforts to change child behavior). Most of these children stay with the conventional group and try to comply, rather than approach and enter a delinquent group. Those children and teenagers who are effectively driven away by rejection may receive an unusually high level of criticism. However, they also may be *rejection-sensitive* people who interpret even ambiguous responses as evidence of intentional rejection. These individuals feel rejected as a result of behavior or speech that would be dismissed as unimportant by most people. Rejection-sensitive adolescents become increasingly disruptive in school and have more absences and suspensions than other teenagers. Their lack of school involvement, or even attendance, frees them from supervision, making it easier for them to engage in antisocial acts (Downey, Lebolt, Rincon, & Freitas, 1998). Experimental work with preadolescents reported a predictable connection between the experience of rejection and the tendency toward antisocial behavior (Nesdale & Lambert, 2007).

A complex outcome such as delinquency is not likely to be caused by a single factor, so it is wise to look beyond peer relationships for causes of antisocial behavior. One such cause appears to be the children's beliefs about their parents' antisocial behavior, such as substance abuse or reckless driving. Children who are not aware of a parent's actions are not in a position to model the parent's behavior, so the children's perceptions of the parent are more important than the parent's actual behavior, at least in research on two-parent families. Children who believe their parents behave antisocially are more likely to do so themselves. As a result, they are more likely to be rejected by conventionally behaved children and accepted by antisocial groups (Dogan, Conger, Kim, & Masyn, 2007).

The similarities between antisocial parents and antisocial children suggest a genetic factor and a learning factor as causes of delinquency. A study of behavior genetics did not report a specific gene or genes that determine delinquency, but a more general tendency toward impulsiveness and irritability may have a genetic cause. Familial tendencies toward alcoholism and antisocial behavior seem to involve some genetic factors (Harden et al., 2007). A biological parent who has a genetic makeup that causes impulsiveness and aggressive behavior (e.g., fragile X syndrome) may pass this genetic material to a child, who will then have an underlying tendency toward antisocial behavior, whether or not the child remains in the custody of that parent. Of course, the impact on the child may be increased if both parents are genetically inclined toward antisocial behavior and if the child lives with them or with other antisocial adults.

Conclusion

Although children may learn undesirable behavior from a delinquent peer group, this learning is only one of many factors that lead to delinquency. Rejection by conventional social groups is an important issue. Lisa should not assume that Wanda can choose to make well-behaved friends because that group may have rejected her previously. It is likely that Wanda has some characteristics that make her acceptable to a delinquent group, and those characteristics may include her family experiences and her genetic makeup.

CRITICAL THINKING

1. In the research reported by Nesdale and Lambert (2007), 8- and 10-year-old children were unhappy and felt impulses toward antisocial behavior when they experienced apparent rejection in a controlled experimental setting. Discuss how these children might be cognitively different from teenagers and whether you would expect teenagers to respond similarly in an experiment. Use information from the article and from a child development textbook as support for your answer.

2. Consider the use of school suspension to change children's behavior. Would you expect suspension to make undesirable behavior more or less likely? Use information from this section and from a child development textbook to form your answer.

3. Read the article by Dogan et al. (2007). What were the characteristics of the families they studied? Did these characteristics limit the extent of the parents' antisocial behavior? Explain your answer.

4. After reading the Downey et al. (1998) article, describe a possible ambiguous situation that a rejection-sensitive child might incorrectly interpret as intentional rejection. Explain your answer.

5. Use information from this section and Downey et al. (1998) to describe methods teachers might use to help an adolescent avoid a sense of rejection.

References

Dogan, S. J., Conger, R. D., Kim, K. J., & Masyn, K. E. (2007). Cognitive and parenting pathways in the transmission of antisocial behavior from parents to adolescents. *Child Development, 78*(1), 335–349.

Downey, G., Lebolt, A., Rincon, C., & Freitas, A. L. (1998). Rejection sensitivity and children's interpersonal difficulties. *Child Development, 69*, 1072–1089.

Harden, K. P., Turkheimer, E., Emory, R. E., D'Onofrio, B. M., Slutske, W. S., Heath, A. C., & Martin, N. G. (2007). Marital conflict and conduct problems in children of twins. *Child Development, 78*(1), 1–18.

Nesdale, D., & Lambert, A. (2007). Effects of experimentally manipulated peer rejection on children's negative affect, self-esteem, and maladaptive social behavior. *International Journal of Behavioral Development, 31*, 115–122.

Rebellon, C. J. (2006). Do adolescents engage in delinquency to attract the social attention of peers? An extension and longitudinal test of the social reinforcement hypothesis. *Journal of Research in Crime and Delinquency, 43*, 387–411.

Claim 47

Young teenagers should be tried and sentenced as adults if they commit serious crimes.

Seventeen-year-old Ali and his parents were discussing at the dinner table a news story about a 13-year-old who had stomped a younger child to death during a "game." Ali felt the boy should be tried as an adult, not adjudicated in juvenile court. "Thirteen is plenty old enough to know right from wrong," he commented. "Besides, if other kids see that he gets off easy after doing this, they'll figure they can do the same thing if they feel like it." Ali's parents were not so sure. His mother felt that people might make the decision to try the boy as an adult simply because they were upset and angry and felt that someone ought to be punished, rather than for any better reason. Ali's father thought that juvenile courts served a good function: Because young teenagers' thinking is not fully developed the boy who had killed should not be treated as an adult.

Who is right?

The question of the right reaction to serious juvenile crime is not just theoretical. At the time of this writing, it is estimated that 73 people are serving life sentences without possibility of parole for crimes committed in early adolescence. What is the right action to take in these cases? Can child development research answer this question?

One consideration is whether all the needed, relevant research exists. Of course there are many studies of thought patterns and emotional responsiveness in adolescence and the early adult years. However, there are still limits on empirical knowledge of the results of different actions taken against juvenile offenders. How are the outcomes different if young people are treated as adults rather than juveniles? Surprisingly—considering how ready people are to draw conclusions on this subject—there is relatively little empirical work on the effects of different treatments (Redding, 2003).

When trying to deal with this difficult, conflicted question, the first step must be to try to understand what is being asked. The most important word involving juvenile offenders is *should*. There are many kinds of *should*, and not all of them can be dealt with through information about child development. Which *should* is being considered here? One possibility is that this is a moral *should*, one that considers how justice can be done. For example, a person focusing on justice might argue that justice demands that anyone who takes a human life must have his or her own life taken in retribution. Or, alternatively, a moral view might state that people older than a specific age are properly treated in one way, people under that age in another. Although psychology and the study of child development can provide information on the ways people think about justice, research studies have nothing to say about moral truths.

Some kinds of moral *should* involve the idea that justice treats some people differently from others. Mentally retarded adults, and, more rarely, mentally ill adults may correctly receive different treatment from others, according to this belief. For questions involving this kind of *should*, the issue about the young teenager may be whether the person's abilities are similar to those of an older person who receives special treatment or whether they are more like those of an adult who receives the full punishment allowed by the law. The study of child development can provide information relevant to the second part of this idea—not the moral issue of how justice is done but the question about similarities between young teenagers and specific others. These similarities can be identified through empirical research.

Another type of *should* involves the best outcome for the community. What type of treatment of the young killer would yield the greatest safety and comfort for other community members? If the young person were adjudicated in the juvenile court, would his later behavior be better or worse than if he were tried and sentenced as an adult? Does one of these treatments make this individual less likely to kill again? And does the example set by the treatment make other young teenagers more or less likely to kill? Are the others deterred from violent acts or encouraged to follow their aggressive impulses? In theory, it is possible for empirical research to provide answers to these questions, but in practice it is quite difficult, in part because there are so few events to study (Redding, 2003).

Finally, *should* statements may involve consideration of the best outcome for the young killer. What if we want to provide the best opportunity for this person to recover from what has happened and recover a healthy developmental trajectory, growing into an adult who can develop his best talents? Is this outcome more likely to occur if the young person goes to juvenile court and receives the intervention considered appropriate there or is it more likely to occur if adult treatment is meted out? Again, these questions have the potential for empirical answers, but because the events are infrequent the practical aspects of such research are challenging (Liptak, 2007). Questions involving types of moral *should* cannot be answered through research. Even questions about the effects of different treatments on the individual and the community are extremely difficult to deal with for a variety of practical reasons, such as frequency of events. (There is some work that looks at the effects of treatments, however; see Eddy, Whaley, & Chamberlain, 2004.) Can the study of child development offer anything of use to this issue? The most valuable information available is probably that pertaining to comparisons between young teenagers and adults. This information can at least tell whether there are substantial differences between the mental lives of teenagers and those of the older people, whom the law considers completely responsible for their own actions.

One important contribution of child development work is information about adolescents' cognitive abilities as they compare to those of adults. This comparison is not as simple as it appears to be, however, because stages of cognitive development are not perfectly linked to chronological age. Although it is possible to describe cognitive characteristics that are typical of a particular age group (Packard, 2007), there are large individual differences, and an individual may not display exactly the same cognitive patterns as his or her age-mates.

Generally, people in their early teens show some of the performance characteristics of *formal operational thought*, but they do not necessarily have abilities equivalent to those of well-developed adults. They are able to hypothesize possible outcomes of an action, but they are more likely than adults to expect the "ideal" outcome out of all the possibilities. Teenagers usually have less experience than adults and may not be able to bring as much information into their decision making. The adolescent criminal might be expected to have a good deal of ability to predict the outcome of an act, but the individual's lack of knowledge and other cognitive immaturity may foster a decision to carry out a serious crime.

The teenager's cognitive ability, although of much interest for this topic, may not be as important as emotional and behavioral factors. Although an adolescent, like an adult, might make a reasoned decision about committing a robbery, murders and rapes are more likely to occur without planning and as circumstances arise. Whether these crimes occur might depend more on emotional characteristics than on the ability to use formal operational thought. The young perpetrator may be drawn into a crime by emotional reactions to the behavior of other people, which the adolescent feels must be addressed—for example, behavior that the individual perceives as disrespectful.

Adolescents are particularly affected by a sense of social anxiety and might find shame to be an unbearable emotion that drives them to attack others. Some individuals may experience social anxiety and shame as if these feelings were threats to their identity and even their existence. They may feel that the only option for self-preservation is to wipe out the source of the threat—the source being a person who seems to be contemptuous or to find the adolescent disgusting. This reaction seems exaggerated to most adults and makes sense only if people comprehend the threat level experienced by these adolescents. The impulse to attack the "threatening" person can be very powerful (Lewis, 1992).

Unfortunately, adolescents may also be less able than adults to resist the impulse to retaliate when *dissed* (treated in what they feel is a disrespectful manner) and less able (as was discussed earlier) to think through the consequences of their actions. What is known about brain development cannot provide a complete explanation of adolescent criminal behavior; however, facts show that adolescents are still in the process of developing brain areas that are involved in controlling impulses. Lack of impulse control is a factor in criminal behavior. Without normal capacities for impulse control, most people would have criminal records resulting from, say, punching people who pushed or impatiently leaving a restaurant without paying a slow-to-arrive bill.

Conclusion

Evidence shows that adolescents' cognitive and emotional characteristics are different from those of the adults for whom the criminal justice system is designed. There has been little research on the outcomes for the individual or the community of treating delinquent teenagers as adult offenders compared with treating them less harshly. The important moral question is one that empirical research cannot answer. Ali's parents are somewhat more in line with what is known about child development, but it is not clear whether they and their son are trying to answer different questions.

CRITICAL THINKING

1. In a child development textbook, or in the book by Lewis (1992), find information about the development of the social emotions. Would a sense of guilt or a sense of shame make adolescents more likely to commit a serious crime? Explain your answer.

2. Describe formal operational thought. How would formal operational abilities make a teenager *more* vulnerable than a younger child to social anxiety? Use information from a child development textbook to support your answer.

3. Read the article by Packard (2007). Describe three cognitive or emotional differences between adults and adolescents as described in the article.

4. Discuss the possible relationship between the experience of social anxiety and the tendency to yield to peer pressure, especially in risky or potentially criminal situations.

5. Locate the term *imaginary audience* in a child development textbook or other source of information. Define the term and explain how this phenomenon of adolescent experience is related both to formal operational thinking and to social anxiety.

References

Eddy, J. M., Whaley, R. B., & Chamberlain, P. (2004). The prevention of violent behavior by chronic and serious male juvenile offenders: A 2-year follow-up of a randomized clinical trial. *Journal of Emotional and Behavioral Disorders, 12*, 2–8.

Lewis, M. (1992). *Shame: The exposed self.* New York: Free Press.

Liptak, A. (2007, October 17). Lifers as teenagers, now seeking second chance. *New York Times*, pp. A1, A24.

Packard, E. (2007). That teenage feeling. *Monitor on Psychology, 38*(4), 20–22.

Redding, R. E. (2003). The effects of adjudicating and sentencing juveniles as adults. *Youth Violence and Juvenile Justice, 1*, 128–155.

Claim 48

Adolescence is an emotionally dangerous time when teenagers are likely to attempt or commit suicide.

Fifteen-year-old Elena and her parents were very disturbed by a series of events at Elena's school. A student in the senior class had been found hanged, and the conclusion was that he had committed suicide. The school called in professional grief counselors and had several meetings for students and parents, in which they discussed some symptoms of depression and suicidal thinking and cautioned parents that some imitations of the suicidal act might occur. When Elena's parents discussed the situation later that night, her mother said, "I'm so scared about this. We've always done everything to protect Elena, now we can't do anything about this. I feel so sorry that she's upset about this boy, but I'm even more worried that there might be more deaths—that even Elena might start to think about suicide now that it's been put in her mind. It seems so unfair that teenagers have to be so vulnerable to suicide when they've hardly started to live."

Of course Elena's mother is worried about her daughter, but is she right in thinking that Elena's age group is especially suicidal?

Disturbing as the idea of adolescent suicide is, and important as preventive efforts are, suicide among adolescents is not as common as it is among older people. The National Institutes of Mental Health reported in 2004 that the suicide rate among adolescents 15–19 years of age was 8.2 per 100,000 people in the age group. For individuals 20–24 years of age, the rate was 12.5

per 100,000. With increasing age, suicide rates increase: The rate for people 65 years and older is 14.3 per 100,000. The highest suicide rate is among non-Hispanic White men 85 years and older. whose rate of 17.8 per 100,000 is more than twice the rate for teenagers (http://www.nimh.nih.gov).

The real danger of adolescence is accidental injury or death, especially motor vehicle accidents. Failure to use seatbelts and alcohol consumption before or while driving are important factors in teenage motor vehicle accidents. In 2002 alone, 5,000 deaths of adolescents 16–19 years old were caused by motor vehicle accidents in the United States. Permanent injuries and disabilities may result from nonfatal accidents, too, and many thousands of U.S. teenagers suffer that fate.

The second leading cause of child and adolescent deaths in the United States is not suicide but homicide. However, much discussion has taken place about the possibility of counting some of these deaths as a form of suicide— *victim-precipitated homicide*—in which individuals carry out actions, such as attacks on others, that are in ways almost guaranteed to bring a fatal response from police. An important issue of adolescent suicide is the role played by depression in triggering suicidal thinking and actions (Liang & Eley, 2005). Girls appear to experience more depression after they enter their teens. That girls are much more likely than boys to attempt suicide without actually dying makes it more difficult to understand the connections between depression and suicide. That drug use and eating disorders are also associated with depression complicates the question even further. In addition, both genetic factors and negative life experiences play a part in depression and therefore may also influence suicidal behavior.

About 7% of high school students in the United States attempt suicide per year. Some of those attempts pose little threat to the person's life, but of course they should not be dismissed as meaningless. Suicide attempts can be predictors of later "successful" efforts, and of course even a weak attempt may accidentally cause death, especially among adolescents who self-mutilate by cutting themselves.

The understanding that adolescent suicide attempts are somewhat predictable has led to a variety of antisuicide efforts by high schools and parent groups. These interventions often involve grief counseling for students distressed by the death of a classmate and educational efforts to emphasize to teenagers that they should not promise to keep secret a friend's suicidal preoccupation.

Currently, the most difficult issue in adolescent suicide studies is whether the use of *antidepressant* drugs increases the risk of suicide among teenagers. Warnings of such a risk were first published soon after the year 2000, and the United States Food and Drug Administration (FDA) in 2004 ordered antidepressant drugs to be packaged with cautions about a possible associated risk of suicide. However, some researchers did not agree with the FDA position. They carried out a meta-analysis, a statistical examination combining a large number of separate studies. The result of the meta-analysis showed a statistically significant increase in suicidal thinking related to antidepressant use, but it was a very small increase. It may be that treatment with antidepressants combines a very small detrimental effect with a bigger beneficial effect.

Some researchers are concerned about the effects of the FDA warning. Parents and mental health professionals have become concerned about the effects of antidepressants on teenagers and have hesitated to use the drugs. Meanwhile, suicide rates for teenagers increased in 2004, the year when the FDA warning began. A 14% increase was reported in the United States, and a 49% increase in the Netherlands (Couzin, 2007). However, two points should be kept in mind when considering the importance of these increases. One is that every natural event, including suicidal behavior, shows spontaneous variations that are caused by multiple factors. Even if drug use and other important factors were held constant, there would still be increases in the suicide rate in some years and decreases in others, so it is not possible to conclude that a change in the suicide rate was caused by a single factor, such as the FDA warning. A second important point is that the percentage of variation has different meanings depending on the frequencies of the events. For example, if only one person commits suicide in a year and two do so the next year, the increase in suicide is 100%—but only one additional death. Infrequent events such as adolescent suicide are easily described in confusing ways when percentage increases or decreases are the measure used.

It is important to realize that not every adolescent has an equal probability of suicide. Certain risk factors allow people to identify individuals with a higher probability of suicidal thoughts and actions. In addition to depression, these risk factors include a history of suicidal thinking, previous suicidal acts, and a history of fighting, especially with threats of or the actual use of weapons (Evans, Marte, Betts, & Silliman, 2001; Perkins & Hartless, 2002).

Conclusion

Suicide rates among teenagers are not high compared to rates of other age groups or teenage death rates from other causes. Elena's mother would actually do better to think about other possible dangers to her daughter and to encourage the high school to work on education about accidental deaths.

CRITICAL THINKING

1. How are statistics about suicides and accidental deaths collected? Explain why the most recent reports are from several years in the past.

2. Read the article by Couzin (2007). Describe the drawbacks of the meta-analysis discussed in this section. What are the advantages and disadvantages of using the results of a meta-analysis to make decisions about treating teenagers with antidepressants?

3. What is the meaning in actual numbers of a 14% increase in teenage suicides? What is the meaning in actual numbers of a similar increase in suicides by non-Hispanic White men older than 85 years of age? To answer these questions, you need to know both suicide rates and the number of each group in the U.S. population.

4. What death rate is represented by 5,000 motor vehicle deaths of adolescents 16 to 19 years old? How does this compare with the suicide rate for this age group (or as near an age group as you can find)?

5. Search the Internet to find media productions, such as films and TV programs, that refer to suicide. What age groups do they focus on and how realistic are they about suicide rates in those groups? Is their view of suicide rates any more or less realistic than views of rape or murder rates? Should high school educational programs take into account the beliefs about suicide that students may have acquired from the media? Explain your answer.

References

Couzin, J. (2007). Study questions antidepressant risks. *Science, 316,* 354.

Evans, W. P., Marte, R. M., Betts, S., & Silliman, B. (2001). Adolescent suicide risk and peer-related violent behaviors and victimization. *Journal of Interpersonal Violence, 16,* 1330–1348.

Liang, H., & Eley, T. C. (2005). A monozygotic twin differences study of nonshared environmental influence on adolescent depressive symptoms. *Child Development, 76,* 1247–1260.

Perkins, D. F., & Hartless, G. (2002). An ecological risk-factor examination of suicide ideation and behavior of adolescents. *Journal of Adolescent Research, 17,* 3–26.

Claim 49

Punishment is an effective way of changing children's and adolescents' undesirable behaviors.

Fifteen-year-old Lance was a high school freshman and thought a book assigned for his English class was boring. He decided to not read the book and not do any of the related assignments. When his mother asked about his English homework, he told her he had already done it—but she went to a parent-teacher conference and found out differently. When Lance's father came home from a business trip, he soon heard the story and decided that Lance must be punished. His father yelled at Lance for quite a long time, then grounded him for a week, so he missed his favorite cousin's big birthday party. What's more, when the report cards came out, Lance had a D in English, which did not please him. During the next marking period, another book was assigned that bored Lance, and he did exactly the same as before. His father decided that because the punishment Lance had received had not worked, a more severe punishment would need to be given.

Was Lance's father right in thinking that a more intense punishment would work when a milder one had not?

The use of punishment has been the subject of years of argument among parents, teachers, and mental health professionals. As is the case for many ongoing disagreements, part of the problem is the definition of the term *punishment*. When this word is used in an unspecified way, neither physical discomfort nor any disagreeable nonphysical experience is particularly implied. The term *punishment* simply refers to the infliction of an experience that the recipient will find undesirable, simultaneous with or following an action of the punished person, and with the intention on the part of the punisher to prevent the unwanted behavior from occurring again. (Note that there is a difference between punishment and the negative reinforcement described by B. F. Skinner. *Negative reinforcement* refers to the removal of an unpleasant stimulus when a desired behavior occurs, to reinforce the desired behavior; it has no direct effect on unwanted behaviors.)

Punishments can range from severe physical pain or even death to social disapproval or deprivation of treats, such as dessert or permission to go to the movies. Some experiences that are intended as punishment—for example, physical pain—may occur in different circumstances, such as sports or medical treatment, and when they occur in those cases they are not considered to be punishment. The essence of punishment lies in the intention with which it is given, as well as in its timing with or following an unwanted action.

Human beings have used punishment for many centuries in efforts to change adult behavior, but little evidence supports its effectiveness. Research on children and adolescents suggests that punishment immediately after an undesirable behavior can stop the behavior in the short term, but physical punishment is associated with, at least, later aggressive behavior by the punished child. Nevertheless, the use of physical punishment remains common (McClure & May, 2008).

Of course, studies of punishment's effects on children or adolescents cannot ethically or practically be conducted as experiments. Instead, researchers depend on quasi-experimental studies that compare outcomes when children are punished to those when they are not. As a result, outcomes of research are difficult to interpret and may be affected by confounding variables. These factors accompany the use of punishment and may cause other events that influence a child's later behavior. For example, parental attitudes might determine both decisions about punishment and other child-rearing decisions, such as those about education. The extensive body of research on child and adolescent punishment has not managed to solve the problem of confounding variables.

Some suggestions about punishment's effect on children may be derived from studies on whether animals learn from punishment. Animal studies can be conducted according to the rules about experiments, so they are much less affected by confounding variables. Although it may not be completely reasonable to try to generalize from animal studies to young human beings, it is possible to implement animal studies that seem to parallel events in human lives. One study focused on a rather practical problem that closely resembled some situations in the correction of children's behavior: how to teach puppies not to eat forbidden objects. The researcher compared two groups of puppies. The puppies in each group received a smack with a rolled-up newspaper if they ate a food they really liked, but they did not receive a smack if they ate a less-preferred food. The difference between the two groups was that puppies in one group were smacked after eating the food, according to the conventional punishment pattern. The other puppies were smacked as they approached the food and prepared to eat it but had not actually chewed or swallowed any food. Later, all of the puppies were tested for their resistance to temptation by being left alone in a room with the favorite food. The puppies that had been punished after eating had poor resistance to temptation and often ate the favorite food but displayed guilt and cringed or hid afterward. Those who had been smacked as they approached the food displayed good resistance to temptation on the whole and did not usually eat even when alone with their favorite food; however, if they gave in and ate, they showed little guilt or fear afterward (research discussed by Walters & Demkow, 1962).

In generalizing from puppies to humans, this study suggests that the most effective punishment is a type that begins when a child or adolescent is starting to do something undesirable. Actually, parents of very young children often use exactly this approach to train their children to stay away from dangers such as a hot stove or an electrical outlet. Later, when older children do things that are annoying or rude but not dangerous, parents are more likely to save punishment until after the act has occurred. Observing these events in everyday life, people can note that most careful parents have no trouble teaching a child not to touch the electrical outlet, but jumping up and down on the sofa is much more difficult to stop, no matter how often it is followed by slightly delayed punishment.

It seems that timing is of the essence in making punishment effective. But timing is hard to control if the punishment used is not a physical one. Being grounded for a week is a punishment that does not begin until the child wants to go out, and much of the punishment is delayed until days after the offense. Parents in the United States use less physical punishment as children become older (in fact, it is considered abusive to use physical punishment with adolescents), so it becomes increasingly difficult for parents to control the timing of the punishment and keep it effective.

Consistency of punishment is also known to be an important factor in effectiveness. As parents turn to nonphysical punishments, such as deprivation of privileges, they also become less likely to follow through on the punishment they decreed. A couple of swats on the bottom are quickly administered and may, or may not, be quickly forgotten by both parties. A week's grounding of a resentful adolescent can take a great deal of determination for a parent to carry out, and after a day or so the offense may be forgiven or even forgotten. These punishments can become empty threats because they are rarely or never completely carried out and cannot be expected to be effective in changing behavior.

Finally, the punishable offenses of older children and adolescents are usually fairly complex. Not doing homework over a period of time involves many instances of failing to do what is required and doing something less appropriate instead. It would be very difficult for a parent to observe a child so closely that a punishment began whenever an act of not doing homework was about to commence. If the punishment were to be given after the whole chain of events is complete, it would be difficult to know which action is being punished. It is not nearly as easy to use punishment effectively as some people may think. It appears, too, that some types of punishment can backfire; for example, in one study of punishment and reinforcement of juvenile offenders, those who were punished had an increase in self-esteem; those who were not punished did not show an increase in self-esteem (Tsytsarev, Manger, & Lodrini, 2000).

Conclusion

Punishment is not an effective way to change behavior unless it is handled with great care, and this is by no means easy to do, especially with respect to the complex behaviors of adolescents. Lance's father will probably find that increasing the severity of the punishment does not have much effect, except to make everyone in the family angrier than they already are.

CRITICAL THINKING

1. Does this section argue for physical punishment as a good choice for parents of children and adolescents? Explain your answer.

2. In a child development textbook, find definitions of *child abuse*. How are these definitions relevant to the use of physical punishment for adolescents? Explain your answer.

3. Read the article by Walters and Demkow (1962). Is it reasonable to generalize from the puppy study described in this section to the use of punishment with school-age children? In what significant ways are children and adolescents different from puppies? Be sure to comment on differences in cognitive abilities, such as theory of mind.

4. Why do you think the puppies that were punished after eating showed poor resistance to temptation? Did they experience positive reinforcement as well as punishment for their actions? Are there similar situations experienced by adolescents? Explain your answer.

5. Name two reasons that might cause parents to continue to use punishment even though it has proved ineffective in changing adolescents' behavior.

References

McClure, T. E., & May, D. C. (2008). Dealing with misbehavior at schools in Kentucky: Theoretical and contextual predictors of use of corporal punishment. *Youth and Society*, *39*, 406–429.

Tsytsarev, S., Manger, J., & Lodrini, D. (2000). The use of reinforcement and punishment on incarcerated and probated substance-abusing juvenile offenders. *International Journal of Offender Therapy and Comparative Criminology*, *44*, 22–32.

Walters, R. H., & Demkow, L. (1962). Timing of punishment as a determinant of response inhibition. *Child Development*, *34*, 207–214.

Claim 50

Children are reaching puberty earlier with each generation.

Becca and Rich were the parents of 7-year-old Megan, who was one of the tallest children in her second-grade class. Even though Becca and Rich were tall, they worried because Megan's height seemed so far above the average. Becca had read that rapid growth in height could mean that a child was approaching puberty, and she was concerned that her child might soon be sexually mature. Their next-door neighbor sympathized with Becca's worries but said, "Yes, she might be getting close to puberty. I read that every generation is becoming sexually mature at an earlier age. It's happening 5 or 6 years earlier than it did 150 years ago. What's going to happen—are we going to have 2-year-olds who need to shave?"

Was Becca right to think that Megan's height meant early puberty? And was the neighbor right in thinking that puberty would continue to be earlier with each succeeding generation?

Changes in physical growth and development patterns over time are referred to as the *secular trend*—*secular* meaning something that occurs over a period of time, not something that opposes religious belief. The secular trend in growth and maturation is a well-established phenomenon of childhood and adolescent growth. During the last 150 years, children in Europe and North America have been taller and heavier at specific ages than their parents' generation was at the same ages. They have also reached sexual maturity at earlier ages than the immediately previous generations.

The idea of children growing more rapidly is a rather scary one. The novelist H. G. Wells wrote a science fiction story about a baby food that caused gigantic growth and the awful consequences of great size and strength governed only by infantile minds. The secular trend worries people, who wonder whether there will be any end to the "progress." Of course, it is also concerning to think about sexually mature bodies with very childish minds.

Some facts about the secular trend can put these anxieties into perspective. The first fact is that changes in growth rates are flattening, with smaller changes during at least the last 20 years. Although there are large differences between the present average height of 5-year-olds in the United States and the average height of 5-year-olds in 1900, the height difference between 5-year-olds in 1970 and 5-year-olds in 2000 was small.

A second fact has to do with historical information about growth, especially about puberty. Although keeping statistics about growth rates is a modern practice, historical material tells something about the timing of sexual maturation. For example, the Old Testament set the minimum marriage age at 14 years for boys and 12 years for girls, figures very similar to present average ages at puberty. It does not seem likely that the Old Testament authorities would have wanted marriages to take place 3 or 4 years before sexual relations were possible. To look at a more recent time, Shakespeare depicted Juliet as wanting to marry Romeo when she was not yet 14 years old—and her father said, "Younger than she are happy mothers made" (although her mother did not approve of this view). Shakespeare may have been wrong, but he obviously felt it was not unusual for a 13-year-old girl to have reached puberty.

Do these historical facts contradict the evidence for the recent secular trend? No, that evidence is well established. In the 19th and early 20th centuries in Europe and North America, children grew more slowly and reached puberty later than they do presently—and, apparently, than they had in previous centuries. Growth rates were lower during the 19th century compared to what they were at other times. A number of factors may have been responsible for the reduction. The Industrial Revolution, with long hours of hard work for children as well as adults, is one factor. Another is 19th century life in cities and industrial centers, with little access to healthy food or clean water. City life at that time also involved high rates of contagious disease because people lived in crowded conditions that made disease communication easy. These risk factors are better controlled in modern times, so general health has improved and growth rates have returned to the human average.

Sexual maturation is considered to occur when a girl experiences *menarche* (the first menstruation of her life) or when a boy begins to produce viable sperm. Obviously, a girl's menarche is much easier to confirm than a boy's maturation. But both boys and girls experience detectable maturational changes before any final step occurs, so it is possible to predict maturation and to collect relevant information before puberty. These maturational changes are on a timetable similar to that of sexual maturation itself, so they provide some important information about the secular trend. A system for measurement of breast and testicle development was developed years ago by J. M. Tanner and is used for research on sexual development.

Surprisingly, the secular trend in these early maturational steps does not seem to be exactly the same as that for menarche. This fact was revealed in studies of *precocious puberty*, the abnormally early occurrence of sexual maturation. Until recently, precocious puberty was defined as involving the onset of early stages (previous to menarche or sperm viability) before 8 years of age for girls and before 9 years of age for boys.

Recent research showed that although the average age at menarche has not changed for some years, some of the preliminary maturational steps occur earlier than they did in the known past. The cut-off points—ages that mark the divide between precocious puberty and normal development—are now considered to be 7.7 years for girls and about the same for boys. These cut-off points are established by finding the 3rd percentile for the chronological age when development occurs for a large sample of children. Thus, only 3% of children show a particular level of sexual development at an earlier age than 7.7 years, and 97% do not show that level until they are older (Parent et al., 2005). Precocious puberty—very early sexual maturation—should be considered as more than a socially awkward event because it is possible for endocrine or neurological problems to cause this developmental event (Nield, Cakan, & Kamat, 2007).

Although growth in height is a predictor of a child's puberty schedule, an increase in fat and relative fat levels are also useful predictors for girls. Girls with higher fat levels are likely to experience menarche earlier (Lin-Su, Vogiatzi, & New, 2002).

Conclusion

Although growth in height is quicker and puberty is considerably earlier today than it was 150 years ago, major changes in the pattern of development seem to have come to a stop, and it seems that the 19th century was a time of slowed growth and sexual maturation caused by poor health conditions rather than the present time being a period of unusually fast growth. However, some of the early steps in sexual maturation seem to be occurring a bit earlier than they did 40 or 50 years ago. In Megan's case, her unusual height for her age may be inherited from her tall parents and not evidence of unusually early development, but if her parents are concerned, they can ask for a medical examination. Measurements of her skeletal development can show whether her development is in the normal range for her chronological age.

CRITICAL THINKING

1. Describe the secular trend for girls' sexual maturation. When did the biggest changes in timing occur? Use information from a child development textbook to support your answer.

2. Read about the onset of puberty in a child development textbook. Explain why girls who grow more rapidly also reach menarche earlier. (The explanation for boys is similar but more complicated.)

3. Look at the work of J. M. Tanner (1989), who developed a system for evaluating the early stages of sexual maturation. What might be some practical and ethical problems of conducting research on this topic? Is it possible that such problems have caused inaccurate measurements of the developmental steps used in defining precocious puberty? Explain your answer.

4. A graph in the article by Parent et al. (2005) shows a comparison of ages at menarche for girls born in the United States and Europe, girls adopted from their own countries to the United States and Europe, and girls growing up in the countries where the adoptees were born. What differences between these groups do you see? What factors might explain the differences? (The article offers one explanation.)

5. The cut-off point for abnormal precocious puberty is the 3rd percentile. Of two children who are very similar in development, can one be considered developmentally normal and the other developmentally abnormal? Explain your answer.

References

Lin-Su, K., Vogiatzi, M. G., & New, M. I. (2002). Body mass index and age at menarche in an adolescent clinic population. *Clinical Pediatrics, 41*, 501–507.

Nield, L. S., Cakan, N., & Kamat, D. (2007). A practical approach to precocious puberty. *Clinical Pediatrics, 46*, 299–306.

Parent, A. S., Rasier, G., Gerard, A., Heger, S., Roth, C., et al. (2005). Early onset of puberty: Tracking genetic and environmental factors. *Hormone Research, 64*(Suppl. 2), 41–47.

Tanner, J. M. (1989). *Fetus into man.* Cambridge, MA: Harvard University Press.

Claim 51

Teenage boys and girls should have about the same level of fat in their bodies, about 10%.

Sixteen-year-old Amy and Julia went together to a gym that had recently opened in their part of town. One of the gym's specialties was calculation of body characteristics such as muscle mass and fat content. Both girls were horrified to find that they had fat levels far above that of their friend Jake, who went with them. Jake's fat level was calculated at about 11%, Amy's at 23%, and Julia's at 24%. Jake was determined to get rid of some of his body fat by lifting weights and dieting. Amy said, "I feel like a monster. How did I get so much blubber on me? I'll just have to stop eating completely until I get down to even less fat than Jake has. Even 10% sounds like a huge amount."

Was Amy right? Were she and Julia victims of the obesity epidemic without realizing it?

Fear of fat has become a critical aspect of popular thinking about physical development. It's true that there are some excellent reasons to be concerned about excessive body fat. The obesity epidemic in the United States is connected with serious physical problems, such as diabetes and heart disease. Unfortunately, attitudes about body fat are also determined by fashion concerns and confusion about developmentally appropriate physical differences. As a result, some parents have fed their babies diets with minimum fat, resulting in dire consequences, such as nervous system damage and even infant death. Teenagers are not as likely as babies to die as a result of the belief that fat must be kept to a very low level, but this belief can lead to inappropriate diet and weight goals, with undesirable physical results.

The claim that boys' and girls' fat levels should be the same is also connected to the belief that boys and girls have the same needs—in essence, that they should be considered the same for most practical purposes because they deserve the same opportunities. But, however admirable the goal of gender equality may be as a social value, problems can arise when the differing realities of male and female developmental patterns through childhood and adolescence are ignored.

To understand comparisons of boys and girls, people need to keep in mind that the two groups are on different timetables as they develop from birth to puberty. A group of girls will reach puberty (as measured by first menstruation) an average of 2 years earlier than a group of boys (whose puberty is indicated by the less easily measured criterion of production of viable sperm).There is good deal of variability (individual differences) in sexual maturation, so this average difference does not necessarily allow people to predict how a certain girl will differ from a specific boy. Some girls and some boys will mature earlier than the rest of their peers, and some girls and some boys will reach puberty later; nevertheless, the average ages at puberty for the two groups are predictably different.

The differences in boys' and girls' developmental timetables mean that girls in their early and middle teens are quite a bit further along toward developing their mature bodies than boys of the same age. A girl in her middle teens may already have been at her final adult height for 2 years, while a boy is still growing. X-ray examination of this girl's bones will show that her bones are completely developed, but an X-ray of the boy's bones will show that their development is not finished. The girl will probably not be at her full adult weight but is likely to be closer to it than a boy is to his adult weight.

Fat plays a role in both males' and females' reproductive lives, so a sufficient amount of fat is needed before puberty can occur. However, the contribution of fat to reproductive functioning is related to specific reproductive hormones, of which the balance is of course different for males and females. Estrogen, the primary female reproductive hormone, is stored in body fat and to some extent produced by body fat.

To be ready for reproduction—to become sexually mature, initially—the female body needs to have a considerably higher level of fat than the 10% or so that is characteristic of the adolescent male. The first menstruation does not occur until a girl has about 22% body fat, and regular menstrual cycles require about 24% body fat. After the onset of puberty, dropping below these fat levels will disrupt and can even prevent menstrual cycles (Tanner, 1989).

Even 10% body fat sounds like a great deal if it is envisioned as a separate part of the body, a sort of gym bag full of fat. But body fat in females is distributed in such a way that a girl with a 24% fat level may look very slim. Most of the fat is distributed evenly under the skin rather than in a lump somewhere. And lumps that are present are generally considered attractive: In the nonpregnant, nonlactating human female, most of the breast consists of fat.

For good health—especially good reproductive health—teenage girls should not try to attain the low fat levels characteristic of boys of the same age. The belief that low fat levels are appropriate for girls may be a cause of anorexic or bulimic eating patterns, which have potentially serious long-term health consequences, including the possibility of impaired reproductive functioning, even after normal eating patterns have returned. And, once again, a slim, attractive appearance is by no means ruled out by a normal female body fat level. On the contrary, although anorexic girls may consider their emaciation to be a mark of beauty, very few other people agree with them.

High fat levels make a difference to high school athletes, both positively and negatively. Athletic performance worsens as boys increase their fat level above 10% and as girls exceed 19% (a level at which normal menstrual cycles do not occur) (McLeod, Hunter, & Etchison, 1983). However, low fat levels cause an increased likelihood of bone fractures, and the long-term effect on the still-growing body is not known (Patel, Greydanus, Pratt, & Phillips, 2003).

Conclusion

Healthy teenage boys and girls have different normal fat levels—lower for the boys, higher for the girls. Girls whose body fat drops below about 24% will not have regular menstrual cycles, whereas boys of the same age will mature reproductively with 10% body fat or less. Amy and Julia need to understand that their own good health and the reproductive capacity that they will probably want later in their lives depend on keeping the appropriate fat level for their age and gender.

CRITICAL THINKING

1. Find information in a child development textbook or in the book by Tanner (1989) about physical development in both boys and girls. Describe the developmental differences between boys and girls ages 1 year, 10 years, and 14 years. At what age are individual differences greatest? Why?

(Continued)

(Continued)

2. How would you expect individual differences in body fat to affect individual differences in menarche or in the establishment of regular menstrual cycles? Would you expect cultural and chance factors to play a role? Explain your answer.

3. Find information in a child development textbook about the effects of unusually late and unusually early puberty on both girls and boys. (Consider only ages at puberty that are within the normal range, not precocious puberty.) Why would the effects be different for boys versus girls? (Don't forget that early puberty in girls may occur as early as 9 years of age.)

4. Describe the symptoms of anorexia, including the effect on reproductive hormones. Why is a low level of body fat connected with a low level of female reproductive hormones? Use information from a child development textbook to support your answer.

5. What would you expect to be the effect of intense athletic training on girls' reproductive cycles? Would you expect a similar effect on boys' sexual development? Explain your answer.

References

McLeod, W. D., Hunter, S. C., & Etchison, B. (1983). Performance measurement and percent body fat in the high school athlete. *American Journal of Sports Medicine*, *11*, 390–397.

Patel, D. R., Greydanus, D. E., Pratt, H. E., & Phillips, E. L. (2003). Eating disorders in adolescent athletes. *Journal of Adolescent Research*, *18*, 280–296.

Tanner, J. M. (1989). *Fetus into man*. Cambridge, MA: Harvard University Press.

Afterthoughts

Some Ideas to Take Into Your Future

Are you now thoroughly prepared to assess all claims about child development? Even if you have carefully worked through every question and example in this book, the answer, of course, is NO. There are a number of reasons why such assessments are difficult and will remain difficult throughout your life. One important issue is that the study of child development is full of unanswered questions; the more professionals learn about it through research, the more new questions arise. The existence of unanswered questions explains why you are likely to find some poorly supported claims in any child development textbook, even though its author has struggled to report the best evidence about the topics. In fact, child development has been a topic of scientific study for a rather short time (Cahan, 2007).

Another reason for the difficulty is that claims can have personal meaning for readers. Many claims involve emotional experiences and personal memories. Most of them are in some way related to moral obligations—how you or others ought to behave toward children and how children should behave toward others. Quite a few claims have a combination of these factors, and they resonate with readers about how their parents treated them (and how they treat their own children, if they have any). The most difficult claims to assess may be those that have to do with what one might call *righteousness*. Many claims about parenting, education, and criminal justice fall into this category.

Assessment of claims about child development also shares some problems with analysis of other scientific claims. Readers cannot directly know or evaluate much of the evidence for any of these claims, so they fall back on other approaches in which critical thinking is difficult. One discussion of this issue made the following point:

> Few of us are qualified to assess claims about the merits of string theory, the role of mercury in the etiology of autism, or the existence of repressed memories. So rather than evaluating the asserted claim itself, we instead evaluate the claim's source. If the source is deemed trustworthy, people will believe the claim, often without really understanding it. . . . Their belief is not necessarily rooted in an appreciation of the evidence and arguments. Rather . . . [they] accept] this information because they trust the people who say it is true. (Bloom & Weisberg, 2007, p. 997)

This tendency can create problems both for your own critical thinking and your ability to change other people's beliefs.

Changing Assumptions and Future Possibilities

Earlier parts of this book mentioned certain assumptions made in the study of child development—for example, that developmentally appropriate practice is an important consideration and that transactional processes are important to development. Though most of these assumptions are still present, professionals need to realize that new assumptions are likely to be added in the future. For example, research and theory in child development are increasingly oriented toward *dynamic systems theory*, a way of thinking that emphasizes the importance of many variables that work together to produce an outcome. An essential aspect of dynamic systems theory is the assumption that in some cases small changes in relevant variables can produce a major outcome change, and in other cases large variations in causal factors may create little or no change in outcome. Dynamic systems theory, like the transactional process approach, emphasizes the idea that development may be based on small changes that accumulate gradually over time (Spencer, Clearfield, Corbetta, Ulrich, Buchanan, & Schöner, 2006).

Using Critical Thinking About Child Development Claims: Personal and Professional Issues

There are real personal advantages for those who have learned to assess claims about child development. Critical thinking about child development can be helpful in life decisions, enabling people to make some appropriate choices for themselves and their families. The ability to assess claims can protect people against confused or even fraudulent persons who want to "sell" their practices or ideas. It can be very gratifying to learn how to assess claims and to practice what one has learned. Unfortunately, this achievement may not mean that one will win more arguments! On the contrary, using critical thinking about common beliefs can be very offensive to opponents who are committed to their unexamined beliefs. Those people can become even more entrenched in their belief system as they hear it assessed critically. This may be the case particularly when there is a connection between religious or political ideology and the claim in question—then the proponent of the belief feels that analysis of the claim attacks him or her at a serious level. Few people are actually objective about popular child development claims, and it is possible that no one is totally objective about all of them.

In addition to the personal advantages of thinking critically about child development beliefs, some related issues are of importance to the entire community, such as those dealing with the concept of *evidence-based practice*. In the mid-1990s, the medical profession began to emphasize the idea of an evidence basis for medicine. Physicians and surgeons felt it was time to reject the traditional reliance on authority and accepted methods and to seek empirical evidence that showed whether or not a practice was both safe and effective. Psychologists and other members of the helping professions soon followed this path and began to demand that interventions be chosen on the basis of research that supported their appropriateness.

The concept of evidence-based practice is now commonly used in education, parent training, and child and family mental health work. Members of these disciplines agree that methods should be chosen on the basis of evidence of their safety and effectiveness. However, this agreement is not as simple or as complete as it might appear to be. Some educators and mental health professionals reject the idea of evidence based on research. Others believe that choices of evidence-based practices should include not only empirical research evidence but also the clinical experience of the professional and the values of the child's family. These factors—experience and values—need to be assessed through critical thinking approaches. The implication that evidence-based practice is objective and "scientific" cannot be accepted unquestioningly when these subjective factors are included.

There is still another problem that demands critical thinking about evidence-based practices. There is really no good general definition of the evidence needed to make a practice legitimately evidence based. What research evidence shows an intervention to be safe? What shows it to be effective? How are these two terms defined? None of these questions has received an adequate answer, so it remains the task of teachers, principals, child care providers, parents, social workers, and mental health professionals to apply their critical thinking abilities when they choose educational programs, discipline techniques, or mental health interventions.

The End for Now—But Don't Get Uncritical!

In conclusion, you may want to keep in practice by pursuing two more questions with your critical thinking skills. First, consider the child development textbook you have been using. What were some topics that were presented with little or no research evidence for the claims made? And, second, what kind of research evidence would you want to require as support for the effectiveness of, say, a child care program or a suicide-prevention plan for adolescents? You may not feel prepared to answer these questions right now, but keep them in mind as you pursue your studies and work at higher levels—you will find these matters simpler with more practice and more information.

Critical thinking about child development issues like these is hard work. But don't forget that your critical thinking skills can make a difference in your life—and in what you can give to your community. Thinking critically is worth the trouble.

References

Bloom, P., & Weisberg, D. S. (2007). Childhood origins of adult resistance to science. *Science, 316*, 996–997.

Cahan, E. D. (2007). The child as scientific object. *Science, 316*, 835.

Spencer, J. P., Clearfield, M., Corbetta, D., Ulrich, B., Buchanan, P., & Schöner, G. (2006). Moving toward a grand theory of development: In memory of Esther Thelen. *Child Development, 77*, 1521–1538.

Index

About the Author

Jean Mercer (PhD, Psychology, Brandeis University), Professor Emerita of Psychology at Richard Stockton College, has taught undergraduate courses on developmental psychology, infant development, statistics, and research methods for 30 years. A past president of the New Jersey Association for Infant Mental Health and a Fellow of the Commission for Scientific Medicine and Mental Health, she has written a general interest book about early emotional development, *Understanding Attachment* (Praeger, 2006), and a textbook, *Infant Development: A Multidisciplinary Introduction* (Brooks/Cole, 1998). She recently served as an expert witness in the trial of a mother who kept her adopted children in cages and claimed she had a book advising this, providing a good example of failure to think straight about child development.

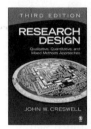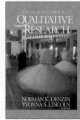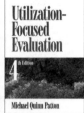